OIL CITIES

Peter T. Flawn Series in Natural Resources

OIL CITIES

The Making of North Louisiana's Boomtowns, 1901–1930

HENRY ALEXANDER WIENCEK

University of Texas Press

AUSTIN

The Peter T. Flawn Series in Natural Resource Management and
Conservation is supported by a grant from the National Endowment for the
Humanities and by gifts from various individual donors.

Requests for permission to reproduce material from this work should be sent to:
Permissions
University of Texas Press
P.O. Box 7819
Austin, TX 78713-7819
utpress.utexas.edu

∞ The paper used in this book meets the minimum requirements of
ANSI/NISO Z39.48-1992 (R1997) (Permanence of Paper).

Library of Congress Cataloging-in-Publication Data

Names: Wiencek, Henry Alexander, author.
Title: Oil Cities : the making of North Louisiana's boomtowns, 1901–1930 /
Henry Alexander Wiencek.
Description: First edition. | Austin : University of Texas Press, 2024. |
Includes bibliographical references and index.
Identifiers: LCCN 2023034360 (print) | LCCN 2023034361 (ebook)
ISBN 978-1-4773-2917-7 (hardcover)
ISBN 978-1-4773-2918-4 (pdf)
ISBN 978-1-4773-2919-1 (epub)
Subjects: LCSH: Petroleum industry and trade—Louisiana—History—
20th century. | Cities and towns—Louisiana—Growth—History—20th century. |
Petroleum workers—Louisiana—Social conditions—History—20th century. |
African Americans—Violence against—Louisiana—History—20th century. |
Oil well drilling rigs—Social aspects—Louisiana—History—20th century. |
Land tenure—Louisiana—History—20th century—Case studies.
Classification: LCC HD9567.L8 W546 2024 (print) | LCC HD9567.L8
(ebook) | DDC 338.2/72809763809042—dc23/eng/20231205
LC record available at https://lccn.loc.gov/2023034360
LC ebook record available at https://lccn.loc.gov/2023034361

doi:10.7560/329177

To my parents

CONTENTS

A NOTE TO READERS ix

PROLOGUE: The Savage-Morrical No. 1 xi

CHAPTER 1. The Boom 1

CHAPTER 2. The Communities 17

CHAPTER 3. The People 35

CHAPTER 4. The Racial Violence of "Bloody Caddo" 55

CHAPTER 5. The Courts of Bloody Caddo 75

CHAPTER 6. The Land 93

CHAPTER 7. The City 119

EPILOGUE: The Bust 135

ACKNOWLEDGMENTS 147

NOTES 151

INDEX 177

A NOTE TO READERS

IN 1909, STANDARD OIL BEGAN OPERATING IN THE STATE of Louisiana via a subsidiary firm known as the "Standard Oil Company of Louisiana." However, in 1911 the US Supreme Court ruled that Standard Oil was in violation of federal anti-trust statutes, further ordering that the company must be divided into several competing entities. As a result of that decision, the Standard Oil Company of Louisiana division became a subsidiary of the newly constituted Standard Oil Company *of New Jersey*.

For the sake of clarity, I will refer to the Standard Oil affiliate doing business in Louisiana over this period as the "Standard Oil Company of Louisiana" consistently throughout the text. This term will refer to both the pre-1911 subsidiary of the Standard Oil Company as well as the post-1911 subsidiary of the Standard Oil Company of New Jersey.

PROLOGUE: THE SAVAGE-MORRICAL NO. 1

IN MAY 1904, J. S. AND W. A. SAVAGE—BROTHERS, OIL field drillers, and business partners—ventured into the rural countryside of Caddo Parish about thirty miles north of Shreveport. Working just outside of "Surry," a quiet rural depot along the Kansas City Southern railroad line, the Savage team erected Savage-Morrical No. 1, the first oil derrick in North Louisiana.[1] In February 1905, their cable-tool drill percussed into an underground deposit of crude at 1,546 feet.[2] A photograph documenting this iconic moment paints a rustic picture of remote woods and primitive living conditions. Next to the wooden derrick stands a log cabin, where Walter Duvall George, a member of the drilling team, lived with his wife, Effie, and son, Walter Duvall Jr. Three women and two boys pose alongside seven male workers; the wives' dignified appearance in white dresses and ornate hats forms a striking contrast to the hard visage each of the men bears. One boy holds what appears to be a hat aloft, triumphant.

There is a frontier quality to the photograph: modern technology taming the wilderness and ushering in a new era, a golden spike piercing the swamp. Framed by the thick North Louisiana woods, the drilling team postures like prospectors who have just discovered a vein of gold in the California mountains. By creating such an image, these drillers and their families depicted themselves as explorers planting the flag of civilization in a rough place. They seemed to have little doubt that oil would transform this desolate stretch of bayou into a productive new space of modernity and wealth, replicating the same dynamics of industrial growth and resource extraction that were spreading across much of early twentieth-century America. This was the first moment of a historic oil boom and the beginning of a new era for North Louisiana.

As word of Savage-Morrical No. 1 proliferated, thousands of prospective workers descended upon Surry and its adjoining lands in the hope of earning the daily wage of three dollars (or more) one could acquire on the rigs. They

FIGURE O.1. *The Savage-Morrical No. 1, North Louisiana's first successful oil well, 1905.*

ranged from farmers with no previous oil field experience to hardened industry veterans arriving from the latest boom. Surry's new occupants began improvising a rough and wholly fascinating new community: Oil City. Life in the nascent boomtown was primitive and dangerous. Residents had to endure mud-laden roads, a lack of potable water, and a riotous social world full of heavy drinking and unrelenting violence. Lines of clapboard saloons, hotels, and other businesses arose to meet the sudden economic demands of so many new migrants. Buildings, such as they were, tended to be crudely built and quickly assembled. The largely male workforce typically resided in dense clusters of tent homes, very often pitched in the shadow of the derrick that employed them.

Oil City was just one of many such boomtowns that would germinate across the countryside of North Louisiana's Caddo and Claiborne Parishes as new oil fields materialized. Communities with names such as Mooringsport, Trees City, Vivian, Belcher, Hosston, Ida, and Homer also emerged to absorb heavy influxes of migrants as wildcatters sought out the region's next major pool of crude. Much like their nineteenth-century antecedents in the oil fields of Pennsylvania, Louisiana's new industrial environments grew atop sparsely populated rural districts.[3] Land prices in what had been quiet, largely agrarian hamlets dramatically spiked after decades of steady decline.

North Louisiana's oil field communities, however, were much more than just cookie-cutter company towns designed to efficiently integrate disparate centers of production into one vertical corporate structure.[4] They were built to reflect the unique values, politics, and prejudices of a specific region of the American South. While these boomtowns all shared oil production as a common economic linchpin, they each developed locally distinct economic and demographic characteristics. North Louisiana's oil field communities were not simply designed from the top down by corporate fiat, but rather grew and developed in conversation with each other: local industry executives, workers, and politicians all helped create contrasting versions of what an "oil boomtown" ought to be.

On one side of Caddo Lake stood the notorious Oil City, which teemed with violence, drinking, and general disorder; just across the water, Mooringsport offered workers access to the same rigs, but with a far quieter social atmosphere, sturdier homes, and more salubrious conditions. Many family-oriented oil men accordingly preferred Mooringsport's distinct vision of a boomtown and its distance from Oil City's mayhem. The company town of Trees City similarly cultivated a space that was intentionally free of drinking, gambling, and violence: a new model of "boomtown" that would attract not just male workers but also their wives and children. And while many of Oil City's men gladly lived alongside saloons and brothels, others sought out a more pious community. In one 1915 photo of Caddo's oil fields, a massive Baptist revival is taking place alongside Caddo Lake. The photograph captures scores of white-clad congregants wading into the water as oil derricks line the horizon, a vivid

FIGURE O.2. *The Mooringsport Baptist Church conducts a baptism ceremony in Caddo Lake, 1915.*

illustration of how economic and social change collided in an evolving boomtown world.[5]

The early twentieth-century oil boomtowns of Texas and Louisiana were economically transformational to many of their new residents, especially rural farmers trapped in the cycle of declining crop prices and debt that prevailed across much of the post-Reconstruction South.[6] Oil fields even became crucibles of economic uplift for many European émigrés who managed to arrive in such a faraway corner of the United States. To the most skilled workers such as Walter George Sr., oil production enabled an ascent into an entirely new life. In 1900, George was boarding as a farm laborer in the small East Texas town of Rusk.[7] Thirty years and several oil booms later, he owned a Shreveport home valued at $15,000 and employed a live-in cook.[8] The arc of Walter George's life reinforces a familiar narrative: that the oil boom offered a collective economic bridge toward a new era of prosperity for all who were willing to work for it.

However, this triumphant mythology about the transformative power of oil also makes an ahistorical presumption: that every individual, irrespective of economic or racial background, had equal access to the uplift which oil production offered. In fact, the economic and racial dynamics in Louisiana before the oil boom directly shaped the allotment of opportunity in the new oil economy. Although oil field wages undoubtedly provided an economic ascent for many farmers and émigrés, those who already possessed land, cash, or capital well before 1904 were the best-positioned to win in the new economy. Stories of rural farmers such as Walter Duvall George striking it rich may dominate the collective memory of North Louisiana's boomtowns, but the biggest winners were the large property owners, cash-rich companies, and white-collar investors with the resources necessary to undertake the considerable expenses of drilling, storing, and refining the oil. Oil City indeed created some new millionaires, but more often it made already wealthy individuals and companies even wealthier.[9]

The nascent oil economy also collided with North Louisiana's intensely white-supremacist government, economy, and society, which delineated sharp racial boundaries onto the new industry. Prior to the oil boom, nearly three quarters of Caddo Parish's population was Black and mainly worked as tenant farmers in the same rural areas as their enslaved ancestors. Following the Civil War, violence and lynchings proliferated across "Bloody Caddo" to reinforce the firm racial divides of Louisiana's cotton fields and government. White planters used threats and violence to keep their Black cotton field hands pliant, productive, and on the plantation. But as oil created a lucrative new source of cash wages, the economic motives behind that racial violence flipped: violence became a means of keeping North Louisiana's massive Black population *away* from the oil fields, so that any new jobs and wealth that oil production wrought would remain exclusively for the white migrants coming into the area. White managers, politicians, and oil field hands all projected their own racial prejudices onto an otherwise inert geological product, ensuring that white-supremacist boundaries would govern who could access the vast wealth from oil.

Individuals living through North Louisiana's oil boom witnessed astonishing changes not only to the region's economy but also to its natural environment. The industry's impact on the landscape was dramatic: oil fires that burned all day and night; rows of derricks pouring saltwater into freshwater lakes and streams; solid earth liquefying and churning into whirlpools. Oil derricks, pipelines, and massive pools of toxic runoff stood right alongside homes, restaurants, and brothels: a constant reminder of the industry that had drawn so many people to this place. But municipal services were largely absent in many of the boomtowns, resulting in rampant fires, impenetrable roads, and significant environmental devastation. As in previous American oil fields, investors regarded North Louisiana's boomtowns as a kind of "ruined locale" that inevitably would be abandoned once the crude dried up, and thus not worth more than a minimal investment in building materials, infrastructure, or general livability.[10]

The enduring fascination with rowdy boomtowns like Oil City also obscures a mundane but critical attribute of North Louisiana's oil boom: that the city of Shreveport was its biggest economic beneficiary. Although tent cities, hard drinking, and "Wild West" tales remain central to historical memories of the region's oil boom, Shreveport's urban offices, hotels, and tree-lined neighborhoods were its true headquarters, drawing, and, even more crucially, *retaining*, the largest share of the oil fields' people and money. Shreveport's political and economic elites disproportionately owned and managed much of North Louisiana's boomtown assets, from the oil field leases to the saloons and hotels adjacent to them.

The 1905 image of Savage-Morrical No. 1 conjured a Manifest Destiny oil field world in which prospectors ventured into the wilderness alone in search of El Dorado. But that hinterland was inextricably tethered to Shreveport's corporate headquarters, political bodies, and credit institutions. Boomtowns such as Oil City were bought, sold, and designed by Shreveport's urban elite: the Savages could not have cultivated that rural frontier without cash from the city's banks, permits from its political bureaucracy, or the land titles exchanged among its business class.

North Louisiana's rural oil fields may have produced the economic value at the core of the oil boom, but it was Shreveport's banks, land managers, and politicians who determined the ultimate destiny of all that money, and they generally allotted those critical resources into making Shreveport, their own community, ever more comfortable and prosperous while the boomtowns continued to languish. Such deliberate actions guaranteed that oil field communities such as Oil City languished in a crude state of disrepair, destined to remain boomtowns forever.

The rough and dangerous conditions of oil boomtowns like Oil City were not simply the inevitable products of the volatile natural resource extraction that underlay its economy. They were social, economic, and political constructions: the products of white supremacy in Louisiana's government and workplaces; of the economic hierarchies that preceded oil production; and of the active choices that North Louisiana's economic and political elites made to divest resources away from the oil field communities in order to enrich urban Shreveport instead. The boomtowns were very much oriented around the oil fields and their attendant natural wealth. But it remained within the agency of the region's people and institutions to improve the conditions of homes, roads, and businesses surrounding the derricks. Violence, tent cities, and environmental catastrophes may have been common traits of North Louisiana's oil boomtowns, but they were neither "natural" nor inevitable: they were man-made.

OIL CITIES

1 / THE BOOM

THE BIRTH OF LOUISIANA'S OIL INDUSTRY WAS PRECEDED by an iconic moment in American energy history—and one that occurred just across state lines. On January 10, 1901, a rotary drill operating on the "Spindletop" field near Beaumont, Texas, struck oil at 1,139 feet.[1] Spindletop was hardly the first successful oil well in the United States, nor was it the first site of production in Texas, where producers had already innovated the rotary drilling technique in Corsicana and Nacogdoches during the 1890s.[2] But the scale of Spindletop's production was unprecedented: as much as seventy-five thousand barrels flowed each day as it emitted a sonic roar that was audible for miles around.[3] Within months, Spindletop had elevated the southwestern United States into the new epicenter of US oil production, displacing earlier plays in Pennsylvania, Indiana, Illinois, and West Virginia.

This new flood of Texas oil fed a rapidly industrializing US market that was consuming petroleum at an accelerating rate. The proliferation of the internal combustion engine made refined gasoline a critical component across the American economy: automobiles, motor-driven farm equipment, planes, and industrial factories now needed oil to function.[4] Spindletop's geological composition was particularly suited for fueling power and locomotion, making railroad and steamship companies one of its largest consumers. The new and plentiful supply of crude not only satiated preexisting economic demand but also incentivized American industry to shift away from coal-fired power and toward oil by the first years of the twentieth century.[5]

Oil boomtowns had existed in the United States prior to Spindletop, but no communities had generated the same level of economic excitement or breakneck expansion. A maelstrom of people and money inundated the nearby city of Beaumont. By early 1901, more than sixteen thousand people had crowded into tents along the hills surrounding the gusher. Entrepreneurial boomers assembled primitive saloons, gambling halls, and brothels to meet the oil field migrants' varying economic needs. Among these nascent businesses, a fortune-teller named Madame la Monte sold her psychic ability to discern where the next big gusher could be found.[6] Even enterprising fraudsters earned their cut of the boom by selling fake oil field stock to credulous investors, a practice so widespread that "Swindletop" became an alternate term for the oil field.[7] The rapid pace of Spindletop's growth, as well as the improvised nature of its homes and businesses, would become a recurring dynamic across the boomtown communities that eventually spread across Louisiana and the oil-producing Southwest.

Just a few months into 1901, 214 wells stood in proximity on the hills surrounding Spindletop.[8] That so many wells lay within the immediate vicinity of each other reflected not only investor enthusiasm for acquiring Texas crude, but also the chaotic "Rule of Capture" doctrine governing oil production in the late nineteenth and early twentieth centuries. Although never codified in US law, Rule of Capture—alternatively known as "Law of Capture"—became a common-law rule that judges used to adjudicate property disputes over oil-bearing lands.[9] Since the earliest days of American oil production, the industry had been plagued by a consistent dilemma: when several investors leased drilling rights above the same pool of crude, which one had legal right to extract the crude below? Rule of Capture ascribes ownership to the party that reduces the underground product to their possession *first*.[10] In practical terms, this meant that the first driller to extract the oil had full economic rights over its value, even with multiple operations competing over the same resource.

Rule of Capture thus forced producers into an economic predicament: extract a salable product now, regardless of the current price, or risk allowing competitors to drain the reservoir from under their feet. Thousands made the self-interested decision to do the former, resulting in dense thickets of competing derricks operating next to each other in pursuit of the same resource. Such practices were individually rational but collectively destructive: by seeking immediate production over steadier, long-term production, drillers were depleting oil reservoirs of their underground pressure.[11] With less pressure to drive crude up to the surface, oil becomes less amenable to drilling, necessitating more expensive pumping to extract the product. This pursuit of immediate production had a predictably deleterious impact on Spindletop. Just one year after the iconic fountain of oil leapt from its hills, the relentless pace of drilling began to deplete Spindletop's underground pressure, resulting in declining production.[12]

Oil industry figures nonetheless remained confident that Spindletop's chaotic, if brief, success could be replicated somewhere else along the Gulf Coast. Speculators, geologists, and farmers alike set about looking for the same indications of underground petroleum that had augured the East Texas strike. Spindletop had become a kind of "training ground" for the oil industry at large, providing the first professional experience to a multitude of workers who ultimately disseminated those practices across the boomtowns that would materialize across Texas, Louisiana, Oklahoma, Arkansas, and beyond.[13] Producing atop Spindletop's "salt dome" geology had also established a set of expectations for how to successfully locate and drill future gushers. Common to the Gulf Coast, salt domes occur when evaporate materials like salt gradually push up through various layers of sediment, fashioning a visible arched structure, or dome, that can encase underground crude.[14]

Lacking modern seismic equipment, speculators and drillers looking for the Gulf Coast's next Spindletop largely sought out such above-ground indications, including arched domes, gas emerging from bayous, or large stretches of barren farmland.[15] Therefore, when gas seepages, the same natural indications that had foretold the Spindletop gusher, became apparent on the hills of Mamou Prairie just outside of Jennings, Louisiana, speculative activity migrated eastward across state lines. According to one source, such discharges had been manifesting in Southwest Louisiana well before Spindletop. In 1938, Jennings native T. C. (Thomas Clayton) Mahaffey produced a short memoir claiming that in April 1893 a German homesteader entered his store and told a remarkable story: after dropping his lit match into a local spring, the German allegedly witnessed a "flash of fire over the water."[16]

Originally from Pennsylvania, where oil production had already been a fixture of the nineteenth-century economy, Mahaffey speculated that the seepages were the result of underground oil reserves. Those suspicions were confirmed when the German drilled two holes into the ground, lit a match, and witnessed gas flares burn all night. Ultimately, though, Mahaffey "forgot all about the gas" until 1901, when Spindletop's seminal gusher sent investors and speculators in search of seepages across the Gulf Coast.[17] Mahaffey would become a significant figure in the development of Jennings's oil production. Along with fellow investors Dr. Avery Wilkins, S. A. Spencer, F. R. Jaenke, and I. D. Williams, Mahaffey formed the S. A. Spencer Company, which leased nearly two thousand acres of the Jennings prairie land where gas seepages had been manifesting.[18]

In need of the expertise and technology to extract the underlying oil, Spencer and Mahaffey went to Beaumont, whose access to Spindletop had transformed the town into a major hub of oil patch investors, labor, and capital. Spencer and Mahaffey acquired the services of wildcatter W. S. (Walter Scott) Heywood, one of four brothers from Ohio with prior drilling experience in California and Texas. The Heywood drillers and the Spencer Company merged to become the Jennings Oil Company and issued stock to fund their investment, primarily soliciting buyers in Beaumont.[19] In June 1901, Heywood transported a sixty-four-foot drilling rig from Beaumont onto an especially promising forty-acre plot in the rolling prairies outside of Jennings.

The lessor of these forty acres was Jules Clement, an Acadian rice farmer who owned much of the rural prairie lands emitting the gaseous seepages.[20] But even as the prospect of untold fortunes beckoned, the farmer allegedly balked at the prospect of transforming his land into a forest of derricks. According to W. S. Heywood's recollections, Clement abruptly locked the gates of his property to prevent the drilling from commencing, fearing that "his cattle would break their legs in the holes [that would come from oil production]."[21] Clement further protested that even if there were good production, he "wouldn't know what to do with the oil."[22] But Heywood ultimately secured Clement's permission to drill, assuaging the farmer's concerns by paying an advance bonus to compensate for any potential damage to his crops or livestock.

By Heywood's telling, Clement's ambivalence was utterly irrational—the quaint, antiquated ideas of a rural farmer unschooled in this modern new industry. However, as other local rice farmers in and around Jennings would later discover, allowing oil production near their crops and freshwater sources would indeed result in significant environmental and economic costs, suggesting that Clement's initial reticence was hardly irrational. In fact, his hesitancy foreshadowed the wider economic and political contests that drillers would encounter in Southwest Louisiana over oil production. Landowning rice farmers had a real stake in the land and were not always eager to unconditionally embrace a new extractive industry.

Clement's initial reluctance now overcome, the Heywood brothers proceeded to drill on their lease throughout 1901. The Jennings prairies may have produced similar aboveground indications as Spindletop, but they contained unique geological conditions underneath. Unlike the more porous limestone that prevailed in East Texas, Jennings's sandy soil persistently caved in on the well and ruined production, prompting Heywood to apply a steel screen that would keep the well clear.[23] And while Spindletop's well became a gusher at around one thousand feet, that depth produced nothing on Clement's land. Heywood convinced his investors to import more drilling pipe that would allow him to reach a depth of fifteen hundred feet, prompting many stockholders of the Jennings Oil Company to anxiously unload their shares. Dissent even emerged among the brothers, with W. S. forced into the position of convincing the others to continue drilling.[24]

At seventeen hundred feet, W. S. Heywood was vindicated. On September 21, 1901, a stream of crude oil emerged from the Jules Clement No. 1 well, becoming the first successful well in the state of Louisiana.[25] Having established the productivity of the site, the Heywood brothers subleased their tract to other

FIGURE 1.1. *A 1907 view of the Jennings oil field shows the oil derricks' proximity. The "ponds" in the foreground are earthen tanks storing crude oil.*

drillers, transforming a rural stretch of prairiel and into a dense industrial forest of derricks. Guided by the same Rule of Capture doctrine, rapid production ensued among drillers trying to extract the most product at the fastest rate. Unable to afford more elaborate storage tanks, many drillers pooled any oil they extracted into massive earthen tanks carved out of the ground. According to Heywood, such earthen pits at one time held seven million barrels of oil, becoming so enormous that armed company watchmen bobbed in rowboats atop the black "ponds" at night to prevent theft.[26] Such recollections may be more folkloric than pure historical truth, but they still capture the dramatic changes that were swiftly transforming Jennings's land and economy.

DRILLING IN LOUISIANA

In the summer of 1902, *Oil Investors' Journal*, an industry newsletter published out of Beaumont, Texas, triumphantly announced, "JENNINGS [*sic*] WHERE THE OIL WELLS ARE." Articles optimistically described the Southwest Louisiana town as a "growing city of five thousand" brimming with "thrifty . . . well-to-do" people and "graceful architecture."[27] The town also boasted an ideal geographic location. Easily accessible to the Southern Pacific Railroad's main line, the Gulf of Mexico, and the Mermentau River, the oil field's crude could reach distant markets either by barge or rail. Although the Jennings boom was "slow in starting," many "Beaumont operators . . . visited the field" to see it for themselves. Local stores even promoted their town's new industry, placing "the gusher picture . . . in every shop window."[28]

This dramatic transition of energy and investment from Spindletop to Jennings presaged a dynamic that would recur throughout the region's oil fields: workers, capital, and technology were always ready to pull up stakes in search of the next, more productive oil field. Rule of Capture incentives only accelerated the pace of such migrations. By engaging in shortsighted, dense production, the industry was in constant need of the next boom as previous sites became depleted and unproductive.

The *Oil Investors' Journal* expressed further confidence that Jennings's success would transform Louisiana into a new center of American oil production. In the September 1902 issue, geologist C. F. Z. Caracristi asserted that the bayou state would "in a few years become a greater petroleum producer than Texas."[29] Others were betting that something even larger lay underground; a "popular belief with oil men and others" held that a massive new pocket of crude lay under the Southwest, an "oil belt . . . of greater magnitude than has heretofore been thought of, [extending] from the South Texas coast eastwardly to and beyond the Mississippi River." The development of such an "oil belt" could produce "oil in quantities sufficient to supply the needs of the world."[30]

Jennings's bucolic setting even seemed to portend economic success. According to the *Oil Investors' Journal*, the wells were surrounded by "wooded ridges" fanned with "Fresh breezes" and "meadow grass" that provided "relief to the workmen, whose hands and faces are tanned brown by the hot sun."[31] Jennings's verdant lands hosted not only the emerging petroleum industry, but also a thriving rice-growing community. Irrigation canals were lined within sight of the oil field, making "one think of California and the great west land."[32] The *Journal*'s heavily romanticized account promoted Jennings as a place brimming with economic and environmental advantages: a ready market of oil-consuming rice producers living in an abundant landscape ready for industry.

Spindletop lay just a few dozen miles from the state line, but Louisiana's political and economic environment would frame the nascent industry in very distinct ways. Since the end of the Civil War and the abolishment of slavery, the Democratic Party had dominated state politics in both Louisiana and Texas, albeit in pursuit of slightly different ideological objectives. The Texans' Democratic platform largely reflected the late nineteenth-century concerns of Agrarian and Populist Democrats: rural farmers distrustful of large corporate trusts, particularly the railroad companies with the ability to set rates on moving staple crops.[33] Those Populist ideals, and distrust of non-Texas corporate entities, would uniquely frame how Texas interacted with its oil sector.

The ascent of Democrat Jim Hogg in late nineteenth-century Texas politics embodied the party's adoption of rural Populist ideals, particularly as it related to regulating large, "foreign" businesses from outside the state. As attorney general and then as governor, Hogg regarded the federal government, railroad companies, and other "extra-Texas" corporate interests as all part of a "malevolent, anti-Texas conspiracy to throttle the state's economic development." State regulatory bodies such as the Railroad Commission were not neutral arbiters, but rather an "offensive weapon" against "non-Texas competition."[34] In 1889, Texas adopted sweeping anti-trust legislation to protect local agricultural producers from competing with the corporate monopolies that had steadily expanded their influence over more and more segments of the US economy since the end of the Civil War.[35]

The Democratic Party's efforts to eliminate any non-Texas economic competition also characterized its regulatory stances on the state's emergent oil industry. After the discovery of oil in Corsicana, Texas had become a major contributor of crude into the US market, as well as host to the refining and transportation capacity in the state's east.[36] The 1889 anti-trust legislation prevented consolidation and integration among the state's oil firms, ensuring that *Texas* producers were largely free of competition. Even Jim Hogg himself managed to profit from the protectionism he helped enact following his retirement from politics in 1895, first as a partner in the Hogg-Swayne oil syndicate and then as a founding member of the Texas Fuel Company, which would become the iconic Texaco.[37] Ultimately, Texas Democrats such as Hogg did not wish to exterminate industrial wealth, but to ensure they would only enrich *Texans* like themselves.

Most notably, the state's anti-trust law ensured that Standard Oil, the most notorious of all "extra-Texas" corporate trusts, was not able to operate in the state. However, that did not stop Standard from trying. In 1900, the US Supreme Court ruled that the locally chartered oil firm Waters-Pierce was secretly functioning as a financial conduit for Standard in Texas and ordered the revocation of its company charter.[38] And yet Standard Oil, via Waters-Pierce, continued its pursuit of Texas oil. After paying $3,300 to the US senator from Texas, Joseph Bailey—ostensibly to settle a personal loan—Waters-Pierce managed with Senator Bailey's help to secure a new corporate charter on the promise that they sever their connection to Standard.[39] But in 1906, the Texas attorney general enacted new proceedings against the company, charging that it had continued to serve as an agent of the Standard Oil trust. The state's efforts to actively reign in Standard and other non-Texas trusts embraced a strategy of using regulatory bodies to maintain a rural, agrarian society while also fostering a "self-sustaining, wholly Texas economy."[40]

Meanwhile, to the east of the state border, Louisiana remained a firm bastion of more conservative "Bourbon" Democratic politics that preached a laissez-faire, pro-business philosophy to the benefit of a narrow class of white elites. Since the end of Reconstruction, a "merchant-banker-planter" power alliance had managed Louisiana's political affairs through a highly parochial and oligarchic system. Using the opaque Democratic Primary process as a closed and tightly managed election, Bourbons filled the state government with officials who dutifully prioritized the interests of large plantation owners and urban merchants. Democrats nominally idealized the self-sufficient Jeffersonian yeoman farmer, but merely as public relations to promote their oligarchic structure before a largely agrarian state. In reality, their policies consistently aligned with the "agrarian monopoly" of wealthy merchants and planters as they bought more and more of Louisiana's farmland, a dynamic that pushed the state's farming yeomen further into tenancy and crop liens.[41]

White supremacy was also a core governing ideology of Baton Rouge's political elite. Bourbon Democrats catalyzed virulent racism into a brutal legislative agenda designed to reimpose political and economic segregation across the state following the end of Reconstruction. Much like other parts of the postbellum American South, Louisiana experienced an extraordinary, if momentary, glimpse of increased racial equity in politics, business, and society following the Civil War. Between 1877 and 1900, Black Louisianans participated in state elections, held public offices, served on juries, and even rode alongside white passengers on city streetcars. Most remarkably, the number of registered Black voters actually eclipsed those of white voters in Louisiana between 1880 and 1896.[42]

However, by the last decade of the nineteenth century, the conservative Bourbons had assumed full control over the levers of state government and severely foreclosed on Louisiana's racial experiment, introducing sweeping Jim Crow legislation mandating racial segregation in public places, transit, and marital relationships. This political assault on Louisiana's Black citizenry culminated in the 1898 Constitutional Convention, in which Bourbons collaborated with more "reformist" white Democrats, their erstwhile political adversaries, to eradicate Black suffrage. Louisiana's amended state constitution adopted ballot "reforms" similar to those in other "Redeemed" Democrat-run southern states, fabricating new property and education qualifications to explicitly disenfranchise Black citizens. The outcome was swift and unequivocal: between 1890 and 1900, the number of registered Black voters fell from 127,000 to 5,000.[43] Alluvial parishes with the highest Black populations, such as Caddo Parish's Red River Valley, lost virtually all their Black voters overnight.

As oil production began migrating from Texas into Southwest Louisiana, the industry operated within this distinct political environment of Bourbon Democratic dominance, where a laissez-faire economic philosophy reigned and the state enforced a firm white supremacy in government, business, and society at large. This fostered an economic space in which private enterprise—even monopolistic concerns such as Standard Oil—could freely invest with minimal government interference. That political context also assured that white managers and workers alike would have a free hand to uphold white supremacy in their workplaces; conversely, vulnerable Black workers trying to maintain their safety and earn fair wages would not be protected by the state. However, these political conditions were not uniform across Louisiana. Local differences would still prevail, as particular "Police Juries," Louisiana's regional governing bodies, still interacted with their constituencies and local industries in very distinct ways.

The oil industry also encountered unique geological and environmental circumstances as it drilled the sandy prairies of Southwest Louisiana. Even the crude itself bore distinct chemical properties, making it better suited to particular materials and industries. While the composition of Spindletop's crude ideally translated into refined gasoline, Jennings yielded a more "aromatic" type that was better suited for the pharmaceutical market. Accordingly, Louisiana's first refinery, which opened in Jennings in 1903, focused on transforming local crude into medicinal products such as "Alboleum," or Russian white oil. The refinery expanded in 1907 to incorporate a chemical plant that produced terpene in addition to other largely pharmaceutical products.[44] Jennings's unique geological landscape thus had a ripple effect on the economy that developed around the oil industry, shaping what kinds of labor, production, and profits could be achieved in the emergent fields.

As Jennings's crude oil production expanded, so did the accompanying infrastructure necessary to its transportation and refining. Louisiana's hydrological system provided a critical means of bringing that product to market. Bodies of water such as Bayou Nezpique, the Atchafalaya River, and the Mermentau River became active barging routes, providing an accessible means of moving fuel from refiner to consumer. In 1905, the firm Carnes, Bass and Bencheinstein began constructing Louisiana's first pipeline for transporting petroleum. The line spanned fifty-eight miles between Jennings and the Atchafalaya River, where the crude was barged to the Plaquemine Bayou and then moved through shorter pipe to the Mississippi River, on which it could access markets both upriver and down. Once this transportation network was completed, estimated the *Oil Investors' Journal*, between five thousand and seven thousand barrels of Jennings crude could move from well to market each day.[45]

But Southwest Louisiana's waterways also created enormous obstacles to production and transportation. As Carnes, Bass and Bencheinstein attempted to complete its pipeline, the region's "low, swampy country" was turning construction into a Herculean task. Pipeliners had to endure water "to a depth of ten and twenty feet" with the last "ength [sic] miles at the east end . . . all swamp." Conditions were so unpredictable that engineers had to suspend construction until

FIGURE I.2. *A 1902 image of a well in Jennings that burned for six days.*

late in the summer, when water levels ebbed. Even by then, the environmental circumstances remained challenging. Workers had to drop pipelines into the water from "barges and boats." And all the while, surrounding vegetation created a thick "jungle . . . the men had to cut their way through."[46]

The environmental issues surrounding oil production in Jennings were most vividly captured in "The Jennings Gusher Fire," a short pamphlet published in 1902 by Holland S. Reavis, general agent for the Jennings Oil Company. Photographs and a brief narrative tell the dramatic story of a massive "gusher fire" that ignited when lightning struck a well on July 15, 1902. The fire burned for six straight days, destroying two twelve-hundred-barrel settling tanks and costing the company between $10,000 and $15,000. Alongside photographs depicting massive tunnels of smoke, the pamphlet described workers hauling water boilers from the Jennings railroad station, a process requiring "twelve and sometimes sixteen horses"[47] to push the massive objects through the mud. A struggle between industry and nature vividly unfolds in "The Jennings Gusher Fire," a far cry from the *Oil Investors' Journal*'s accounts of fresh breezes and wooded ridges.

THE PEOPLE OF JENNINGS

Jennings's oil production may have attracted waves of new jobs and companies, but those changes did not occur within an economic vacuum with no vestiges of industry. Since its 1883 Anglo settlement, largely by midwestern (namely Iowan) farmers, Jennings had been a center of industrial agriculture, achieving higher rice production through technological innovation.[48] In the 1880s, midwestern transplant Maurice Bryan successfully modified the "twine binder" method (typically used for cultivating wheat) to harvest Jennings rice, mechanizing and expanding a process that had previously been done by hand and sickle. Contemporaneously, irrigation companies were building new networks of canals and pumping stations to provide more consistent water sources. Such acts of engineering expanded production and resulted in higher yields, pushing the acreage of Jennings rice lands under cultivation from roughly 1,000 in 1884 to 201,685 by 1899.[49]

Jennings's burgeoning centers of oil production thus had to coexist with an already dynamic economy of industrial agriculture, and initially that new energy economy complemented preexisting industries. Locally produced fuel oil became cheap, accessible energy to a variety of businesses associated with the production and transportation of rice, including canal-building operations and mills.[50] Nearby rice irrigation pumping plants also became significant local consumers of Jennings fuel. According to the *Oil Investor's Journal*, every such plant within a thirty-mile radius of the fields used oil burners by 1902, allowing them to achieve greater production at a lower cost.[51]

Oil production also offered the prospect of steadier wages to farmers accustomed to seasonal production. When oil derricks sprouted on adjacent lands, local rice farmers rushed to finish their annual harvest so they could earn cash wages in the new local business.[52] Farmers who owned land in and around the oil-producing Mamou Prairie could easily sell or lease their property to oil wild-catters under highly favorable terms. Other locals simply chose to invest in oil stocks as they continued to cultivate rice, using the new industry as a means of financing a preexisting one rather than as a replacement.[53]

However, oil and rice production increasingly began to compete for space and resources across Jennings. Accordingly, new environmental and economic contests emerged across the prairies and bayous, particularly with respect to water. In 1906 the Jennings oil fields began producing large quantities of salt-water, a worthless byproduct that drillers sought to hastily expel. Producers did so by releasing the discharge into nearby bayous, invading a crucial source of freshwater to rice irrigation.[54] Increased canal digging had provided rice farms with better access to more distant water sources, but now it inadvertently exposed them to the industrial consequences of oil production as well.

Rice farmers responded to these hydrological threats by mobilizing. In 1906 the Heywood Brothers received a letter from rice producers in western Acadia Parish threatening legal action if their oil wells did not stop sending saltwater into local waterways: "We will be forced to begin proceedings at once unless the operators upon the field will agree to discontinue the drainage of Salt Water into the above named Bayou without litigation." The Heywood Brothers evidently did not take the threat as idle and resolved to store their saltwater product during the May–September rice irrigation season, retrofitting earthen tanks "at a great expense."[55] In a 1909 letter, W. Scott Heywood further described the saltwater issue as a "great hardship" that "retards development greatly from April until September."[56] And this was just one episode. In 1907 and 1909, rice farmers in Crowley, just outside of Jennings, signed similar petitions to the district attorney when saltwater runoff invaded Bayou des Cannes, a water source their farms accessed via the Abbott-Duson canal.[57]

The rice farmers' political mobilization was remarkably successful, coalescing into new regulatory statutes from state agencies. In 1910, the Louisiana Conservation Commission established a new "hold-and-release" policy mandating that oil field operators find methods to contain their saltwater between September and March—water-pumping months for rice producers.[58] During the winter months, when the rainier climate would dilute the runoff's salinity, producers would be allowed to discharge the saltwater. The Conservation Commission eventually earned a reputation for uneven, and perhaps even corrupted, regulation. But on this occasion their edict regarding saltwater successfully deterred producers from using waterways as industrial dumping grounds.

That Louisiana's laissez-faire political system would intervene underscored the significant political and economic clout that rice farmers could wield in the southwestern corner of the state. Economically well-established prior to oil production, Jennings's local farming communities represented a formidable constituency for the industry to face in the courts and in local government. But such economic and political roadblocks to oil production were largely unique to this corner of Louisiana. Oil producers would scarcely encounter such burdens when they eventually migrated to the northern reaches of the state, which would offer a far more acquiescent political and economic climate for the industry.

THE END OF JENNINGS'S BOOM

Much like Spindletop, in Jennings the advent of oil production brought excitement and opportunity, but also a new atmosphere of economic and social volatility. W. Scott Heywood recalled a "wild boom . . . of saloons, dance halls, honkey-tonks, gambling houses, boarding houses, restaurants . . . and all classes of people, with fights, murders and everything that usually goes on in a boom of that kind." He further described an incident in which a landowner refused a pipeline crew the right of way through his property, only to find the workers digging under the cover of night. The landowner promptly gathered a mob bearing "hammers, stones, clubs" to halt the process.[59] According to one contemporary editorial, the prospect of oil work even paradoxically attracted individuals with little motivation to work:

> There is a good number of loungers and idlers hanging around the corners today, especially around the depot. This morning a business man was heard to offer some of these loungers twenty cents per hour to work. Their reply was, "We don't care to work." Some of them are filthy and dirty and not fit to appear in public. We have a great many visitors in town now, and we should make it appear to advantage.[60]

However, there is evidence to suggest that such tales of boomtown violence were overstated and that, in fact, violent crime in Jennings remained relatively stable during the oil migration.[61] There were a variety of reasons for this relative calm, the most notable of which was the presence of robust municipal and civic organizations that preceded oil production. Unlike many other boomtowns to come—notably, Oil City—industry figures did not encounter an ill-funded, provincial local government without the resources to manage the multitude of civic challenges that an oil boom presents.

Even within the first years of the Jennings discovery, business and government officials were already keenly aware of the industry's volatile and fickle nature. Civic and commercial leaders accordingly sought to temper their town's rough-and-tumble boomtown identity by promoting Jennings as a stable and wholesome place to live and work that would thrive with or without oil. In 1903, the town of Jennings published "The City of Jennings, Louisiana," a pamphlet that presented their town as an economically diversified, safe place to do business, both in the present and in the years to come. Describing Jennings as "the Coming Metropolis of Southwest Louisiana" and a "City with a Brilliant Future,"[62] the document enumerated a diverse array of local businesses: insurance brokers, liveries, banks, clothiers, and rice mills among them. Photographs depicted the ornate brick buildings and comfortable homes their proprietors had built. This promotional document made the case that, despite the happy presence of oil money, Jennings was by no means an *Oil Boomtown* of booms and busts, but rather a prosperous and stable community.

Depictions of the elaborate new businesses that oil production funded may have been promotional, but they were not exaggerations. J. M. Hoag grew up in boomtown-era Jennings and recalled the transformative changes that oil brought to the community: a new country club with "a huge wooden building" was "brought on by the oil discovery," in addition to an indoor swimming pool, a bowling alley, and a dance floor. Jennings even boasted an opera house, where a young Hoag went to see "Goldilocks and the Three Bears"—much to the chagrin of a local Methodist minister who would publicly chastise locals for attending the "sinful" theatrical productions. But alongside those tony theaters and country clubs, the grime and filth of oil production remained ever present. According to Hoag, her father used to take children from the local orphanage to the stagnant pools of saltwater runoff, where he let the young orphans swim in the briny ponds to alleviate mosquito bites or scratches.[63]

Jennings released another promotional pamphlet in 1907, once again cheerfully reporting even more economic and civic growth—albeit with an undercurrent of anxiety about the future. Just a quarter century earlier, Jennings had been just a "prairie, over which roamed herds of cattle and horses." But now the "Queen City of Southern Louisiana" stood as home to "five thousand prosperous, contented, happy people!" The pamphlet artfully conveyed that transformation through photographic collages and romantic histories. A pair of panoramic images compared dusty, remote Main Street in 1891 to the same space in 1906, where streams of people now walked alongside dramatic new brick buildings and a widened road.[64] Glossy photographs also captured innovative rice threshers, irrigation plants, and newly dug canals bringing ever more wealth and production to Jennings. Much like in the 1903 pamphlet, civic boosters conjured Jennings as the "Rice *and* Oil City of Southwestern Louisiana," with a diversified economy in which modern technology was buoying all its industries, old and new.

However, on the topic of Jennings's most prominent business, the document assumed a more defensive posture, asserting that its oil field "is the greatest in the South if not in the world," an objectively dubious statement at the time. But the author did acknowledge the existence of dissenting voices who would question the "durability of the Jennings Oil Field." Dismissing such speculation as the idle "chatter" of "speculators and jealous knownothings," the author asserted that, based upon unspecified "geological data," the Jennings oil field would remain a "very good producer for years and years to come, outlasting easily the present generation of mankind . . . especially the fraternity of croakers, wanderers and salt-water sharks."[65] That a promotional civic document would adopt such an acerbic tone only underscored the latent unease that existed about the future of Jennings's oil production and its role in the local economy; ostensibly produced to illustrate the vibrancy and diversity of the town's economy, this 1907 document does precisely the opposite by obliquely acknowledging the centrality of oil.

Indeed the "fraternity of croakers, wanderers and salt-water sharks" was eventually validated, as Jennings's crude production would ultimately peak by 1906. The wave of businesses, people, and enthusiasm that had arrived in the wake of the Jules Clement No. 1 began to subside. J. M. Hoag recalled that when "the oil started to slow down . . . the money mongers left with it."[66] The opera house, country club, and various hotels catering to well-heeled oilmen vanished. Although Jennings's preexisting rice mills and railroad depot positioned the town to maintain some of its economic vitality, the heady oil rush days were over. Despite the civic boosters' deluded efforts to make the boom more permanent, Jennings discovered the same truism that many other resource boomtowns before them had already learned and would continue to learn: their newfound wealth ultimately rested upon a temporal and fickle product.[67] In August 1909, *Oil Investors' Journal* reported a strange "mad dog" epidemic in which dogs around Jennings's remaining oil wells were mysteriously dying. "Poor old Jennings," the piece facetiously lamented. "We knew she had gone to the dogs as compared with the glorious days of 1904, 1905 and 1906, but we didn't know it was so hard on the dogs!"[68]

Jules Clement, lessor of Louisiana's first successful oil lease, by all accounts became very wealthy from the years of oil royalties. According to Clement's 1957 obituary, the Jennings farmer was still drawing money from the lease he signed fifty-six years earlier.[69] But census records indicate that any wealth that Clement may have accumulated did not drastically alter the fabric of his family's life. In 1920 and 1940, he remained in the same corner of Southwest Louisiana, still listed as a farmer.[70] Assuming Clement amassed a great deal of wealth from Louisiana's inaugural oil well, he did not use it to acquire a fundamentally different lifestyle. That decision would stand in contrast to the oil lessors of North Louisiana, many of whom used their newfound wealth to flee industry boomtowns such as Oil City in favor of safer, more sanitary, and more cosmopolitan trappings.

The year 1906 was not the end of Jennings's oil industry. As demand improved and drilling technologies advanced, investment would ultimately return to its prairies by the end of the 1920s, albeit at a more modest pace.[71] But the rapid migration away from Jennings still very much reflected an industry that was largely focused on booms rather than more efficient, steadier production. Technological limitations and perverse Rule of Capture-driven incentives pushed drillers to accumulate as much oil as possible, often at the expense of long-term production. With such a dense sea of competing derricks pumping alongside each other, any firm choosing to produce more gradually was effectively ceding product to its competitors. Immediate extraction was paramount. Therefore, when Jennings peaked, the industry began to pivot its capital and money toward the next boom: North Louisiana.

2 / THE COMMUNITIES

TO WHAT DEGREE DID OIL CREATE OIL CITY AND ITS SUR-
rounding boomtowns? The emergence of Louisiana's oil economy was
undoubtedly the major agent of historic change, generating the wealth and
jobs that attracted migrants from across the United States—and indeed from
around the world—to such a remote corner of North Louisiana. Oil City's
spatial language very much reflected the volatile nature of its principal business: hastily built shacks and tents exemplified the need to house people
quickly and cheaply, given the expectation that the community would probably cease to exist once the oil wells diminished. Meanwhile, the sea of largely
male workers fed a rowdy social atmosphere of drinking and violence that
became synonymous with the notorious boomtown world.

But a closer examination of North Louisiana's boomtowns reveals that oil
was not the only historical force shaping the emergence of these communities.
Boomtowns were not solely developed for optimal access to the rigs, but also
to express social and political values. While many of these new communities
coalesced around the oil fields, others specifically coalesced *away* from the violence, drinking, and primitive housing that communities like Oil City exemplified. One company town was even born as a social and economic *reaction*
against the boomtown model: it was a new kind of oil field community where
families could pursue wholesome lives among tree-lined streets free of saloons
and brothels, and perhaps of racial miscegenation.

Oil field communities like Oil City were not simply "natural" reflections of
the oil business, but deliberate social, economic, and political creations—and
deliberate acts of *indifference*. The violence, drinking, and lawlessness that prevailed were not inevitable, but rather the product of a lack of investment and
political will. Even though Oil City's tents and shacks reflected an implicit
pessimism about its civic future, the town still could have been configured
into a different kind of community, a fact demonstrated by "alternative"

communities like Mooringsport and Trees City that were developed nearby with specific social and economic agendas. Oil may have brought people to North Louisiana, but social and political values still dictated the precise shape and form of the communities they occupied.

THE BIRTH OF "OIL CITY"

Before oil production lured thousands of migrants into North Louisiana, the place that would become "Oil City" was just a remote stop along the Kansas City Southern railroad. One 1904 map of Caddo Parish contains no "Oil City," just a small dot on its approximate spot about thirty miles north of Shreveport listed as "Surry." Alternatively recorded as "Sury," "Surrey," or "Annias," the small hamlet subsisted on a modest sawmilling economy, sending its locally sourced logs to depots in Shreveport via the KCS rail line. The 1900 federal census listed railroad workers, wheelwrights, farm laborers, and log haulers among its sparse residents.[1]

By 1904, oil industry speculators began betting that this remote corner of the American South could replicate the success of Jennings and Spindletop before it. Geological indications that petroleum lay below the North Louisiana and East Texas border had been apparent since 1870, when a water well feeding a Shreveport ice manufacturer began emitting flammable gas.[2] In the spring of 1904, Dr. Frank H. Morrical of Beaumont, Texas, became the first investor to bet on the potential of North Louisiana's oil fields, signing sixteen leases with Caddo Parish landowners on behalf of the Shreveport-based Caddo Lake Oil and Pipeline Company. Dr. Morrical must have been a shrewd negotiator, as the leases he brokered would pay landowners a one-tenth royalty in addition to a $100 annual sum, both of which were below the customary one-eighth royalty and typically higher bonuses that lessors would have expected in similar contracts.[3]

A peripatetic doctor originally from Virginia, Dr. Morrical previously spent time in Chicago, Missouri, and East Texas before going into the oil business alongside drillers W. A. and J. S. Savage, brothers with experience in the West Virginia and Texas fields.[4] The Savages' migration across West Virginia, Texas, and Louisiana mirrored oil production's dynamic mobility—and the industry's ability to quickly pivot its capital and labor onto a new landscape. Morrical and the Savage brothers came into Caddo Parish having already achieved considerable success drilling other sites, particularly the Sour Lake and Spindletop fields of Texas, leading one contemporary oil operator to observe they had enjoyed "more good things than anybody in the business."[5]

In May 1904, the Savage brothers began drilling on one of the rural leases Morrical had acquired near Surry, where they erected the Savage-Morrical No. 1, North Louisiana's first oil derrick.[6] Sources differ on the initial success of Savage-Morrical No. 1. One newspaper account from February 1905 reported a strike at 1,546 feet, causing Shreveport to become "mildly excited . . . owing to the fact that many persons in that city own land near the well" and that the price of adjoining lands had "gone up with a whirl."[7] However, in a 1911 report to the American Institute of Mining Engineers, geologist Walter Hopper offered a far milder assessment. By Hopper's account, the Savage-Morrical No. 1 produced only a small amount of oil before being abandoned in January 1906.[8]

Although Savage-Morrical No. 1 did not produce an immediate bonanza, the Savage brothers' spike unleashed a flurry of new speculative activity in and around Surry. Drillers began to establish the outlines of a new reservoir: the Caddo oil field. An enormous pool of crude largely concentrated between Clear Lake to the northeast and Caddo Lake to the southwest, the Caddo field rapidly became Louisiana's most explored source of supply. In 1908 the Caddo field collectively produced just under half a million barrels, still a pittance compared to Spindletop's ceiling of seventy-five thousand barrels per day. But in the following year, Caddo's figure doubled, and its growth continued over the succeeding years. Six years after the Savage Brothers erected the region's first derrick, *Oil Investors' Journal* declared a new epicenter of Louisiana's oil industry: "Caddo Now Center of Interest." The article also referred to the burgeoning new community of oil field workers that had sprung up alongside it: *Oil City*.[9]

As production soared across Caddo Field, so did the demand for housing across the adjoining Oil City. In 1907, Caddo Parish land fetched an average of $25 to $50 an acre; just one year later, that figure reached $500 to $1,000 per acre.[10] To meet such heavy demand, a new class of developers began subdividing land around the derricks, drawing new lines that would further transform the sparsely populated depot of Surry into the densely packed Oil City. Caddo Parish landowner John S. Noel was among the early developers who ushered in such dramatic changes to North Louisiana's economic and community life. In 1900, Noel was a merchant, planter, and lumber investor who owned a slice of rural lands alongside the Kansas City Southern rail line.[11] By 1907, the influx of oil migrants had increased the value of that land exponentially, prompting Noel to subdivide his auspiciously located property into 180 lots that he could sell into the boom.[12]

The "Plat of Oil City" Noel submitted to the Caddo Parish surveyor in Shreveport for approval in 1907 offered an embryonic look at Oil City's urban contours. The document's clean, elegant perimeters belied the frenzied and chaotic boomtown that would come to occupy the property: each geometric lot would become the offices, saloons, pool halls, and hotels that would assume the economic and social fabric of Oil City. Until his death in 1920, Noel sold his Caddo Parish land plot by plot to aspiring business owners, many of whom became iconic figures in the Oil City community. In 1911, Noel sold lot 23 of Block "B" to James K. Norman and his wife, Ida, future proprietors of the Norman Hotel, a prominent space for oil field workers to live and socialize. The original sale stipulated that Norman would not "allow any intoxicating liquors to be sold or gambling to be carried on," parameters to which he and his wife did not adhere.[13]

During the last decade of his life, Noel's investments enabled him to fully transition from rural planter to Shreveport real estate speculator, joining the ranks of other middle-class industry figures who ascended into the city as oil became the preeminent local business. More broadly, Noel's move away from his rural property and into the urban business world reveals two bordering communities under transition. In 1900, the value of Noel's land resided in its railroad access, an ideal point to transport and broker raw agricultural goods. However, as thousands of migrants suddenly descended upon the oil derricks, an even better opportunity materialized in subdividing and selling those parcels to the variety of hoteliers, barmen, and other investors looking to profit from that new population density. These dynamics were at the core of Surry's evolution from a quiet, rural town into Oil City, a dense boomtown—as well as Shreveport's budding role as an urban enclave for ascendant, middle-class investors such as Noel who stood to benefit from that transition.

AT HOME IN OIL CITY

Production and land prices rose so rapidly that new living quarters had to be erected quickly and efficiently—very often at the expense of domestic comfort. For many individuals looking to work in the oil fields, simply pitching a tent alongside the derricks was standard. John F. Law grew up with a roughneck father in the Caddo oil fields and described their neighborhood as a "settlement of shacks" alongside the rigs.[14] Claude McFarland labored on the rigs and recalled workers "had to live where they worked," estimating that by about 1910, somewhere around five thousand men were living "all over the woods in tents."[15] McFarland's figure may have been exaggerated, but his recollection, inflated or not, nonetheless captured the desperate and improvised housing situation that many Caddo oil field workers encountered.

Such hastily built clusters of tents offered virtually no distance between the modest domesticity of home and the industrial churn of oil production. In 1907, prominent Caddo Parish landowner William Pierce (or W. P.) Stiles leased his

3,254-acre property to Mike Benedum and Joe Trees, experienced drillers from Pittsburgh who operated as Benedum and Trees. Much of the production on Stiles's lease emerged from "Stacy's Landing," a sloping piece of shoreline adjacent to Jeem's Bayou. Stiles's land was "wild . . . some of it almost impenetrable . . . country" covered in high grass, fog, and lacking any roads or trails.[16] A 1910 image captured the remarkable hybrid of home and work life that Benedum and Trees employees endured on Stacy's Landing. Shrouded by trees and derricks, a collection of densely packed white canvas tents clung to the hillside just meters from the water—a precarious spot given the area's tendency to flood. Taken from the opposite side of Jeem's Bayou, the photograph also revealed a skiff floating just offshore, an indication of how workers might have reached the other side of the bayou, where downtown Oil City and the Kansas City Southern rail lines lay.

Another aerial shot of Stacy's Landing depicted an extraordinary feature of this industrial home-work space: a small patch of gardens right alongside the derricks, and mere yards away from a sprawling earthen tank bearing oil, saltwater, or some other viscous drilling product.[17] Given the garden's modest size, it is likely that employees used it for their own consumption, an indication that oil production did not overtake all uses of the land. The garden also underscored the scarcity of fresh produce, much of which had to be either transported from Shreveport or locally sourced alongside the noxious liquids of oil production.[18]

FIGURE 2.1. *An undated image of a typically primitive North Louisiana oil field tent home. From left to right: Belle the dog, Gordon, Myrta, and Mrs. Hal Boylston.*

Stacy's Landing provided a vivid illustration of how home and work life during the oil boom very often collapsed into one bizarre space of industry and proto-domesticity.

Many worker tents were exclusively canvas and rope, designed to easily construct and deconstruct as needed. But others contained wood bases and sturdier tops, reflecting a desire to live within some comfort—and perhaps for a relatively longer period of time.[19] While Oil City remained a heavily male space of oil field workers, wives and children were at times present in the tents as well, making the tent's comfort and livability an even greater priority. Florence Hartman spent much of her childhood in a tent along Caddo Lake and retained strikingly warm recollections of her family's domestic space: "it was real comfortable . . . it had a wooden floor." Hartman's mother would even periodically host small dinner parties for four to five oil workers who lived in the adjacent boardinghouse.[20] One 1920 photograph of an Oil City family's tent displayed one such improvised domestic space bearing a wooden foundation and a canvas roof. In the foreground two women, a young boy, and "Belle" the dog posed.[21]

BUILDING (AND REBUILDING) LAND AVENUE

As cheap living quarters sprouted alongside the oil fields, so did a dynamic commercial district on Oil City's Land Avenue. This sprawling, mud-laden boulevard hosted a row of hastily built wooden shacks that ran parallel to the Kansas City Southern railroad tracks. One 1912 image of the avenue captured a smokehouse, a billiards hall, and an attorney's office, reflecting its position as a mutual center of both recreation and business. Another photograph from the same year revealed a line of saloons and restaurants as dozens of men milled along the dirt road. At the avenue's center stood a leafless tree, to which, at least according to many local histories tinged with romanticism, law enforcement officers would tie drunks until they sobered up.[22]

The cheaply made wooden shacks that proliferated along Land Avenue became severely flammable powder kegs. Major fires broke out along Oil City's main thoroughfare in 1909, 1911, 1917, 1922, 1926, 1936, and 1939. Tom Moore knew of one barber shop that burned down five times.[23] Moreover, the boomtown's cheap architectural standards and lack of insurance made such events not only more prevalent but also more destructive. The 1909 blaze "virtually wiped out" the town, destroying thirteen buildings, including three hotels and the post office, causing more than $30,000 in damages.[24] Two years later another blaze struck, causing $25,000 in damages, with little to no insurance to buttress the owners against the losses. On this occasion, the blaze was alleged to be a deliberate act: "Incendiarism is suspected," reported the *Thibodaux Sentinel*.[25]

FIGURE 2.2. *A 1912 image of Oil City's Land Avenue. According to legend, law enforcement tied up drunks to the tree in the center of the road.*

Every such incident reexposed the consequences of Oil City's poorly made and poorly insured housing stock. The 1922 fire destroyed three city blocks of "frame buildings," most of them "comparatively new, having been erected since a disastrous fire that swept the same portion of Oil City four years ago."[26] Once again, "there was very little insurance" among the affected businesses. Dramatic photographs of the 1922 fire captured crowds of people desperately carrying boxes of goods away from the wood-framed shops and onto the KCS rail line at the center of town, where presumably they would be safe from the flames. A 1926 inferno would ultimately become the most destructive of Oil City's many fires, rendering "37 buildings" into a "mass of smouldering [*sic*] ruins," at a staggering cost of $750,000.[27]

One serious impediment to combating fires in Oil City was the inaccessibility of municipal fire services, most of which lay twenty-four miles south in Shreveport. Although Shreveport and the rural boomtowns were relatively close in mileage, virtually no traversable roads connected them. Each time a blaze erupted, machinery and manpower had to navigate those swampy, mud-laden twenty-four miles while precious moments passed and flames engulfed more buildings. In 1922, Shreveport firefighters arrived "about five minutes" before the flames reached the town's brick buildings, preventing "much heavier losses." Four years later, the Shreveport Fire Department rushed to the scene

FIGURE 2.3. *Business owners and families along Land Avenue frantically move household items onto the Kansas City Southern railroad tracks to escape a 1922 fire, one of many that occurred along the major thoroughfare.*

of a fire, only to find themselves stymied by Oil City's crude infrastructure once they arrived: "there being no water mains, it was difficult for firemen to battle the flames." Eventually the firefighters obtained water from a nearby pool, but only after "one of the trucks was mired" in Oil City's notoriously muddy roads.[28]

The absence of Shreveport's firefighting equipment prompted locals to fight blazes with whatever means they could. When a "chemical engine" arrived in Oil City to extinguish the 1917 inferno, firemen were surprised to discover that "the workers and others of Oil City had gotten the blaze under control."[29] But such ingenuity could not overcome the inescapable reality that Oil City lacked the requisite firefighting technology and personnel to mitigate the town's severe fire vulnerability. When another fire struck in 1936, Oil City was still precariously reliant on Shreveport's firefighting force, whose arrival "prevented the fire from spreading in two directions."[30] No matter how quickly firemen arrived from Shreveport, there would inevitably be precious minutes wasted as the inferno consumed yet another wood-framed building.

Moreover, the occurrence and severity of these fires was not simply bad luck, but rather the reflection of a particular boomtown mentality that governed the development of Oil City. Many investors and business owners simply regarded the community as little more than a temporary investment to make money while the oil flowed; builders accordingly favored quick and cheap construction over well-insured, sturdier structures. A. B. Hanner, who arrived in Oil City in 1919, recalled asking a fellow oil worker why the town was "all little shot-gun houses" and offered so few well-made buildings: "They really don't want to stay here, the town is so rough they don't want to raise their families here. They just build little ole cheap houses and go off and leave them."[31] This dynamic was not exclusive to Oil City or Louisiana: city planners in the oil boomtowns of nineteenth-century Pennsylvania similarly resigned themselves to the transient nature of their boomtown settlements, a presumption that came to be reflected in their hastily constructed structures and minimally planned townscapes.[32]

Oil City's severe flammability and generally primitive conditions were a direct consequence of that "boom management" style of oil field city planning.[33] Business owners were unwilling to invest and insure property in what they regarded as an ephemeral community. That reluctance became a self-fulfilling prophecy, making Oil City more fire-prone, less habitable, and ultimately less likely to attract longer-term occupants and industries.

LIFE AND DEATH IN OIL CITY

Violence and murder were endemic to life in Oil City. Countless inhabitants of North Louisiana's oil boom days vividly recalled its brutality and ubiquity. "It was a pretty rough town in those days," as Walter Duvall George Jr. recounted.[34] "You could get killed real easy," another Oil City native lamented.[35] Tom Moore saw three dead men after the "law got in a fight with them."[36] Margaret Bateman (née Pace) remembered a pool hall shooting and the image of people hand-cuffed to a telephone pole.[37] Mike Benedum and Joe Trees witnessed a series of five brawls break out at the Oil City railroad station as participants wielded "knives, brass knuckles, clubs and other weapons."[38] One former oil field gauger could recall an evening in which he was momentarily mistaken for another individual and almost shot because of it. When the shooter, a gambler, located his intended target, he shot and killed him.[39]

Such historical accounts and oral histories often describe those rowdy oil boom days with a tinge of "Wild West" romance: the pool hall fights, card games, and shootouts become nostalgic tall tales from a bygone era. But such romanticized accounts of Oil City transform the community's staggering violence into one-dimensional, cartoonish scenes that are stripped of all historical weight. A more critical examination of those "Wild West" tales reveals a darker, far less charming truth about Oil City: that death and violence plagued its streets; that law enforcement was largely powerless to stop it; and that such conditions were neither a natural nor inevitable boomtown condition, but the direct and intentional product of civic disinvestment, apathetic public officials, and ineffective—and perhaps corrupted—law enforcement.

Numerous interviews and accounts allege that Caddo Parish law enforcement officials applied the law in Oil City unevenly at best and corruptly at worst. Police had precious few men or resources, or lacked "sometimes the nerve," to tackle the "influx of outlaws, gamblers and rowdies" coursing through Oil City. As the oil boom grew, "the regular law . . . almost ceased to exist," making "assault and homicide . . . daily occurrences."[40] Willis P. Butler, the Caddo Parish coroner during the early oil days, offered an even more blunt assessment of the community's public safety: "Oil City was noted for having no respect for the law. The law was handicapped. The outlaws were running the place."[41] Officers were so outmanned that oil companies sometimes had to hire their own private security forces. In 1910, the Benedum and Trees drilling team brought in Pinckney "Pink" Taylor, a former Texas Ranger and San Antonio police officer, largely to act as a courier for company payroll as it traveled from Shreveport to Oil City.[42]

At least one lawman, deputy sheriff Will George, was reputed for attacking illicit behavior, if overzealously. Even within a community so notorious for its violence, George, ostensibly on the side of law and order, was infamous for his extreme methods. As John F. Law put it, George was a "rough man" operating in "rough times," often striking people in the head with a flashlight to make his point.[43] Tom Moore recalled George clearing out drunks from the pool hall with beatings rather than the threat of jail.[44] But the violent circumstances in which he worked ultimately consumed Deputy George. He died in 1945 after an intoxicated night watchman shot him in the Caddo Parish oil field town of Belcher.[45] Howard R. Hughes Sr., oil field inventor and eventual founder of the Hughes Tool Company, and father to the even more iconic Howard Jr., briefly held the positions of deputy sheriff and postmaster for Oil City. He would ultimately look back on the job with terse bitterness: "I never held a public office, except that of deputy sheriff and postmaster at Oil City, La. Therein I lost my religion."[46]

RENO HILL

Oil City's downtown also played host to a notorious, if commercially dynamic, marketplace of underground tastes operating alongside the oil rigs. Just east of the Kansas City Southern line and parallel to Land Avenue lay "Reno Hill," a sprawling ten-acre assemblage of bars, hotels, and tents that sold drink and sex to the oil workers. In a shrewd marketing tactic, Reno Hill's businesses were color-coordinated, with the exterior hue of each matching its title: The Red

Duck, the Yellow Head, the Brown Hen, and the Gray Goose (or the Blue Goose, as Tom Moore remembered it) among them. A fence encircled Reno Hill's establishments, inspiring a perversely fitting nickname for the district: "the Barn Yard."[47]

The alleged arson of 1911 centered in the notorious area, which one newspaper described as "being the scene of a great deal of the lawlessness . . . in the oil field." The same article listed a series of "hotels" and barrooms destroyed by flames, the monikers of which betrayed the neighborhood's unsavory character: "the Stag hotel, Delmonico hotel, Joliff's pool hall, Jackson's near-beer place . . . McCabe's near-beer establishment, and two vacant houses."[48]

Reno Hill's "houses of ill repute" were wildly popular among the oil working set. D. R. Beamer was a young man of twenty when he began to spend time in Reno Hill and retained vivid memories of its alluring sights, sounds, and procedures. He remembered ascending to a big dance hall as derrick "flares all over the hill" framed the scene. As he approached, an "old grandma" would pursue men and "get them to make a date," although Beamer declined to repeat precisely what she would say. The big dance hall was a kaleidoscope of "all rough necks and all these women around there and an old tinkly piano going and dancing." "Oklahoma Mamie" was the ruthless proprietor of one such Reno Hill establishment, where she would stand "in the corner by a barrel of empty beer bottles." On one occasion, Oklahoma lost her temper and began indiscriminately throwing beer bottles—"boy, her aim was marvelous!"—and consequently cleared out the dance hall.[49]

Although liquor consumption was illegal in Caddo Parish, an elaborate bootlegging ring smuggled spirits into the community and did a swift business in Reno Hill. Cleo Norris estimated that at least ten bootleggers—one of whom he knew—and five whiskey stills operated in Oil City. He observed that locals didn't "pay a whole lot of attention to the federal law."[50] Bootlegging apparently became so entrenched in the local economy that its partisans rioted when law enforcement officials tried to shut it down. In November 1910, "Pink" Taylor attempted to arrest Thomas Hickey, the head of a notorious Oil City bootlegging ring, but ended up having to use deadly force:

> He warned Hickey to submit to the law, but [Hickey] resisted. Hickey broke away from Taylor threw his right hand to his hip pocket as if to draw a gun . . . Taylor drew his gun and fired, the bullet going through Hickey's body.[51]

In the ensuing days, as Hickey recovered in a hospital, an estimated seventy-five of his underworld associates expressed solidarity with their boss by "shooting up" the town and threatening to burn Oil City as "Men, women and children ran into store or homes and barred the doors and windows."[52] The rioters ultimately did "more talking than execution," however, and were brought under control when Taylor and Caddo Sheriff James Patteson Flournoy arrived armed with Winchester rifles.[53] While the riot may not have amounted to much violence or death, it still underscored the depth of Oil City's liquor business: that seventy-five bootleggers would openly threaten violence and brandish weapons revealed that its practitioners were highly protective of their lucrative business, and perhaps believed themselves to be immune from any legal ramifications.

The bootleggers may have had good reason to think that to be true. In response to Reno Hill's underworld dealings, law enforcement was apathetic at best and corrupted at worst.[54] When an interviewer asked Oil City native Tom Moore whether law enforcement knew about the pervasive drinking, he claimed that bootleggers in the Hart's Ferry area "paid the laws off." Moore claimed the same apathetic law enforcement standards applied to gambling as well: "they gambled too!"[55] D. R. Beamer, an Oil City resident who worked for Texas Company, faulted even higher authorities for corrupt activities, accusing the Caddo Parish courthouse of getting "a rake off from all the prostitution, gambling and so forth." Beamer further claimed that Pink Taylor, the righteous officer who broke up the 1910 bootlegger riot, actually lived with a sex worker named Dorothy Jackson.[56] There is no other evidence that would confirm such a relationship, but there is clear evidence of Jackson's profession. In 1914, Jackson was arrested for running a Reno Hill prostitution and bootlegging operation.[57]

Reno Hill's barrooms and "houses of ill repute" might seem like a quaint and colorful vestige of the wild oil boom days, but they were also shrewd, profit-driven businesses operating within an elaborate nexus of trade and smuggling. The madams and bootleggers set up shop in Oil City precisely because it was an ideal market for their products. The boomtown's populace was a disproportionately young group of male wage earners, most of whom were either unmarried or apart from their spouses. Reno Hill offered those workers a respite from the oil field's hard labor, locating its bars and dance houses within easy access of the job site. Indeed, they were right next to it: when you exited a Reno Hill establishment, "out at the back were flames from the oil wells."[58] With few roads leading in and out of this remote corner of North Louisiana, oil workers without the ability to easily leave were left to patronize whatever businesses were nearby. In effect, the proprietors of Reno Hill had a captive market that was demographically and economically aligned with their business model.

Sex worker jobs were very often the best, if not the only, opportunity that women had to materially benefit from the oil boom. Indeed, there was a real economic logic to the profession: it was hardly coincidental that one sexual encounter with a Reno Hill sex worker cost the same (three dollars) as the common daily pay for a (white) oil worker. In fact, many sex workers arguably did *better* than their male counterparts on the oil patch, charging ten dollars for an entire night.[59] These women understood that they possessed an economic asset in a space that was flush with cash. And one that retained a very fungible economic value, as one sex worker artfully illustrated to John F. Law: "she had something to sell when cotton and corn wouldn't!"[60]

ESCAPING OIL CITY

Although Oil City did attract some wives and children to its tent communities, the boomtown's pervasive violence and drinking very often deterred families from settling there, even for a brief period of time. Oil City "was a dirty place," recalled Florence Hartman, who was a young girl when her family moved to a tent alongside Caddo Lake. "We just never were much around Oil City," she added, as it was "rough and rowdy." Keeping wives and young daughters away from Reno Hill was especially paramount. Hartman never laid eyes on the notorious Hill, but she was very much aware of its reputation: "they had plenty of girls . . . and fellas liked to go up there."[61] Bill Snead's father refused to live in Oil City precisely because "Reno Hill was filled with women that he didn't want his wife or his daughter associating with."[62]

Many who brought wives and children to North Louisiana chose to settle in nearby communities that could still offer access to the oil fields, but at a sufficient distance from Oil City and its conditions. Mooringsport became one such satellite boomtown, attracting many family-oriented oil workers, such as Bill Snead's protective father.[63] Located along the shores of Caddo Lake, Mooringsport was just a few miles south of Oil City but was comparatively far quieter and safer. Contemporary photographs captured a lakeside town of ample wooden homes framed by picket fences with no apparent centers of vice in sight.[64] Mooringsport was an oil boom community that developed not simply for access to the fields, but as a *reaction* to the social conditions of Oil City—an intentional effort to build a different kind of boomtown.

The determination of many families to seek a "safer" domestic experience in Mooringsport may have also had racial undertones. Interviews with Caddo Parish natives suggest that part of Mooringsport's appeal to more "family-friendly" migrants was that it was regarded as an all-white community.[65] Reno Hill was a space for not only vice but also racial transgression, where Black and mixed-race sex workers could mingle with white patrons, a dynamic that many white oil workers would have regarded with contempt. Areas of Mooringsport may have been considered all-white, but Black communities still resided there, albeit in cloistered pockets. Records from the 1920 census note clusters of Black residents living within Mooringsport, primarily married families with men who worked in the oil fields, in railroad yards, or on nearby farms.[66] Mooringsport was even home to Huddie William Ledbetter, or "Lead Belly," the iconic Black outlaw and bluesman. White migrants may have regarded Mooringsport as an exclusively white enclave, but that perception could not erase the fundamental existence of local Black residents.

In spite of, or perhaps because of, Reno Hill's popular establishments, a deep-seated religious movement developed in North Louisiana's boomtowns. Christian revivalism, especially of the Baptist variety, manifested around the oil field towns. Faith communities organized despite the absence of brick-and-mortar churches, often meeting "out under a tree or maybe in a tent."[67] Big tent revivals took place in Oil City, Mooringsport, and Vivian.[68] Even the fetid bayous that curled around the oil fields became improvised sites of religious conversion. In 1915, the Mooringsport Baptist Church held a baptismal ceremony on the shores of Caddo Lake. A photograph of the event captures hundreds of participants dressed in white and black lining up to be dipped into the water. A cluster of oil derricks framing the horizon presides over the sacramental scene.[69]

Not surprisingly, advocates of revivalist Christian faith found Oil City's leisure-oriented residents to be tough souls to save. Bill Snead argued that Oil City's irreligious people were not necessarily sinners but just busy, reasoning that it is hard to be religious when a man is working twelve-hour shifts.[70] In 1912, Shreveport's chapter of the Gideon evangelical organization distributed thirty Bibles to the Norman Hotel in the hope of reaching the migrants who resided therein.[71] But efforts to revive the souls of Oil City remained frustratingly slow. A newspaper story from the same year noted that Methodist minister Thomas Jefferson Holladay had opened a church in Oil City but was able to secure only one parishioner in six months, then subsequently added only one a month: "He acknowledged it was a hard field."[72]

But many such attempts at conversions were indeed successful and long-lasting. Charlie Spikes, who grew up in the oil company town of Trees City, was saved along with thirty other souls in the baptismal waters of Jeem's Bayou in June 1932. He could still remember those details because he recorded them on the 1,053rd page of his dog-eared Bible:

CHARLES WINFRED SPIKES DOB 9-16-19
CONVERTED JUNE—1932 (SECOND BIRTH)
Revival Meeting—REV. E. A. INGRAM
(30 Baptisms)
Trees Baptist Church
Trees, LA
Baptisted [*sic*] in Jeems Bayou

Spikes's notations, written with evident pride, appear just below one of the Book of Malachi's last admonishing passages: *For, behold, the day cometh, that shall burn as an oven; and all the proud, yea, and all that do wickedly, shall be stubble.*[73] Even in oil field communities so notorious for violence and drinking, or perhaps *because* of it, evangelical faith became an important source of communal identity. Given all the degenerate behavior taking place nearby, parables of good and evil surely assumed a real urgency. For the ministers preaching to their oil field congregants, Oil City and Reno Hill offered a very compelling and tangible illustration of those who do wickedly and "shall be stubble."

TREES CITY: A NEW KIND OF BOOMTOWN

The drinking and violence that overwhelmed Land Avenue and Reno Hill even began exerting an adverse economic impact on oil field operations, exasperating industry executives. Saloons, brothels, and other such establishments were "as close to the wells as possible," often to the detriment of their workforce's safety and productivity.[74] Given the physical dangers of oil field drilling, functioning with less than a fully conscious mind or body could produce all kinds of workplace disasters. Fatigue or drunkenness could result in the destruction of a well, or even the loss of human life.[75] Drilling partners Benedum and Trees soon discovered that Reno Hill's temptations were slowing operations on their W. P. Stiles lease. The pair often had to suspend operations on their derricks due to the "condition of the driller," at enormous economic cost.[76]

Benedum and Trees sought to eliminate such behavior from their work sites through an ambitiously wholesale approach: creating an entirely new community for their workers to live in. In 1909 the partners began to construct "Trees City," a clean, safe, and wholesome alternative to the riotous corridors of Oil City and Reno Hill. Ironclad rules governed its streets: there were to be no "bad women" or drinking and, according to Claude McFarland, no "billy goats" or bull dogs, apparently an effort to keep the area free of unruly domesticated animals. Those who failed to live up to these rules, especially the ban on drinking, met with swift retribution: there was "a man who would beat you," by McFarland's recollection.[77] Benedum and Trees reasoned that such an environment would not only discourage bad behavior among their workers, but also encourage wives and children to settle as well. Having more domesticated households would thereby encourage a more virtuous workforce that would be less prone to the temptations of Reno Hill and the economic consequences that accompanied them.

Trees City's layout articulated a spatial language of domestic purity and civic permanence—a challenge to the ephemeral boomtown model of Oil City.

FIGURE 2.4. *Trees City, a Caddo Parish company town designed to encourage oil field workers to live quieter, more domesticated lives.*

Consisting of fifty stately brick homes laid out evenly on geometric streets, the company town offered an escape from the flimsy tents encircled with mud and violence that roiled the other boomtowns. In one remarkable 1918 photograph of Trees City, a collection of mothers and children all robed in unsoiled white play on a swing set as oil derricks peek over the horizon.[78] This image perfectly encapsulates the idealized universe Benedum and Trees sought to create: an unsullied space of healthy family life buoyed by a productive oil economy.

Trees City even hosted an array of businesses to provide residents with wholesome leisure activities: a hotel, a church, a pool hall, and a dance pavilion were all available to residents.[79] The local pool hall became a particularly important space of social and economic activity, as well as a de facto mail sorting and distribution center until a formal post office was built in 1912.[80] Two doctors and a dentist also served the community. In 1914, Stiles even built an "air dome" that displayed movies.[81] The elaborate collection of nearby services and leisure activities were by design: they were a means of ensuring that locals stayed *within* the confines of the community, did not stray to Reno Hill, and only spent their wages at Trees City's establishments.

Nurturing Trees City's unique network of local commerce was not only a means for Benedum and Trees to improve their workers' productivity, but also a business opportunity for W. P. Stiles. As the town's landlord, Stiles was shrewdly turning these oil workers, and the businesses they patronized, into tenants, effectively recapturing their wages in the form of rent. Rather than spending money toward a sexual encounter in Reno Hill, employees put their money back into the Trees City business ecosystem, which ultimately went back to Stiles. If Trees City could fulfill its ultimate vision of a more stable and permanent oil town, then Stiles could further enrich himself through a long-term rise in land value. Just as he had gamely pivoted his property into oil production, Stiles saw a new opportunity to benefit from its potential value as boomtown real estate.

The development of Trees City demonstrated that oil was not necessarily the singular historical force creating the spatial contours of new communities, and that many boomtowns were the products of cultural agendas, not simply economic necessity. Trees City was not so much an oil boomtown as a *critique* of one: the brick houses and anti-vice prohibitions were an ideological counter to the boomtown archetype, and a bet that oil workers would make a longer-term investment in a clean, wholesome environment. But economic incentives nonetheless remained at the core of this project. Despite its utopian language of social betterment, Trees City remained a fundamentally profit-driven endeavor to build a more stable, productive workforce that would enrich its investors.

The divergent formations of Oil City, Mooringsport, and Trees City challenge the notion that oil field boomtowns would inevitably mirror the rough conditions of the oil field: dirty, ephemeral, and plagued with violence. Although North Louisiana's boomtowns undoubtedly possessed many of those attributes, they remained acts of social and economic engineering. Oil City's primitive conditions were *made*, and not simply the "natural" extension of oil production. The violence, drinking, and lawlessness that prevailed reflected a deliberate lack of investment and civic infrastructure; Oil City's poorly made (and poorly insured) housing stock reflected a similar pessimism that ensured those conditions would remain indefinitely. Why invest in a boomtown that would eventually cease to exist?

While Oil City developed as a quick and efficient means of housing new migrants, Trees City and Mooringsport also emerged as cultural antidotes to those conditions: they were communities that offered far more than just an easy access point to the derricks. Many of North Louisiana's migrants sought an escape from the boomtown's violence, primitive conditions, and perhaps even its perceived racial fluidity. New types of boomtowns thus coalesced as a social and civic challenge to preexisting forms of community building, even if their fundamental raison d'être still centered on the economic productivity of energy production. Oil fundamentally impelled the need for new communities in North Louisiana, but the particular contours of those communities ultimately reflected the economic and civic decisions made, and not made, by its residents.

3 / THE PEOPLE

OIL WAS THE COMMON THREAD AMONG OIL CITY'S BOOMING population—the singular force that brought so many people to what had been a quiet, rural outpost of the American South. North Louisiana's oil boom was a particular godsend to the region's farmers, who were enduring falling crop prices and the loss of farmland. However, the profile of poor rural farmers abandoning their old work in favor of a new life does not uniformly apply to every migrant who reached Oil City and its surrounding communities. To be sure, oil offered a new economic future for many of the rural farmers who reached North Louisiana's boomtowns. But for others, the new industrial economy was not a permanent replacement for the farm, but rather a temporary source of income to *preserve* it. Moreover, oil production did not wholly supplant older forms of work, but very often coopted them, retrofitting well-established tools and infrastructure from the railroads, sawmilling, and hauling into the oil patch.

The new residents of North Louisiana's oil boomtowns were also strikingly diverse in their professions as well as in their regional and ethnic makeup. Migrants arrived from across the American South, Southwest, Midwest, and Northeast; immigrants from Ireland, Sweden, Bulgaria, and Russia came as well. Men constituted the largest proportion, a natural reflection of the oil patch's workplace personnel, but women were very much present in North Louisiana's boomtowns, and a select few of them may have even worked in the oil fields. A collection of enterprising and ruthless women also created Oil City's parallel economy of sex work, luring female workers, either voluntarily or otherwise, into the community. Sex work became a dynamic trade in the oil boomtowns, reliant on the cash wages being generated on the derricks but operating within its own distinct zones and under its own unique set of economic rules.

Examining the people of Oil City and North Louisiana's oil boomtowns also underscores the power of wealth to beget more wealth. While the daily wages of North Louisiana's oil fields provided a fount of economic opportunity to its migrants, the greatest individual beneficiaries were the people with preexisting resources: capital, land, and wealth that enabled them to take the necessary risks and access the requisite technology to fully benefit from oil production. Studying the people of North Louisiana's oil boom therefore tells a broader story about industrial capitalism and its tendency to enrich the already rich.

WHAT BROUGHT YOU TO OIL CITY?

We got hungry.[1]

As Caddo Parish native Cleo Norris plainly stated in a 1999 interview, his family migrated to North Louisiana's oil boom for nothing less than economic survival. Norris had spent his youngest years in Clay County, Arkansas, where his father tried his hand at sawmilling and then at farming—a "big mistake because he wasn't no farmer."[2] Knowing other families who had made the same journey from farm to oil field, the senior Norris moved his family to Oil City in 1926. Before drilling the first successful well in Caddo Parish, Walter Duvall George had also been a farmer in Rusk, Texas. But when Spindletop's oil wells began spewing crude in 1901, he took a pair of mules to East Texas, inaugurating a dramatic change in his life. This arc from rural farming to the oil rig would be a common path among North Louisiana's boomtown migrants, even if that transition was often fleeting.

Oil City's new economy attracted migrants from across the nation—indeed, from across the world—but especially from the American South and its rural agricultural populations. In the preceding decades, political and economic changes had significantly reduced the financial viability of Southern farming. Following the emancipation of enslaved labor, the value of farmland across the South plummeted. Between 1860 and 1900, the price of Louisiana's farmland alone fell by $137 million. As a consequence, Southern farmers, especially cotton producers, endured a disastrous combination of declining land values and rising indebtedness. In desperate need of cash, many landowning farmers sold their properties, resulting in a dramatic shift in the ownership of farmland.[3]

A buyer's market ensued as cash-hungry farmers across the South sold off their land to eager investors, most of whom were urban merchants. Scores of farmers suddenly became tenants on their own land and subject to a "crop lien" debt system in which they pledged their future crop in exchange for cash on hand. But overproduction across the South pushed agricultural prices steadily downward over the latter half of the nineteenth century, reducing the value of farmland crops and thereby increasing debt levels. The price of cotton, the cornerstone of North Louisiana's antebellum and postbellum economy, fell to 4.6

cents per pound by 1894, down from the 1870s price of 13.8 cents. This only intensified the economic crisis for agricultural producers.[4]

The farmers of Louisiana's heavily agrarian economy endured a seismic transition in land and economic power. Between 1880 and 1900, Louisiana experienced a 23 percent rise in farmer tenancy. Much like the other rural regions of the South, Louisiana's farmland became an abstracted financial investment for distant landowners, a "money crop extracted by landlords, living in towns." Indeed, the state's "proportion of absentee ownership . . . was the largest in the South" and second only to Wyoming nationally.[5] Even within Louisiana, the northern regions, including Caddo Parish, experienced the worst relative decline in farmer landownership, dropping 32 percent from 1880 to 1890. This ascendant "agrarian monopoly" came to dominate the state's economy and government, and would wield a heavy influence in the development of North Louisiana's oil industry.[6]

Amidst stagnant crop prices and high tenancy rates, the emergence of North Louisiana's oil economy was a welcome development to many of the region's cash-starved farmers. By 1909 the Caddo Parish oil fields were producing more than a million barrels of crude annually through the activities of 163 wells, each of which provided its own cluster of jobs and wages. Every derrick employed roughly five people: a driller, a derrick man, a boiler man, and two helpers. Helpers and derrick men could expect to earn three dollars a day, drillers up to five or six dollars and maybe more.[7] Skilled workers with the ability to construct wooden derricks commanded an even higher salary. John F. Law's father transitioned from roughnecking to rig building in 1918, at which point he earned, by Law's recollection, twelve dollars a day, perhaps an exaggerated figure, but still likely indicative of a highly competitive wage.[8] Black workers, however, earned significantly less, assuming they held any positions on the derrick at all.

Despite its attendant volatility, oil production offered a brighter future to a generation of small farmers seeking to escape their declining fortunes.[9] Farmers from around the South and Southwest flocked to North Louisiana to fill those positions. Carl W. Jones, who went on to become a successful Caddo Parish driller, grew up on a cotton and pea farm in Queens City, Texas. After moving to Vivian, just north of Oil City, he encountered a community full of similar country folk: "Pretty well all nesters . . . like myself . . . they were from up there in the country and looking for a job." Many such "farm boys" Jones encountered regarded the oil industry as a bridge into a new life and were "anxious to learn . . . to get out of that pea patch."[10] The term "oil patch" even allegedly derived from the *pea* and *cotton* patches they replaced, underscoring the close historical proximity of agriculture and petroleum production in the early twentieth-century American landscape.[11]

But for many such families, Caddo Parish's boomtowns were not a final landing spot, but merely one layover in an ongoing pursuit for better wages and better times. In one 1913 photograph, young Kitty and Hugh Sneed sit atop a wooden fence framed by sights of Mooringsport, just south of Oil City; derricks dot the horizon against a foreground of wood-frame homes next to Caddo Lake.[12] The Sneed siblings, wearing fine white clothing, paint a portrait of childhood tranquility and domesticity. But this comfortable moment of respite belied their family's continuous migration through farming and oil communities.

In the 1900 census, their father, Sebrone or "Sebe" Sneed, had been a farmer in Travis County, Texas, only to reappear as an oil field teamster in Jennings ten years later.[13] By 1920 he had moved his family again, from Mooringsport to Shreveport, where he worked in an unnamed oil field occupation.[14] Sebe would ultimately settle in Shreveport, working in the oil business until his death in 1963.[15] The image of his children reposing, seemingly at home, by the oil fields was just a momentary break in the Sneed family's restless and peripatetic history—another illustration of the oil industry's highly mobile nature and its tendency to keep its workforce in a state of perpetual migration.

One 1922 case held before Louisiana's Supreme Court dramatically illustrated how North Louisiana's oil fields acted as an economic lifeline to

FIGURE 3.1. *The Sneed family in Mooringsport, May 1913.*

destitute farming families across the South. In December 1919, Roy A. Gregory left his rural Arkansas farm for Caddo Parish, where the seventeen-year-old became an employee of Standard Oil. Roy did so with his impoverished family in mind, intending to remit a daily wage of $4.25 back to his parents and siblings. Court records detailed the "very poor" and "needy circumstances" the Gregory family suffered, which paralleled the broader economic malaise sharecroppers were enduring around the South:

> They have no stated income and no property, except 40 acres of woodland, which produces no revenue. They lived on a small hill farm in Arkansas, which is owned by a near neighbor and which they cultivate on the share system . . . The father is in his declining years, able to do but little work . . . Roy left home . . . to seek employment where wages were more attractive and he could furnish more assistance to his parents . . . he told his father and mother and the owner of the farm, that he would send to his father $35 each month out of his wages, to assist them in employing a hand to take his place in the farm work for the coming year.[16]

But Gregory's parents would never see any of the wages he promised to remit. On January 26, 1920, after just one month of employment with Standard Oil, Roy and another individual died after a small boat capsized while carrying them across Caddo Lake to their job site.

Roy's parents subsequently filed suit against the Standard Oil Company of Louisiana, arguing that under Louisiana's Employers' Liability Act of 1914, they ought to receive compensation for the lost wages Roy would have provided. The plaintiffs depicted themselves as desperately reliant on young Roy, "dependents to a minor son, who had contributed his labor in making a crop which went to their support and then left home to seek employment, promising to send a state amount each month." For their part, Standard Oil challenged the idea that Roy's parents were financially reliant on his labor, claiming they were not actually receiving "aid or contribution, either material or pecuniary" from their young son.[17]

The court sided with Gregory's family. No compensation was specified in the decision, but the justices cited an earlier case in which a mother similarly dependent upon her son's labor was awarded $3,500 when he died while working on the railroads. By the time of the 1930 census, Roy's parents appeared to be living in similar circumstances, still working on their rural Union County farm.[18] But their son's fatal determination to migrate to North Louisiana's oil fields would assume a bitter irony. Just months after Roy perished, his hometown of Union County, and more specifically the Arkansas town of El Dorado, would become the next major center of regional oil production, bringing many of the individuals who had been working in North Louisiana back to the remote farming district Roy had *left* in search of oil money.

While Roy Gregory's tragic story involves only one person and one family, it still illuminates some of the broader motivations that drove migrants away from their farms and into North Louisiana's boomtowns. Gregory had no intention of making Caddo Parish a permanent home, merely a source of cash to remit back to Arkansas. Even as the oil industry was transforming the region's economic landscape, Roy and his family did not seem to be interested in a new kind of life, only in the cash necessary to keep their increasingly precarious *old* way of life afloat. Such motives certainly helped explain why boomtowns such as Oil City were mired in such states of disrepair: why invest in a community that is little more than a temporary source of income? Gregory's story also weighs against the historical narrative that Louisiana's oil industry created a one-directional bridge for rural farmers to replace the "pea patch" with a new middle-class, wage-earning life. To Roy and his family, North Louisiana's oil boom was not so much a bridge to a better life but rather a new foundation for an old one.

The oil boom generated wages not only for drillers, roughnecks, and those who worked directly on the rigs, but also for those offering corollary products and services. Records from the 1910 census for Oil City and its surrounding environs reveal a dynamic ecosystem of businesses catering to the ascendant new industry and its migrants. Local employers included "tailor shop," "telegraph," "railroad," "pool hall," "restaurants," "shoe shops," "meat market," "bakery," "livery stable," "machine shop," "butcher shop," and "lumber yard."[19] Tom Moore came to Oil City in 1913 not to work in the oil fields, although he would do so eventually, but to "peddle turkeys" to residents.[20] Oil companies' housing camps also employed full-time cooks and washers to serve its residents.[21] Caddo's oil fields were undoubtedly the primary force that transformed quiet "Surry" into bustling Oil City, but they were not the only direct sources of employment.

Many of Oil City's residents successfully retrofitted old forms of labor into the new oil economy. In the decades prior to 1904, North Louisiana had been a center of sawmilling, given its abundant supply of local cypress and timber. Many of the individuals who had worked in transporting and milling logs continued to ply those skills in the oil fields. Jim Douglas Dunman had been in business hauling logs in Caddo Parish with his team of mules, work that paid him a dollar a day plus board. But the advent of oil production presented a new, more lucrative opportunity for his skill set. For a higher salary, Dunman began using his mules to haul boilers, pipe, and timber that would become derricks.[22]

Even as the region's economy drastically changed and expanded, the simple ability to move heavy things from one place to another remained a highly valued asset. All that changed were the products being moved and the wages being offered.

Preexisting infrastructure was similarly repurposed to suit the emerging oil economy, particularly North Louisiana's elaborate rail lines. When pre-oil Surry maintained a more rural, agrarian economy, the Kansas City Southern railroad had been a crucial link between North Louisiana's raw materials and distant markets, moving sawmilled wood and cotton from the fields to Shreveport's warehouses. By the first decade of the twentieth century, the same KCS line remained, but was primarily in the business of moving Caddo Parish crude from derrick to refinery. Prior to the 1910 completion of Standard Oil's Louisiana pipeline, "practically all oil shipments" were made by the Kansas City Southern Railway.[23]

When wells became productive, oil field managers typically built pipelines to loading racks scattered along the KCS line, which in turn loaded crude onto railcars for transportation to secondary buyers or to refineries. Railroad lines moved 830,827 barrels of oil out of the Caddo field in 1909, the vast majority of the roughly one million barrels produced that year. By 1911, five loading racks served Caddo Parish, each of which bore the capacity to load twenty to sixty railcars with crude. Railroads were not only crucial agents for transporting North Louisiana's oil but also eager consumers of it. Oil City became a significant source of locomotive energy for the Kansas City Southern Railway, supplying the line with 257,461 barrels of its crude in 1909. That same year, Texas and Louisiana rail companies burned 16,500 barrels of Caddo Parish fuel oil per day.[24]

Many of Oil City's migrants were not farmers new to the oil patch, but rather veteran oil workers in search of the next boom. These "boomers" brought with them technical experience, oil field tools, and an awareness that constant migration was a necessary component of the business. Carl W. Jones recalled many of Oil City's workers had also been present during the early Spindletop days.[25] W. J. "Bill" Snead's father, Mike, who ran a teamster business hauling oil field equipment, was a classic "boomer" of the time, gradually charting an eastward course as the oil strikes rose and fell across the Texas and Louisiana fields of Spindletop, Hackberry, Sour Lake, Jennings, and Oil City. Prior to Spindletop, Mike Snead had been a struggling Texas farmer looking for a new source of income. By the time he reached Oil City, he had become a seasoned oil field migrant. Once Oil City declined, Mike continued his remarkable migratory pattern, hauling his teamster business to Louisiana and Arkansas's next boomtowns: Homer, El Dorado, and finally Rodessa by 1935.[26]

With so many unaccompanied men arriving in Oil City, in all likelihood for temporary stays, boardinghouses became essential dwelling places. The Norman Hotel was one of Oil City's most prominent such establishments. After a fire destroyed the original structure in 1909, the hotel was rebuilt as a handsome, two-story brick house, a sturdier design that may have contributed to its survival during another fire two years later.[27] In 1910 the Norman hosted twenty-three boarders, most of whose occupations appeared in the census as "oil field laborer," and all of whom appeared as unmarried.[28]

The hotel's residents hailed from a wide variety of states: Indiana, Oklahoma, Texas, Kentucky, Iowa, Ohio, Arkansas, Alabama, Illinois, Louisiana, and Georgia among them.[29] Such boarding establishments were especially important for single men in bachelorhood or living apart from their families, offering a more cost-effective option, but also a level of social fraternity through a collection of young men living alone, together. The Norman was also renowned for its nightlife. An undated photograph of a Caddo Parish road sign advertising the hotel offered a succinct pitch: "1 MILE, NORMAL HOTEL BAD WHISKEY."[30]

Stories of Oil City's wealth even attracted émigrés from outside of the United States. Census records for 1910 captured a remarkably global collection of people living as boomtown neighbors. Theodore Mikoff, a fifty-four-year-old widower, managed to arrive in Oil City from Bulgaria. Despite his apparent inability to speak English, Mikoff worked as a laborer in a lumberyard. Not too far away lived Patrick Moran, who emigrated from Castlebar, Ireland, in 1905 with his wife, Mary, and worked as a wooden tank builder.[31] Moran quickly assimilated into the migratory patterns of his new business, taking his tank-making abilities to the oil fields of Goose Creek, Texas, and El Dorado, Arkansas, where he died in 1925 at the age of forty-four.[32] Next door to Moran lived Al Johnson, a forty-two-year-old Swede who worked as a tie maker for the railroads.[33] White Southern farmers escaping the "pea patch" might have been the archetypical Oil City "boomers," but foreign-born immigrants were very often their neighbors.

Moran and Johnson also lived alongside Isaac Muslow, a merchant in the grocery business and a Russian immigrant. Muslow's remarkable trek highlighted both the logistical networks and economic incentives that drove people from as far as Eastern Europe to such a remote corner of North Louisiana. Muslow was born in 1872 to a Jewish family in Czarist Russia (in the present-day Republic of Georgia). At sixteen he immigrated to New York City, where he had family connections.[34] One year later, Muslow was in New Orleans working as a grocer, acquiring skills he then parlayed into a job as the commissary aboard a train that ran from Port Arthur, Texas, through Shreveport and Oil City. By 1910 he was living in Oil City and running the Pine Island Mercantile grocery business. When Muslow died in 1926 at the age of forty-eight, he had become an accomplished businessman with diversified interests in mercantile sales, oil field hauling, farmland, and oil royalties.

Isaac Muslow's remarkably successful integration into North Louisiana's oil boom was, in many respects, a unique circumstance. Muslow already had family connections in the United States and had the ability to read and write English, advantages that many immigrants might not have possessed. But his story also illuminated the economic and infrastructural forces that brought people to Oil City. Muslow's migration began in urban centers, first in New York and then New Orleans. He was subsequently able to access Oil City via the railroad, exposing him to this rural slice of Louisiana and the economic opportunities it presented. Muslow's success also underscored the significance of bringing a set of preexisting skills or assets to the oil boom. The Russian émigré shrewdly leveraged his experiences as a grocer into the oil field marketplace, enabling him to access the wealth being created in his adopted boomtown community.

THE WOMEN OF OIL CITY

While Oil City's workforce was overwhelmingly male, women were indeed present in the boomtown's homes and businesses. Nettie "Lou" Bell's father, William Thomas Bell, was a prominent participant in the Caddo field, patenting the "oil saver" method of preventing oil pipe leaks in 1917. But according to Bell, her mother Annie (née Daniel) and father were "partners" in the oil business. Annie apparently worked the fields alongside her husband, firing steam boilers, checking water pumps, and driving mules.[35] No census records for 1910 or 1920 corroborate that claim—the 1930 census lists Annie as living in Shreveport with William, having no occupation—but she was indeed present in Oil City during the boom years.[36] In one photograph taken sometime in the 1910s or 1920s, Annie poses on Hart's Ferry Bridge in Caddo Parish with cypress trees and an oil derrick behind her.[37] Her starched white dress seems to project a life of domesticity, but that should not preclude the possibility that she worked alongside her husband on the oil patch.

With the possible exception of Annie Bell, most women did not work directly on the oil patch, but rather occupied a variety of more tangential economic and domestic roles. Benjamin F. Wood, a native of Missouri, lived in Oil City and worked as an engineer for a pumping plant. But he also relied on the wages of his daughters, twenty-two-year-old Clara and twenty-year-old Myrtle, who worked jobs as "sales ladies" at an unnamed store. Boarders at Norman Hotel included a sizable collection of male oil field hands, but also a contingent of women working a variety of occupations: cook, laundress, chambermaid, teacher, and seamstress among them. Notably, three individuals listed as servants in the hotel were Black women.[38] The Norman itself was run by the husband-and-wife team of Ida and James K. Norman.

Aside from domestic roles, sex work offered another means for Oil City's women to financially benefit from the oil boom, if obliquely. Much like the boomers they served, many of Reno Hill's women were driven from impoverished rural communities in search of money. Just as Roy George sought out the oil field's cash wages to buoy his struggling rural family, many sex workers regarded their employment as a way to remit money home. Tunnell Day knew women "from poverty" who would send earnings back to their family farms in East Texas and Arkansas.[39] Some madams actually promoted their inventory of rural ingénues, advertising them as "Fresh Country Butter."[40] Unfortunately, many such girls discovered their new job was neither as lucrative nor as glamorous as they might have imagined. Bob Anderson remembered "some country girls [who wanted] to go to the city and they go and find out it's not the bright picture that they thought they was [sic] going to run into."[41]

To capture the oil money as it rose and fell, many sex workers lived an accordingly itinerant life, alternating between the oil boomtowns of Louisiana, Texas, and Oklahoma as the towns rose and fell.[42] By D. R. Beamer's reckoning, some would stay "a long time, year or more," but most were "more or less transient . . . [1 month] to 3 months."[43] Since the oil business was their most reliable source of clients, it was essential to match its migratory patterns. In some cases, Oil City sex workers entered into lasting relationships with their patrons. Alex Rice, D. R. Beamer, and Tunnell Day all knew of women who ended up marrying local oil workers, although they did not specify whether the husbands had been former clients.[44]

The question of how much agency Oil City's sex workers possessed over their own bodies and the economic value they represented is difficult to conclusively answer. Caddo Parish native Bob Anderson felt that "most of them just voluntarily [came] . . . for some reason or the other."[45] But that is the perspective of an older white man with little direct knowledge of the struggles these sex workers faced. It is probable that not one but many motives existed: perhaps some women consciously, if unhappily, entered the trade strictly for the money; some were indebted, coerced, or otherwise forced into the work; and some became madams to acquire property, wealth, and status. Unfortunately, the extant records largely preserve the recollections of white male patrons and not the sex workers themselves, leaving a crucial, indeed the most essential, perspective conspicuously vacant.

Accounts of Oil City's sex trade reveal a stark power disparity between many female employees and employers. D. R. Beamer witnessed one such newcomer being initiated into Reno Hill's underground economy. As a younger man, he knew a madam by the alias "Oklahoma Mamie" who maintained a bizarre "mother complex" type of affection for him, but also a firm sense of proprietary ownership over her workers.[46] In one instance, the "motherly" Oklahoma offered him a perverse opportunity:

> there's a girl down there, a country girl, she's about 17 and she came here today. She's never had any intercourse with a man, but she come down here because her folks were poor and she heard she could make a lot of money here and she's determined to do it . . . come on, I'll take you over and you can be the first . . . That was something![47]

Packaged as a colorful vignette from a wild past, Beamer's story actually tells a hard and uncomfortable truth about Oil City's sex trade: that economic incentives drove female madams to voraciously sell young, desperate girls to prospective clients. This undercuts the idea that all women in the sex trade existed on the same economic and social plane.

Beamer's story also demonstrates the limits of any historical equivalences that may have existed between the poor rural men coming to Oil City to pursue oil work and the poor rural women coming to Oil City to pursue sex work. This young girl of seventeen may have seen the same rural poverty that led many men to the nearby oil fields, but her bodily sacrifice was inimitable. The physical and mental labor that Oil City's female sex workers had to endure to earn a wage had no parallel in the oil field. Nonetheless, the economic ties that bound oil field work to sex work remained indelible: the fortunes of the latter remained dependent on the former. When things would decline on the oil patch, Reno Hill felt it. Or, as Cleo Norris elegantly put it, "you know the boom is gone when they start pulling up pipe and the prostitutes leave town."[48]

UNIONIZING THE OIL FIELDS

Although the wages of North Louisiana's oil fields were a very welcome infusion of money into the region's economy, its workers were making increased demands through collective bargaining. Unions had attempted to organize Texas and Louisiana's oil field workers since 1902, when the International Brotherhood of Oil and Gas Well Workers began to seek new members in Spindletop. A ten-day strike in 1905 forced the J. M. Guffey Company to reverse a planned wage cut for its Texas workforce.[49] However, for much of the following decade, significant union activity was largely absent from the Texas and Louisiana oil fields, much to the delight of its managerial class.

The spring of 1917 brought a new wave of unionism across North Louisiana's boomtowns. Over the course of several weeks, local workers formed new chapters of the Oil Workers International Union (OWIU): a Mooringsport local in May 1917, a Vivian local in July 1917, and an Oil City local in April 1917.[50] Oil City's Local 15505 would ultimately become the largest oil field union throughout the Arkansas-Louisiana-Texas fields, boasting 330 members and a central union hall for gatherings. In the absence of strong workers' compensation from employers, the union financed a sick and death benefit fund; it also encouraged members to pay their poll tax so they could vote. Shreveport also became the site of Local 101 in 1919, which ultimately gained around 300 members. Local 101 even reflected the city's more urbane atmosphere by providing a private club where members could socialize, play dominoes, or even enjoy its bathhouse facility.[51]

The sudden unionization of North Louisiana's oil fields directly, and intentionally, coincided with the US entry into World War I in April 1917. Workers were eager to leverage the federal government's urgent need for crude oil to gain increased pay and more reasonable working hours. Throughout much of 1917, union representatives had been repeatedly pressing employers across Louisiana and Texas to formally adopt their demands. But the oil companies would not even acknowledge the unions' legitimacy. Ross Sterling of the Humble Oil and Refining Company, who spoke on behalf of the producers, saw "no reason why we should confer with outsiders or strangers upon matters which concern our employees." Management also characterized the budding oil field unions as secretly beholden to the powerful and notorious Industrial Workers of the World (IWW, or "Wobblies" as they were widely known), or even as German saboteurs working to disrupt American production on behalf of the Kaiser.[52]

The industry's eroding labor relations culminated on November 1, 1917, when 9,326 oil workers across seventeen oil fields in Louisiana and Texas walked off the job. Strikers demanded that ownership formally recognize their unions, establish an eight-hour workday, offer a more generous bonus system, and raise their daily wages from $3.60 to $4. More than half of Louisiana's 3,744 strikers were in the North Louisiana oil fields, including 470 in Mooringsport, 425 in Trees City, and 1,100 in Oil City.[53] The strike produced a swift reaction from the US government, which could ill afford to subtract any raw materials from its war machine. President Woodrow Wilson brought his powers to bear and mobilized the US Army to ensure that production would continue unabated throughout the strike.[54]

The First Mississippi Infantry promptly arrived in Oil City to protect the derricks from sabotage and maintain production. Ultimately, five companies of soldiers were dispatched to "prevent destruction of property or violence" at the hands of the strikers, illustrating the importance to the federal government of preserving the oil fields' productive capacity.[55] Rumors that Gulf Coast refiners were also preparing to engage their own sympathetic strike further underscored the need for employers and the federal government to assert order over the levers of production.[56] Contemporary sources differed on whether employers were prepared to use strikebreakers. One newspaper reported, "No strikebreakers will be employed,"[57] but a commanding officer of the occupying soldiers confirmed the opposite: that "the oil companies would attempt to operate the fields with nonunion labor and requested more troops to prevent anticipated bloodshed."[58]

With so many US troops now stationed in Oil City, federal officials became alarmed by the proximity of their soldiers to Reno Hill's intemperate establishments. Consequently, the US War Department sent an order for local officials to "cleanse" the district to protect any soldiers stationed there from its depravity.[59] On November 5, 1917, Oil City's deputy sheriff was given instructions to shut down the vice district "following a conference between the sheriff's force and the Caddo Parish district attorney."[60] The sheriff and district attorney released a joint statement asserting that "'Reno Hill' should be closed for the safety of everybody," in particular the soldiers "on duty in the field." The order would impact forty to fifty sex workers operating in at least five Reno Hill brothels. After years of tacit toleration, if not corrupted participation, from Caddo Parish law enforcement, anti-vice laws suddenly applied to Reno Hill with vigor: "after today those who persist in operating will be arrested," the sheriff warned.[61]

Despite employer fears of striker violence and subversion, workers were largely peaceful, even coming to the aid of occupying troops when yet another fire broke out in Oil City.[62] When the War Department sought to "cleanse" Oil City of Reno Hill's temptations, strikers were eager to position themselves as being orderly and anti-vice. During a public meeting with the sheriff, Tom Hughes, striker representatives averred that "no whiskey, gambling or immoral houses [should] be allowed in the field," assuring the audience that workers would commit their help in the "clean-up movement." Sheriff Hughes warmly credited the strikers "for the way they are behaving," adding that he was "confident that they will cause no disorder."[63] One notable exception to the general tranquility, however, was in Oil City, where a worker was allegedly shot under ambiguous circumstances in the strike's immediate aftermath.[64]

Over the following two months, neither strikers nor producers would budge from their bargaining positions, prompting the occupying soldiers to remain in North Louisiana throughout November and December, including the holidays. Contemporary articles described how the Shreveport Methodist Church provided a large Thanksgiving feast for soldiers who were still stationed by the oil fields.[65] That December, President Wilson ordered the Presidential Mediation Commission to investigate the situation and produce a set of recommendations that could provide a resolution. To the shock of management, the commission ultimately proposed a series of changes broadly aligning with the union's demands: an eight-hour workday, union recognition, and an end to the intimidation of union members.[66] Elated by the report, the union ended their strike in late December under the presumption that management would promptly adopt the commission's recommendations.

However, management simply refused. On January 2, 1918, representatives from 241 oil companies representing 95 percent of the entire region's oil production met in Houston to collectively denounce the commission and refuse to implement any of its findings.[67] Despite the report's unambiguously pro-worker conclusions, its recommendations were ultimately nonbinding. Moreover, management's position was buoyed by its ability to sustain pre-strike levels of production using nonunion workers who were able to work under the watchful protection of federal soldiers. Oil companies even perversely benefited from an ongoing drought across West Texas, which provided a large pool of farmhands eager for cash wages.[68] Therefore, with production steady and no further government intervention forthcoming, management felt no real pressure to reform its labor practices.

The 1917 strike was ultimately a colossal failure for the nascent oil field unions of Texas and Louisiana—and a total victory for producers. In addition to securing none of their demands, one quarter of the fields' strikers lost their jobs. Much of the union's failure can be attributed to its inability to convince Texas and Louisiana refiners to strike as well, a decision that could have applied more pressure on management. In subsequent years, the region's oil companies sought to blunt the appeal of unionization through new stock purchasing plans, housing programs, and even their own *internal* unions to preempt the influence of independent outside shops. Such efforts were broadly successful, with union membership remaining low across the Texas and Louisiana oil fields until the New Deal.[69]

Ironically, the most significant change that the 1917 strike wrought was the eradication of Oil City's Reno Hill, a dramatic loss for the boomtown's largely woman-run shadow workforce. In order to present their cause as "orderly," workers were willing to participate in the "cleansing" of sex work, an industry they had previously worked alongside, and that many among them had *patronized*. The end of Reno Hill also further underscored the general apathy of Caddo Parish legislators, regulators, and law enforcement toward the rural boomtown. Illicit sex work and drinking would only come under real scrutiny from the War Department, a federal entity. The eradication of Oil City's vice district was not even to protect Oil City and its thousands of residents, but rather on behalf of federal soldiers temporarily occupying the community.

THE WINNERS OF OIL CITY'S NEW ECONOMY

While the advent of oil production offered a crucial lifeline to destitute Southern farmers, landowners who had already found success in North Louisiana's pre-oil market of agriculture and sawmilling were in the best position to most directly profit as Louisiana's new industrial economy emerged. Just as workers retrofitted old tools and technologies to earn an oil field wage, those with ready access to land and credit stood to gain the greatest share of the oil fields' bounty, via royalty profits from production on their property.[70] As Louisiana's oil industry migrated north, Caddo Parish's rural farms became the center of intense bidding wars. Prominent farmer and landowner W. P. Stiles's transition into oil leasing illustrates how old, pre-oil money was very often the most effective means of attaining new oil field wealth. Sometime after 1900, Stiles moved from a farm in Ellis, Texas, to Caddo Parish, where he purchased an enormous tract of rural farmland. As Caddo Parish official Willis P. Butler would later recall of Stiles, he "owned the whole town."[71]

In the succeeding years, Stiles would shrewdly adapt his land's function to suit the economic times. In the early 1900s, low prices and boll weevil fears pushed many cotton farmers out of the business, leaving their fields "to a great extent deserted." Idle farmhands became low-cost labor for sawmills, transforming East Texas and North Louisiana into "one vast logging camp [as] small mills dotted the entire country." Stiles accordingly transitioned his Caddo Parish farm into a profitable sawmilling business. But his landownings were large enough to maintain cotton interests as well, allowing him to nimbly pivot back to agriculture when the Panic of 1907 reduced demand for logged wood.[72]

Possessing such a lucrative asset would serve Stiles especially well when the new oil economy arrived, as he was once again able to transition toward the next big opportunity. As the owner of 3,254 acres of Caddo Parish farmland, Stiles attracted a bevy of investors prospecting for new fields. On December 2, 1907, Stiles leased the drilling rights of his acreage to Mike Benedum and Joe Trees. Stiles's extensive holdings perfectly aligned with the drillers' investment strategy in North Louisiana. While other firms were leasing smaller ten- to thirty-acre parcels, Benedum and Trees hoped to acquire more than one hundred thousand acres for drilling.[73] Given that roughly one in nine wildcat wells were successful at the time, acquiring such an expansive lease would maximize the odds of production.[74]

W. P. Stiles's eager transition into the new oil economy also illustrates an important contrast between the pre-oil economic conditions of Jennings and Oil City, and how those conditions created distinct business climates for the industry. Jennings's land primarily belonged to a wide collection of small land-owning rice farmers such as Jules Clement, many of whom already enjoyed steady livelihoods and were accordingly less desperate for cash wages or royalties. Southwestern Louisiana thus became the site of more legal and economic contests between the oil industry and its more economically stable landowning farmers.

In contrast, North Louisiana's "agrarian monopoly" meant that a smaller cluster of wealthy merchants and planters such as Stiles were the primary lessors of oil production. With crop prices low across the South, planters like Stiles were eager to find more profitable sources of income. Wealthy white landowners were also the biggest, indeed, the only, political constituency in local Parish politics, meaning that if they were happily profiting from oil production, then little political intervention would be forthcoming. All these factors made North Louisiana comparably fertile territory for landowning lessors and oil industry drillers to do business.

Drilling was arduous on the Stiles lease, however. By the end of 1909, Benedum and Trees's well had reached a depth of two thousand feet, but had yet to find production, to that point costing the duo $100,000 with nothing to show for it.[75] But on November 12 the W. P. Stiles No. 4 hit production at a depth of twenty-three hundred feet, subsequently generating more than two thousand barrels per day.[76] By the following spring, No. 4 had become enormously profitable, earning $40,000 for its owners in February 1910 alone and an estimated $50,000 to $60,000 in March. Benedum and Trees subsequently ordered a fifty-five-thousand-barrel steel tank from the Petroleum Iron Works Company, a manufacturer located just outside the drillers' hometown of Pittsburgh. Acquiring such a costly investment illustrated the leaseholders' supreme confidence in the future productivity of Stiles's land and their financial ability to acquire such elaborate technology.[77]

Benedum and Trees's success resulted in a frenzy of leasing on and around Stiles's land, much of which occurred on the adjacent lakes and bayous.[78] In 1909, the Caddo Levee Board, the state authority that managed Caddo Lake, leased its lake-bottom acreage to the Gulf Refining Company, the first time it would administer an oil lease on its lands. Gulf's primary objective was to "offset" the prolific Stiles wells, or siphon away their wells' underground oil through production on nearby property. The Producer's Oil Company attempted a similar gambit by penning their own lease with the Caddo Levee Board along the Stiles property as well.[79] The explosion of such "offset" wells around the Stiles lease reflected the Rule of Capture incentives that drove multiple producers to hastily extract the same reservoir of crude from adjoining land. To keep crude flowing through their own wells, Benedum and Trees had to respond in kind, swiftly erecting a new derrick just eighteen hundred feet west of Stiles No. 4.

The production coursing along Jeem's Bayou attracted financial overtures from some of the nation's most powerful and august oil firms. In the spring of 1910, Standard Oil began making solicitations about building a spur from their nascent Louisiana pipeline into the burgeoning fields along Jeem's Bayou. Rumors even circulated about their intentions to acquire Benedum and Trees's leases outright. That year, *Oil Investor's Journal* reported that "Eastern officials of the Standard"—an evocative phrase that would have conjured power, wealth, and intrigue to its readers—visited the Trees property, prompting "talk at Shreveport of a deal by which the Standard will get in on production in this territory."[80]

Standard Oil's solicitations toward Benedum and Trees quickly soured into mutual resentment, however. Trouble ensued when the drillers began selling oil to local cotton mills and Beaumont refiners for $0.70 a barrel, half of the $1.40 per barrel rate that other producers were offering.[81] The iconic oil company was eager to access the Stiles fields, but also indignant that Benedum and Trees would dare to undercut their product in the marketplace. Victimized by their own price strategy of ruthlessly undermining competitors, Standard responded with characteristic guile. One of the Kansas City Southern's board members was a Standard executive as well, a duplicitous tactic that Standard frequently employed to lever influence over the critical transportation segment of the business.[82] That director successfully prevailed upon the KCS to stop transporting oil produced by Benedum and Trees on its railcars.[83]

Mike Benedum would later claim that he summoned higher powers to resolve their dispute with Standard. According to interviews he provided for *The Great Wildcatter*, Benedum secured a meeting with Theodore Roosevelt to protest Standard's monopolistic behavior. Benedum's account paints an almost cartoonish scene of him arriving at the White House in the typical oil field attire of "high-topped boots and . . . flannel shirt," apparently to the president's delight. As Benedum described his ongoing price war with Standard, Roosevelt became increasingly agitated, at one point colorfully swearing. At meeting's end, Roosevelt advised Benedum to meet with a particular executive of the Kansas City Southern, who promptly corrected the "awful mistake" they had made in pricing.[84] By this vague narrative, which lacks specific dates, Benedum and Trees could only resolve their dispute with Standard Oil through the personal intervention of Theodore Roosevelt.

Benedum's account is not completely implausible, given his status as a wealthy and influential oil man of the time, and Roosevelt's well-documented contempt for Standard. But it also reads like a facile regurgitation of Rooseveltian myth: the swearing, unpretentious Teddy busting a nefarious trust to the benefit of the (comparably) little man with typical bravado. Moreover, the story's chronology does not align. Roosevelt was in office until early 1909, at which point Benedum and Trees were still struggling to produce their first well on the Stiles lease. It was not until the end of 1909, when William Howard Taft occupied the White House, that Benedum and Trees would achieve robust production and attract the attention and ire of Standard. For much of 1908, the most plausible moment in which a meeting with Roosevelt could have occurred, Benedum and Trees had little product to sell in Louisiana, let alone to fight over with the world's largest oil company. Benedum's alleged encounter with Teddy reads as highly dubious.

Regardless of this vignette's reliability, Benedum and Trees did eventually transact with Standard Oil. In November 1910, after an elaborate series of negotiations, the pair sold their Caddo Parish interests for $6 million. Benedum and Trees regarded the sale as a great victory, while also acknowledging that it was probably inevitable. Challenging environmental circumstances and the construction of worker housing on the Stiles land had resulted in "staggering" costs and higher debt levels, making them "vulnerable on the financial front." Selling out provided Benedum and Trees a way out of their debt—and a tidy profit of $2 million. They also understood that trying to beat Standard Oil was ultimately a losing proposition. As Benedum observed, Standard would never stop until "they can buy it at their own price," and if "we let them do it, we have no one to blame but ourselves . . . The showdown is coming soon, and we had better get ready for it." As they so often did, Standard indeed won in the long term. By Benedum's later estimation, Standard would have made roughly $185 million in gross income from their Caddo Parish interests by 1952.[85]

The mutual success of Stiles, Benedum, and Trees was not just a product of luck in the oil patch, but also a reflection of the financial resources that all parties could bring to bear. The property and wealth W. P. Stiles had accumulated in North Louisiana's preexisting economy crucially facilitated his success in the new one: he became an attractive oil lessor precisely because he had so much land to spare. For their part, Benedum and Trees were able to develop those leases because of their own pool of financial resources. Had a more modest wildcatting operation with less access to credit tried to drill the Stiles lease, it might not have had the time or the money to burn $100,000 before achieving any production. But even reasonably well-capitalized firms like Benedum and Trees were unable to match the infinite resources of Standard Oil, which could leverage their financial clout to buy out every competitor sooner or later, ultimately making the market's largest, richest firm the greatest beneficiary of Stiles's property.

The achievements of W. P. Stiles and Benedum and Trees were therefore not so much a story of oil miraculously creating new wealth, but rather of old riches simply begetting new riches. Caddo Parish's class of merchant-planters who already possessed large tracts of land now had the greatest ability to acquire oil royalty wealth. And the oil companies with the best access to credit and technology, Standard Oil preeminent among them, had the greatest ability to take risks, acquire the widest portfolio of leases, and stay on course during the often laborious and cost-intensive drilling process. North Louisiana's oil boomtowns were undoubtedly economic lifelines to many of the region's indebted and desperate farmers. But the people and firms who had already won in the pre-oil economy remained the best positioned to win, and to profit, in North Louisiana's new economy.

4 / THE RACIAL VIOLENCE OF "BLOODY CADDO"

BLACK LABOR WAS INSTRUMENTAL TO THE ECONOMIC development of North Louisiana's Caddo and Claiborne Parishes during the nineteenth and early twentieth centuries. Antebellum slaves performed the arduous work of clearing the Red River valley's thick swamplands for cultivation and then toiled on the enormous cotton plantations that took their place. By the dawn of the twentieth century, many of their descendants were still sharecropping on the same plantations to which their ancestors were bound. Intimidation, whippings, and murder became common methods of ensuring the nominally "free" Black workers would remain low-cost bonded labor for North Louisiana's vast cotton plantations.

Racial violence was especially prevalent in Caddo Parish, inspiring a notorious but fitting moniker for the district: "Bloody Caddo." When the Equal Justice Initiative compiled a list of lynchings that occurred across twelve Southern states from 1877 to 1950, Caddo Parish registered in second place nationally with fifty-four victims.[1] However, as oil became North Louisiana's primary economic engine, the number of lynchings perpetrated against Black residents declined across the state, even in Bloody Caddo. Despite the enormous amount of money being produced on the derricks, virtually no lynchings occurred on or around the oil fields. What accounts for this seemingly paradoxical development?

The advent of oil production in early twentieth-century Louisiana coincided with an inflection point between older methods of grisly plantation "justice" and more "modern" systems of courts and juries. Louisiana's rising class of urban-industrial elites, including oil industry figures, advocated for a new "reformist" legal system to supplant rural mob violence with urban due process—in part to promote Louisiana as a modern, progressive place to do business. While the postbellum cotton plantation gentry derived their economic and political power from the lynch mob, the state's budding managerial class regarded courts and local parish governments as the best instruments of maintaining order and ensuring further economic expansion. There was one notable exception, however, to the decline in mob violence amidst the oil boom: a lurid, highly public 1916 lynching that centered on one of the most prominent oil field families of Caddo Parish.

But the decline of lynchings in North Louisiana did not create an era of equal economic opportunity on the oil patch. White managers and, often, white coworkers actively sought to prevent Black workers from filling any of the oil field's lucrative positions. Even when Black workers were able to secure work, they typically assumed the lowest-paying, most dangerous positions. And while lynchings were rare on the fields, white oil workers continued to apply the *threat* of violence to guarantee they would be the only beneficiaries of North Louisiana's geological wealth. Warnings were levied against not only Black workers but also white employers who sought to leverage the region's cheap and plentiful Black labor.

Despite the pervasive threat of white violence, Black workers remained very much a part of North Louisiana's economic fabric: as manual laborers, sex workers, oil field workers, and, in more specific cases, beneficiaries of oil royalties. Oil even created a modest collection of Black fortunes in North Louisiana. Huey Long once quipped, probably with some hyperbole and contempt, that "there are negro wood choppers in this country worth a million dollars."[2] Those fortunes did not just improve the conditions of the landowners, but also contributed to Black schools, Black churches, and Black community centers. Lynching and terror were endemic to the history of this rural slice of the American South, but they did not solely encapsulate the story of how oil impacted the lives of Black Louisianans living through Bloody Caddo's boom days.

Although oil production helped elevate more "modern" forms of justice, violent animosities still cast a long shadow over North Louisiana's oil boomtowns. Willis P. Butler, who served as the Caddo Parish coroner in the 1920s, recalled the racial violence that permeated North Louisiana's boomtowns. "Oil City was my worst spot," he told an interviewer in 1977. "Shootings were common . . . I had more coroner cases—shooting and killing up there than any part of Caddo Parish." Butler estimated these occurred at a rate of around "one or two per day." Racial hatred seethed across the boomtown community, he said: "Didn't many colored people want to live there. They were scared." Butler would later recount one night in which he investigated a multiple homicide in a remote section of Caddo Parish. He vividly recalled being "surrounded by negroes and a dead negro on the porch. Nobody knew anything about it. And the gas flares were burning everywhere."[3]

The first wave of enslaved Black laborers came to North Louisiana after 1836, following the Army Corps of Engineers' successful clearing of the Red River's "Great Raft," an enormous logjam of wood and debris, thus making the river accessible to the Mississippi River and its lucrative transportation routes. Shreveport and its surrounding Red River valley subsequently developed into a major center of agricultural production and distribution, especially for cotton. With much of the southeastern United States experiencing soil exhaustion after a century of tobacco planting, white planters flowed west to participate in the booming cotton economy. Enslaved workers were vital to this laborious work in North Louisiana, with antebellum-era plantations housing an average of seventy-nine enslaved people along the fertile Red River valley.[4]

Accordingly, the demographic rates grew considerably faster for primarily enslaved Black Louisianans than for white residents. In 1840, Caddo Parish was home to 2,416 whites, 29 free Black citizens, and 2,837 enslaved Black people. By the dawn of the Civil War, that number reached 4,733 whites, 69 free Black citizens, and 7,338 enslaved. Even following the abolition of slavery, the population growth of Black North Louisianans continued to outpace their white counterparts by wide margins. In 1880, the Black population in Caddo Parish reached 19,283, nearly three times the 6,922 white residents.[5] Many of those Black residents were now participants in a new postwar "sharecropping" economy that had become the primary method of producing Red River valley cotton. Black labor still picked cotton, but now did so as nominally free employees of their erstwhile white planter owners.

However, this new world of "free" and emancipated labor still bore much of the inequity and violence that bolstered the old slave economy. In theory, Black residents of North Louisiana were free to sell their labor to the highest bidder; in practice, North Louisiana's white planters used whippings, beatings, and threats to keep their Black workforce on the same cotton fields to which their ancestors were bound. Sharecropping also offered the prospect of Black workers literally *sharing* in the profits of cotton production. But again, in practice, this new form of labor more resembled its antebellum precedent, with white planters either refusing to provide Black workers their rightful share of the harvest or forcing sharecroppers to buy food and goods exclusively from their own storehouse at exorbitant rates explicitly designed to recapture their earnings.[6] North Louisiana's cotton plantations were now animated by a new form of bonded, unfree labor to keep its Black workers in the fields.

But even though the role of Black Louisianans in postbellum Louisiana continued to largely resemble their antebellum position, a "social demoralization" still roiled many Southern whites who resented losing their tools of economic and social mastery.[7] Unaccustomed to having its position in society challenged, Caddo Parish's white planter class chafed at the dramatic changes brought by the end of the war. Suddenly, the region's vast Black community was no longer enslaved to the cotton fields, and even sought political power. Planters regarded anything resembling racial equality in the workplace or in government as diametrically opposed to their own prosperity and security; racial hatred created the irrational perception that Black uplift would inevitably result in calamity for the white race.[8]

Consequently, North Louisiana's planters and their white allies began to employ any means they had to reassert control over the region's society and government, including violence and murder. Lynchings against Black communities exploded across the state, in particular its northern parishes. Reconstruction-era Louisiana became notorious for racial killings, compiling 3,494 homicide victims between 1865 and 1876, 81.9 percent of whom were Black. Within that murderous vortex, Caddo Parish's Red River valley accounted for 1,538—or a staggering 44 percent—of those statewide homicides.[9] Moreover, that figure likely undercounts, given the numerous murders that were never reported to officials. Upon even closer inspection, the region's murder rates amount to a collective act of ethnic cleansing: 10 percent of the *entire population of Black men* in Caddo Parish was murdered by white people over this postwar period. The disproportionate level of mayhem in and around Caddo Parish inspired the dark, but very appropriate, epithet: Bloody Caddo.[10]

The motive behind these acts of mob violence and murder was very often political. Suddenly facing the prospect of Black candidates, political parties, and even elected officials, white agitators sought to intimidate and brutalize Black voters and their prospective leaders. The White League, a paramilitary force that attacked and intimidated Black GOP leaders across the South, opened a chapter in Caddo Parish in 1874 in advance of that year's election.[11] Highly public lynchings became a key instrument for eliminating Black political leadership, deterring further Black activism, and conserving racial "purity" at the ballot box.

Such efforts to inhibit Black political mobilization were strikingly effective. Although Black citizens constituted 75 percent of Caddo Parish's population in 1878, the white-supremacist Democratic Party assumed full control of the state government.[12] These extralegal methods of preventing Black political participation became codified into Louisiana's electoral process following the 1898 state constitutional convention, which formalized the notion that voting and serving in public office were exclusively for white Louisianans.

Murders also functioned as highly public assertions of white economic power. White planters sought to reimpose old forms of "plantation discipline" in which the Black population's labor and social activities were under white control. Lynching parties often resulted from disputes in the fields and served as a reminder of white employers' continued authority, even if their Black workforce now assumed a relatively "free" position in Louisiana's economy. Maintaining a stable and docile workforce in the cotton fields was paramount: Black workers daring to seek opportunities elsewhere faced intimidation, whipping, and beating. White plantation hands also murdered many Black sharecroppers who had simply demanded a fair settlement of their crops.[13]

The 1901 killing of John Gray Foster, a wealthy Caddo Parish planter, was a particularly notorious dispute between a white landowner and his Black workforce that ended in a highly public series of lynchings. Contemporary newspaper accounts described how a disagreement between Foster and his Black laborers boiled over: a "bad feeling" had prevailed "between the negroes and overseers on the Foster plantation and Foster was appealed to settle the differences." As Foster approached a "negro cabin . . . he was fired upon and killed."[14] One week later, a white mob of two hundred strong forcibly removed two Black suspects, the preacher Frank "Prophet" Smith and F. D. McLand, from their cells in a Shreveport jail and hung them on the road.

The deaths of these men very much embodied the old forms of "justice" that prevailed in postwar Caddo Parish: a white rural populace impatient with the wheels of due process and eager to enforce its own racial supremacy in a ritualized and highly public manner. Shreveport deputies had been nominally protecting Smith and McLand, but ultimately were unable, and perhaps unwilling, to protect the Black suspects from vigilante justice. The mob believed Smith and McLand to be leaders of a "negro Mafia, a fanatical, semi-religious society which had in view the murder of whites."[15] But another account ascribed an entirely different motive behind Smith's "preaching." Styling himself as "Elijah the Prophet," Smith had allegedly warned of "dire disaster" to "ignorant Blacks" if they did not flee Houston for North Louisiana. Two hundred Black workers followed his millennialist message, only to discover he was "an agent for planters who were short of help" and needed Black labor.[16]

Regardless of Smith's true motives, his murder reflected a paranoid white populace that believed its economic and social position to be a precarious one. White planters remained deeply reliant on Black labor, but also desperate to assert their racial mastery over such a large population of non-enslaved workers. Contemporary newspaper accounts were perversely complimentary of Foster for being "a good friend of the negroes," and for his ability to "get more negroes to work for him than any other man in North Louisiana." While his neighbors were desperately seeking labor, Foster would have "all the hands he wanted and they would work for him like they were driven slaves."[17] Foster's death resonated with the broader anxieties that many white planters experienced over managing such a large pool of free Black labor, and their lingering desire for a pliant Black workforce they could *control* rather than employ.

In 1896, the same climate of racial terror claimed the life of Isom McGee in the remote Claiborne Parish hamlet of Homer, just east of Caddo Parish. The son of enslaved parents, McGee had worked for a local white family until buying a roughly ninety-one-acre portion of their farm in 1889.[18] But in 1896, a mob lynched McGee for the alleged rape of a white woman—or perhaps for achieving too much economic success.[19] In a 1921 interview, Lillie "Gussie" Taylor, McGee's stepdaughter, recalled "feeling the fear of being alone in a community where prejudice was growing all the time." Along with her mother and stepdaughter, Taylor fled to Hope, Arkansas. Her stepfather's land technically passed into her ownership, but Taylor "did not consider [the land] worth anything."[20] Just a few years later, she would discover that this small family farm could make her potentially the wealthiest oil heiress in the world.

THE OIL FIELDS OF BLOODY CADDO

Even as North Louisiana evolved from agrarian cotton production to industrial oil extraction, the nascent economy continued to be characterized by acute racial segregation, albeit in a form that inverted the workplace dynamic of postwar Louisiana. While lynching and violence had functioned to keep black workers *on* the cotton fields as bonded sharecroppers, white oil workers were now in competition with local Black workers and instead sought to keep them *away* from the oil fields and the plentiful wages they offered. Bloody Caddo's long-standing racial animosities enforced sharp demarcations in the new industrial workplace, dictating who could and could not be hired on a rig. As thousands of white migrants became salaried roustabouts, roughnecks, and drillers, white managers relegated Black workers to the most unskilled, peripheral work—if they got any work at all. At times this contest pitted white workers, who resented low-wage Black competition, against their white managers, who were often eager to employ cheap Black labor.

Such trends were hardly unique to North Louisiana. A 1966 Ford Foundation study examining the impact of race in America's oil industry discovered persistent bias throughout the twentieth century, especially with regard to "the attitudes prevailing in many southern towns." Rotary drilling, the predominant method in North Louisiana's fields by the 1920s, necessitated a team of about six workers performing skilled work for accordingly high pay. However, those jobs were all but unavailable to the Black workforce, with few "negroes [working] as drillers except in odd laboring jobs." As late as 1940, Black workers occupied fewer than 1 percent of oil exploration and production jobs across the American South.[21]

But North Louisiana was unique in one important respect. While many other oil fields had "few if any Negroes residing in neighboring areas" prior to production, Louisiana's oil boomtowns had a large Black population that was there before the boom.[22] So as oil production soared, racial animus collided with simple demographics. Frank Dunn, who worked just across the state line at Spindletop, encountered the same collision of prejudice and economic opportunity in Texas. He recalled white employers being worried about Black workers "taking up jobs that some white man probably would be glad to have." Managers who dared to employ Black labor consigned that workforce to the most dangerous, menial, and low-paying tasks. As a result, any Black laborers who managed to secure work on the iconic East Texas gusher were given the least desirable posts, a deliberate measure to, as Frank Dunn recalled, keep "the nigger away from the field" and its best wages.[23]

Despite the perpetual influence of racial animosity across North Louisiana's oil fields, the number of lynchings *declined* as the industry expanded. This would seem like a counterintuitive outcome: why would Bloody Caddo's restive, violent white populace stop performing acts of violence precisely as such a lucrative new industry was growing? This seemingly paradoxical development reflected a broader political and economic contest over how to deliver "justice" in early twentieth-century Louisiana, waged between those who favored the postbellum methods of ritualistic violence and lynching that traditionally prevailed in rural-agrarian regions and those who supported more "modern" forms of due process and courts, which were favored by the state's growing urban-industrial class of businessmen and their political allies.[24]

Following the end of enslaved labor, North Louisiana's white planter elite and rural white working class mutually regarded the state's justice system as too abstract and unpredictable. In contrast to the state, white mob violence offered a far more reliable guarantor of economic and racial authority over North Louisiana's now "free" Black workforce. Lynching enabled Cotton Belt landowners to effectively govern their fields as private legal fiefdoms in which they were judge, jury, and executioner. However, by the first years of the twentieth century, the center of Louisiana's economy was reorienting away from rural staple crop production like cotton and toward urban industrial production. As a new class of merchant capitalists swelled in cities like Shreveport, those middle-class professionals, many of whom had migrated from outside of Louisiana, sought to challenge the "white planter prerogative of violence" toward its Black subjects.[25]

As business-minded elites gained wealth and influence in Louisiana, they promoted a more bureaucratic justice system of due process composed of municipal police, lawyers, and judges: a more "modern" approach than the rural savagery of mob rule and lynchings. Urban business organs such as the Shreveport Chamber of Commerce and the Caddo Bar Association each passed resolutions condemning mob violence.[26] Advocating for reform remained very much an act of self-interest: just as lynching and mob rule maintained the docile rural workforce that was necessary for cotton production, a more stable and regularized justice system would present Louisiana as a "modern" and progressive place to do business, critical to attracting new investment and new workers to its growing urban-industrial landscape.

To encourage more industrial activity in their state, Louisiana's Democratic political class began parroting this reformist language and challenging the primacy of lynching as a means of applying justice. In 1905, Louisiana's governor, Newton C. Blanchard, made a speech castigating mob rule and lynching in the state, not out of sympathy for its numerous Black victims, but because it was retarding Louisiana's "economic and social progress" and preventing the capital investments and immigration its new industrial leaders sought. Just one year later the governor personally intervened to prevent the lynching of Charles Coleman, a Black man accused of murdering a white teenager. To prevent future lynchings, Blanchard further empowered local enforcement to prosecute mob vigilantes and sent militia members to protect the accused, actions that state officials in the late nineteenth century had been loath to do.[27]

Anti-Black lynchings very much continued to occur throughout the first decades of the twentieth century throughout North Louisiana, including a notable surge during and after the First World War. However, the broad numbers of mob violence fell consistently, if modestly, from a rate of 6.4 annual lynching victims during the 1910s to 3.6 annually in the 1920s. Such a trend reflected the broadening economic and political influence of Louisiana's urban middle class and the reformist legal system they sought to advance; it also illuminated the waning power of Louisiana's white plantation elite and the twilight of its rural fiefdoms. But even if the state's new methods of justice offered a break from the savagery of the past, the outcomes were largely the same: state-sponsored executions and legally enforced "Jim Crow" segregation over public spaces simply offered a more "modern" and efficient means of upholding white supremacy for a new class of managerial elites. Charles Coleman may have escaped the mob's lynch rope, but not the state's: he was executed after a brief trial and conviction.[28]

Moreover, the broad decline of lynchings across the state during North Louisiana's oil boom did not translate into a total absence of racialized violence in the fields; the specter of white violence against Black workers and their allies remained ever-present in the workplace. Racially divided employment patterns reflected not only an employer's personal racism, but also fears of how other white employees would react to the prospect of Black coworkers. Black laborers were often cheap and performed some of the hardest work on the oil patch, attributes that were attractive to cost-conscious managers. But the mere presence of cheaper Black labor could raise the ire of particularly virulent white coworkers. And the spatial proximity inherent to oil work would have made such antipathies unavoidable. Unlike a large factory in which Black and white labor could theoretically occupy separate quarters, oil field workers primarily oriented their tasks around the derrick itself. Even the more peripheral manual work that Black laborers tended to perform—digging earthen tanks, hauling pipe, clearing land—could only be so far from the actual rig. The rural isolation of North Louisiana's boomtowns heightened tensions as well, making the presence of Black workers impossible to conceal from white-supremacist coworkers.

Resentment often boiled over into outright violence. Mike Benedum recalled that his Caddo Parish labor force occasionally had a "bad white element." Not only would they reject oil field jobs they considered beneath them, but they also would not let anyone else work in their stead. On one occasion when Benedum's team needed workers to swiftly dig an earthen tank to capture oil spewing from a well, the white laborers refused to work. In desperate and immediate need of storage, Benedum looked to hire out "some negros [*sic*] over there [from] a ranch" to perform the job. As the Black ranch hands began digging, seven or eight of the white workers approached to prevent "any of these damn-niggers working around here."[29] An Irishman Benedum had deputized to maintain order warned the mob to disperse and drew a revolver. The rioters advanced apace, prompting the deputy to fire and wound several of the men.

Benedum and Trees employees rushed the injured men to a hospital, where they ultimately survived. The riotous workers were subsequently arrested, but since there was no "jury that wasn't afraid," Benedum remembered, they were put "on the side of the road with a ball around their legs, and they were there for three months." Benedum's recollections are cryptic but seem to suggest that justice would have been elusive against a group of white men defending their race before an all-white jury. In that context, three months on a work gang was perhaps the only possible legal outcome. While the deputy seemingly acted in defense of the Black workers, Benedum's bold actions were primarily on behalf of the white rancher who loaned them: he had promised the rancher to protect his Black labor.[30] This was not an act of charity; the intersecting economic interests of two white employers saved these Black ranch hands.

Even white oil patch workers alleged to be supporting Black workers over their own race became the targets of violence. In July 1920 a Claiborne Parish court convicted Tom Shannon, a white contractor on the Homer oil field, for murdering twenty-eight-year-old William H. "Pete" Dunson, also a white oil worker. In the preceding months there had been "trouble between the drivers of the two races," prompting the local sheriff to deputize several "employers of negro drivers to keep the peace and protect the negroes."[31] Shannon, an employer of Black drivers, had assumed one of those deputized roles, so when Pete Dunson "had an argument with a negro workman," Shannon confronted Dunson and shot him in a field.[32] Coroner Willis P. Butler listed "Traumatization by Firearm (Homicide)" as the cause of death, which occurred on May 21, 1920.[33] It is unclear whether Shannon was simply protecting an employee and his economic assets, or consciously defending a Black man from the threat of violence.

Testimony from Shannon's post-conviction appeal to the Louisiana Supreme Court captured how incensed the white oil field workforce had become over Dunson's killing, with many agitating for violence against the Black men Shannon protected. Oil field laborer H. A. McDonald overheard his fellow workers saying that "[Dunson's] death was caused—[by] those negro drivers out there." Coworker Burt Pixley openly discussed ridding the field of Black drivers: "They were going to cause trouble in the field if we didn't get shed [*sic*] of them." Elmer Aycock told the court that Shannon's actions aroused a "good deal of feeling among the oil field workers," with one man purportedly threatening to "go . . . out there to hang him [Shannon] . . . and run the negroes off" before a group of people at a country store.[34]

As it turned out, T. A. Reynolds, the man Aycock recalled threatening violence against Shannon, was a juror in the trial that convicted his former coworker. Shannon appealed his conviction in 1921 on the grounds that as a juror, Reynolds "had a fixed opinion . . . [that] was prejudiced against the defendant," particularly for the racially transgressive nature of the murder he committed. Defense lawyers cited Aycock's testimony as evidence that Reynolds wanted Shannon to be "hanged or mobbed" before the trial even began, negating his impartiality as a juror. The prosecution readily acknowledged Reynolds's fury over "Mr. Shannon . . . taking up for the negro drivers," but argued that such racial animus was separate from the question of his suitability as a juror, as Reynolds had expressed "no opinion about [Shannon's] guilt or innocence."[35] Ultimately, the Louisiana Supreme Court upheld the lower court's guilty verdict, ruling that Reynolds's open hostility for Shannon and his Black workers did not taint his neutrality as a juror.

The outcome of Shannon's case reflected a legal system caught between two worlds. While nominally a "modern" form of justice grounded in due process, North Louisiana's courts still retained strains of the old methods of plantation justice. At no point in the proceedings did the prosecution directly attack Shannon for murdering a white man in defense of a Black man. But the unveiled contempt that witnesses and a juror expressed toward those Black workers Shannon protected was a not-so-implicit indictment of the act he committed.

That T. A. Reynolds could openly attribute Pete Dunson's death to the oil field's "racial mixing" and remain a duly appointed juror demonstrated the acceptability of that view in Louisiana's legal system, and the likelihood that white oil workers daring to protect the lives of Black workers over their own race would have little recourse in the state's "modern" justice system.

As the oil boom accelerated across North Louisiana, regional chapters of the Ku Klux Klan were also rapidly appearing across its cities and towns. With its elaborate ceremonies and bureaucratic hierarchy, the Klan sought to blend the structural ethos of modern industrial corporations with raw violence and intimidation to govern "proper" racial behavior and promote Anglo-Saxon power. With its long history of fierce racial conflict, Louisiana quickly became one of the most notorious realms of the Klan's "Invisible Empire." North Louisiana became a particularly critical power center of Klan activity, stretching from its urban "throne city" of Shreveport to the region's wider hinterland of oil communities.[36] By 1923, local "klaverns" had been established in two rural boomtowns: klavern #41 in Vivian and klavern #63 in Homer.[37] Further east in Morehouse Parish, the Klan even successfully recruited a collection of oil and gas workers into their ranks.[38]

If anyone objected to Klan activities in rural boomtowns, they would have found little recourse with Caddo Parish officials in Shreveport. The state's courts and police were filled with Klan members.[39] Meanwhile, the state government was run by individuals who at the very least tolerated the Klan, or, at worst, were active participants in it. W. Scott Wilkinson served as a Democrat in the Louisiana House of Representatives between 1920 and 1924 and knew many "prominent—very fine citizens of Shreveport that belonged to [the Klan]."[40] He admiringly described Klansmen as "high-type men . . . concerned against having the white women molested by the Negro men," adding they conducted themselves in a "very orderly way."[41] The Klan sought to promulgate their dark influence across every corner of North Louisiana's oil boom, from Shreveport's urban corridors of commerce and politics to the more rural centers of natural resource production.

However, the early 1920s would ultimately stand as a high-water mark for Klan power in Louisiana. The same reformist movement challenging the prevalence of lynchings also began to confront the Invisible Empire's quiet influence over the state's government and society. The political reaction against the Klan in Louisiana was triggered by a 1922 incident in which a petty conflict between rival factions in Morehouse Parish prompted a group of armed Klansmen to abduct and brutally murder several members of a prominent white family. The lurid case horrified the Louisiana public, perhaps because the Klan had murdered *white* victims, and prompted the state's governor, John M. Parker, to forcibly denounce the organization. Distrustful of his own state's law enforcement personnel, Parker reached out to the Department of Justice in Washington for assistance in investigating the case. The governor also refused to promote several district judges due to their Klan membership and even took the remarkable step of appointing a Jewish sheriff in Morehouse Parish.[42]

Two years later, anti-Klan initiatives became key issues in the state's gubernatorial election, with the top two candidates both supporting legislation to curtail the organization's political and social power. The third candidate, Huey Long, instead focused his attacks on Standard Oil and the economic influence of monopolies while remaining politically agnostic on the Klan, largely to avoid antagonizing white voters in North and Central Louisiana. Henry Fuqua, a Protestant from Baton Rouge, won on a promise to "unmask" the Klan and ultimately signed legislation mandating that private organizations publicly submit membership lists to the state. Despite the ascendency of a reformist governor, however, deep wells of pro-Klan sentiment remained in Louisiana's state government, particularly within Northern parishes like Bloody Caddo. While Fuqua ascended to the governor's mansion, the Louisiana House of Representatives elevated J. Stuart Douglas of Caddo Parish, a Klan advocate, as its speaker.[43]

Unfortunately, many firsthand recollections of Klan activities in North Louisiana's oil boomtowns offer only romanticized perspectives. John F. Law, who grew up in Oil City in the 1910s and 1920s, recalled all the things the Klan "did good." If a man "wouldn't work and support his family, they'd come to him" and administer a "whooping."[44] Law heard of one wayward man being whipped "like a mule" and another being tarred and feathered. Walter Duvall George Jr., whose father drilled Caddo Parish's first well, similarly admired the Klan for ensuring "people didn't carouse" and for "[taking] care of their own." When the interviewer asked George to elaborate, he demurred: "I don't know much more."[45]

The younger George's reticence to speak about racialized violence is striking. He would have certainly known more on the topic, as his own family participated in a notorious 1916 lynching in the oil field community of Vivian, which lay just north of Oil City. Although the rise of oil production in North Louisiana coincided with a broad decline in lynchings, one glaring exception centered on George's parents: in particular, the wife of Walter George Sr., Martha (née Jones), or "Effie" as she was also known. In August 1916, Effie accused a Black man named Jesse Hammett of "entering [her] bedroom . . . armed with a butcher knife and making an attempt to criminally assault her," a charge to which Hammett allegedly confessed. The George family had apparently employed Hammett for many years. Newspaper accounts also highlighted a particularly remarkable detail: Hammett had "nursed [Effie] as an infant."[46] This detail was potentially spurious: Hammett was only five years old at the time of

Effie's birth and infancy, making him an unlikely nursemaid; however, this narrative at least suggests that Hammett and the George family maintained a very close relationship prior to the accusation.

The dramatic narrative of Hammett's murder illuminated the ongoing tensions between a new, more "modern" system of legal due process trying, in this case unsuccessfully, to wrest power from traditional forms of mob "justice" that still held sway among so much of Louisiana's rural white working class. After the alleged incident occurred in the early hours of Friday morning, Hammett was arrested by a team of Caddo Parish sheriffs, to whom he apparently confessed at 11 a.m. on Friday. As word of the confession spread across Vivian, a mob of white Caddo Parish locals began to coalesce around the jail where Hammett was held. While the oil fields' working class was eager to enact their own swift and deadly justice, Vivian's business and political elite sought to intervene and prevent Hammett's lynching. Various "substantial men" of the community, including the mayor, J. T. Smith, a deputy sheriff, and even Effie's parents, all addressed the fiery lynch mob, asking them to disperse and allow the legal system to proceed.[47]

Although the sheriffs were keeping Hammett under custody in Vivian, they planned to transport him south to Shreveport for prosecution. But as the mob's size steadily grew, the sheriffs had to abruptly flee the jail with the suspect and seek refuge in the thick woods outside of Oil City. The team stumbled upon what appeared to be a vacant home and barricaded the doors as one of the sheriffs hid with Hammett inside a kitchen pantry. Meanwhile, a white mob composed of people from Vivian, Oil City, and even the supposedly tranquil, rule-abiding community of Trees City combed the woods in search of the Black suspect. As the sun rose on Saturday morning, August 26, a group of 150 assailants finally located the hideout and forcibly confiscated Hammett from the overwhelmed deputies. A few hours later, at 1 p.m., the mob strung up Hammett by his neck on a telephone pole in the center of Vivian as more than a thousand spectators watched.[48] As with many other American lynchings of its time, a photographer captured both the mutilated body swinging from the pole and the enormous swell of people watching below.

In the aftermath of Hammett's execution, Vivian's political and business elite expressed deep regret. Mayor Smith felt that he spoke for the "sentiment of the better class of citizens, the stable business and professional men of the community" by saying the lynching was a "splotch on the town's name." Meanwhile, none of the more than one thousand witnesses identified the main assailants, vaguely characterizing the perpetrators as "outsiders, non-resident[s]" of Vivian.[49] Jesse Hammett's murder demonstrated the continued proximity between new methods of "justice" and the grisly violence of the plantation. Despite the relative decrease in mob violence against Black men during North Louisiana's oil boom, white lust for swift, extralegal killing remained ever-present, even as the state's justice system increasingly assumed a veneer of "modernity."

BLACK WORKERS ON THE PIPELINES

Lower pay, harsher conditions, and fewer opportunities for upward mobility were also standard for Black workers building Louisiana's earliest system of oil pipelines. In 1909, when the Standard Oil Company of Louisiana initiated construction on its enormous four-hundred-mile line connecting North Louisiana's wells to its growing Baton Rouge refinery, Black labor was essential, especially for the most odious and strenuous tasks. Before any pipes went underground, a largely Black "right of way" team used saws and axes to manually clear trees, vegetation, or anything else along the line's route.[50] Simultaneously, a separate crew of Black workers unloaded twenty-foot-long, six-hundred-pound segments of steel pipe from railroad stops and placed them along the newly cleared right of way.[51]

With these enormous steel lines in place, skilled teams of "tongsmen" began the elaborate process of connecting and burying the lines. Much like the roughnecks and drillers on the rigs, tong gangs were the highest-paid and highest-skilled positions on the team. Accordingly, they were exclusively white. As the tongsmen connected the piping, Black laborers performed menial, and even extraneous, tasks. During the blistering Louisiana summers, one team of six Black workers spent their days holding a wood-framed strip of canvas to shade white tongsmen. "It sure helped a lot," recalled grateful pipeliner J. B. Barnett.[52] White employers regarded the Black workforce as little more than cheap economic parts, even in death. When accidents killed white employees, Standard Oil paid all the funeral expenses. When a Black laborer died on the job, the company unceremoniously buried the corpse along the pipeline's right of way.[53]

Racial disparities also delineated the workers' quality of life away from the pipelines. Employee housing consisted of racially segregated sixteen-by-twenty-foot tents that were constantly being deconstructed, moved ahead, then reconstructed as the line progressed forward. White camps had wooden floors and free access to an entire culinary team: "a head cook, a pastry cook and a second cook and usually about four flunkies to peel potatoes and wash dishes."[54] Numerous former pipeliners recalled the food's surprising quality: "just as good as could be, the very best," declared John Crump.[55] However, Black workers had neither floors in their tents nor access to free meals. Already paid half the wages of their white counterparts, Black pipeliners were often obliged to buy their own food at country stores nearby. At times they resorted to hunting for their own meals, with each Black worker "catching his rabbit where he could."[56]

FIGURE 4.1. *A team of Black workers retrofit Standard Oil's Louisiana pipeline to protect its steel from the soil's natural acidity, 1914.*

Despite the harsh working conditions and inferior pay, "Negro labor was plentiful," recalled white pipeliner Fred Bimel. But as on the derricks, a volatile tension existed between the manager's desire for cheap labor and white pipeliners' virulent hatred for Black competition. Given the precarious price of cotton throughout much of the 1910s, employers could draw from a large pool of underemployed Black farm labor. One pipeliner estimated that Black workers received "two or three times more than negroes working at other places" at the time.[57] Bimel recalled managers could easily offer "more money than the farmers were paying," adding that "we had a hard time keeping them away from us,"[58] reflecting white anxieties about employing too much low-cost Black labor.

Black labor was cheap, but always rife to upset the delicate racial equilibrium of the workplace. Bimel felt that his team "never had any race trouble," but later acknowledged that conflicts did arise: "we had to fight the civil war over a few times."[59] Local planters allowed their Black workforce to pursue new economic opportunities on the pipelines, but never to the detriment of their own fields' productivity. Plantation men periodically rode out to the pipeliner camps on horseback carrying six-shooters: a warning to their Black farmhands to be "back on the farm Monday as they wanted to start plowing."[60] Like the armed men on horseback, Louisiana's old farming economy was never far from the pipelines, contributing a bottomless supply of Black workers to cheaply perform its most laborious tasks—that is, before returning to the fields.

Pipelining was an entirely new type of industrial labor in North Louisiana, but many vestiges of the old cotton fields still governed its workplace. White pipeline managers even sought to re-create aspects of the plantation to ensure their Black workers would remain pliant and productive. One Black pipeliner named "Old Henry Lowry" earned an extra $0.25 per day for leading his compatriots in work tunes that would mimic old plantation songs: "he would sing when the work would begin to lag and the others would join in and they would all be singing and the work would be going great."[61] Songs were particularly useful as they performed "any kind of work that lent itself to rhythm."[62]

The content of Old Henry's songs mostly eluded his white coworkers: "it was hard to tell at times just what they were singing," acknowledged Smith W. Day, but "it would sound like a holy roller meeting."[63] Fred Bimel recalled songs to be about "what they were going to do on Saturday night."[64] Old Henry was paid, albeit sparingly, for singing his "holy roller" songs. But his white employers did so to conjure Louisiana's bygone antebellum economy, when a planter could truly *possess*, rather than employ, his Black workforce.

Despite all the efforts to keep the oil boom exclusively white, Black Louisianans still managed to build an identity as Black oilmen, even if it was often more aspirational than actual. Music was one such outlet for expressing the hopes and frustrations of Black communities living through the oil boom across the Southwest. Texas bluesman Blind Lemon Jefferson performed "Oil Well Blues" as an ode to the industry; Louisiana Creole singer Amede Ardoin contributed "Waltz of the Oil Fields" to the canon of oil field blues tunes. And in 1947, Houston native Eddie "Cleanhead" Vinson recorded the raunchy and self-assertive "Oil Man Blues," which equated the longing for oil wealth with sexual gratification: "I'm an oil drillin' daddy, and your ground looks very rich." Vinson's playful eroticism was evidently too sexually and racially transgressive for contemporary radio stations, which refused to play "Oil Man Blues."[65]

North Louisiana's oil boomtowns became particularly rich sources of inspiration for pieces of Black musical and cultural self-expression. In 1940, folklorist John A. Lomax traveled to Mooringsport, the Caddo Parish "City of Derricks," to find relatives of local blues legend Huddie Ledbetter, better known as Lead Belly. But Huddie's Uncle Bob insisted that Lomax also meet a lesser-known musician in the family, his grandson Noah Moore. On October 10, 1940, Lomax recorded Moore performing "Oil City Blues," a nine-minute eponymous ode to the boomtown, where Moore knew he could find the "brown skin gal a waitin' there for me." The bluesman describes standing on the corner, "'til my feet got soakin' wet . . . tryin' to make friends with every Oil City girl I met."[66]

Moore's song implies a nostalgic familiarity with Oil City, a hometown to the singer. But there is also a longing, a searching for that "brown skin gal" who perhaps does not exist. Moore's narrator is in Oil City, but also perpetually traveling—on the corner, on the road—and never seems to settle. "Oil City Blues" captured the strange duality of life in Louisiana's boomtowns as a Black man: you are present, but constantly searching, and never truly safe and at rest in an economic and social world of hostile white men. However, the very existence of Black music indigenous to Louisiana's oil boom still revealed a community unwilling to be silent participants.

THE BLACK SEX TRADE

If Black Louisianans had limited ability to prosper in the economy of oil production and pipelining, they had relatively more success in a parallel industry: the sex trade. While unable to earn the same three dollars per day on the derrick as their white counterparts, Black workers could access some of that money through North Louisiana's raucous and more racially transgressive brothels. Sex work in the boomtowns was a very dangerous profession. But it was paid labor that Black workers could perform more freely than oil field labor, and, in many cases, where they could attain much greater success.

Unlike the oil fields' heavily male workforce, the sex trade provided unique opportunities for Black *women* looking to acquire a piece of the oil boom. "There were lots of colored girls down there," remembered former chief of Shreveport Police Bob Anderson. He recalled the popular Octoroon Club as being "one-eighth Negro," presumably referring to the demographic ratio of its employees.[67] Shreveport native W. H. Griffin bluntly remembered "more nigger women than there was [sic] white women down there."[68] Some Black sex workers were even "kept by white men" on a kind of perverse retainer: they lived in their madam's house and served other men, but "'cleared the decks' for the men who kept them." One "prominent oil man" of Caddo Parish allegedly "kept a colored girl in the servants' house on his place."[69]

Despite the transgressive sheen of North Louisiana's sex trade, racial ideologies still very much shaped economic outcomes. As with Black oil workers, Black sex workers fetched a comparably smaller wage. White prostitutes could attract three to five dollars for one encounter or ten dollars for a whole night. Black sex workers, in contrast, could only fetch one dollar per session. But Griffin remembered this racial disparity not as a disincentive to patrons, but as an economic opportunity: "I went to bed with a lot of them nigger women myself.

We didn't have much money, you'd go to bed with one of them nigger women for a dollar." Asked whether the Black sex workers were good-looking, he equivocated: "Most of them wasn't real black."[70]

The intricacies of race further governed which individuals could patronize which sex worker, and which could transgress those racial boundaries. W. H. Griffin remembered mixed-race women running businesses that served an exclusively white clientele: "places run by yellow skinned Niggers just running it for white men." However, that racially fluid atmosphere did not apply to Black patrons. Griffin noted that if any "Nigger men got in there they came in by the backdoor, didn't let anybody see them." A former bell boy at Shreveport's Washington-Youree Hotel used to witness the same double standard. As Black men walked by white brothels, prostitutes used to call out to them, but they "were afraid to go in."[71] White patrons racially crossing for sex could be exotic and mischievous, but ultimately acceptable. Black patrons attempting to visit white sex workers, however, remained far too subversive for Bloody Caddo's codes of racial and gendered conduct.

The desirability of Black women to white oil workers such as W. H. Griffin presented an opportunity, if a distasteful one, for those Black women to economically participate in the oil boom, and not just to earn money, but to be *employers*. Willis Butler recalled "colored women" running "2 or 3 of the best kept houses" in Shreveport.[72] Mary Marks, aka "Baby Jane," became a particularly famous "Negro woman" purveying girls in the city. According to Bob Anderson, Marks was "Black as the ace of spades" and constantly donning "red wigs, yellow wigs, purple wigs." Baby Jane's dramatic ensembles brought in a flood of money from the oil patch. When oil field workers visited her establishment, "Baby Jane would take care of them men . . . She was very popular."[73]

Even amidst North Louisiana's strictly observed racial codes, the comparably fluid standards of its rowdy underworld stood in sharp contrast to the oil fields. Black men near the rigs were constant objects of fierce contempt and mostly alienated from the oil economy. But Black *women* could be perceived as glamorous and transgressive, and thus comparably freer to earn, although they earned less than their white female counterparts. White oil workers' desire for racial exoticism arguably gave many Black women equal, and perhaps even greater, access to North Louisiana's oil wealth than Black men. This is not to idealize the experience of Black sex workers. Exploitation, lower pay, and dangerous working conditions were all too common. But it is hard to identify economic equivalents of "Baby Jane" or other Black-owned brothels in the oil industry, where Black men could hardly dig ditches without facing the threat of violent reprisal.

For North Louisiana's Black population, the region's oil boom was a distinct break from the past, but also a persistent reminder of the white-supremacist ideologies that continued to govern its economic and legal institutions. Oil may have transformed North Louisiana's stagnant farmlands into a teeming center of industrial production, but that new economy was mostly inaccessible to the region's largest demographic of people: Black sharecroppers. The very families whose labor had been so instrumental to North Louisiana's agrarian economy for almost a century were suddenly alienated from its newest means of production.

One fortunate byproduct of these economic changes was the relative decline in Bloody Caddo's ferocious mob violence. The oil industry's influence helped usher in a more "reformist" justice system that produced a significant decrease in anti-Black lynchings. But even the "modern" system that replaced it simply provided a more efficient means of executing Black defendants and legally enforcing "Jim Crow" across North Louisiana's workplaces, ultimately benefiting the state's elite white managerial class far more than its Black citizenry.

The Black experience during North Louisiana's oil boom illuminated a critical dynamic of America's early twentieth-century oil industry and of industrialization more generally: the birth of new forms of production did not eradicate old racial prejudices, but rather created new, more "modern" outlets for them. Indeed, the oil boom's enormous financial stakes only accelerated the need for white Louisianans to assert strict racial boundaries over the economy, albeit under the guise of a more "reformist" justice system. The correlation between new petroleum wealth and the more intense "Jim Crow" divisions that characterized Bloody Caddo would echo across the oil fields of Oklahoma and East Texas over succeeding decades, ensuring their economic beneficiaries remained almost exclusively white well into the mid-twentieth century.[74] Even as the oil patch transformed North Louisiana's landscape, old boundaries of the *cotton* patch continued to delineate lines of wealth, power, and labor.

5 / THE COURTS OF BLOODY CADDO

THE ADVENT OF NORTH LOUISIANA'S OIL INDUSTRY POSED an enormous threat to the state's economic and racial order. By its geological nature, oil had the unique capacity to cross social boundaries: *anyone*, white or Black, could theoretically discover oil on their property and draw profit from it. Rural acreages that had sold for hundreds of dollars only years prior were now worth millions. Even Black families who owned modest North Louisiana farms were suddenly poised to earn untold oil riches. The same land that hosted a sprawling slave economy, and the comparably degrading sharecropping system that succeeded it, now had the potential to create a new class of Black wage earners, and, perhaps even more astonishing, Black *millionaires*. For Black landowners, discovering that oil lay under their property was just the beginning. Maintaining control over that land and the precious wealth underneath it was a far longer, and far more perilous, journey.

Black landowners who discovered oil on their property had to navigate a legal and economic system that regarded the notion of Black oil millionaires as comical at best and repellent at worst. The power of Louisiana's courts over the industry reflected the state's "reformist" movement toward more legalistic due process over rural mob justice to adjudicate business disputes. However, shades of the old plantation model of "justice" remained embedded within this nominally more "modern" new model. Predatory lawyers, speculators, and drillers used all types of intimidation—economic, legal, and physical—to impose racial boundaries on this highly profitable, but at times too racially transgressive, fount of wealth. And yet to successfully compete before white judges and white juries, Black claimants still had to rely on white attorneys, many of whom were more interested in siphoning royalties for themselves than offering sound legal counsel to a Black client.

Two legal dramas revealed how long-standing racial hierarchies intersected with North Louisiana's lucrative new industry and shaped its economic and social boundaries. The case of Lillie "Gussie" Taylor offered a particularly vivid example of a Black landowner seeking remedy in Louisiana's white-run legal system. In 1896 a Claiborne Parish lynch mob murdered Taylor's stepfather, Isom McGee, forcing Gussie, her mother, and her stepsister to flee the state. Twenty-three years later, a group of Shreveport attorneys informed Taylor that the land she had been forced to abandon was now worth untold millions in oil royalties. The attorneys offered to win it back for her—in exchange for one-half of the share she stood to inherit. A byzantine legal battle ensued that would not only arbitrate the rightful heir to this rural patch of farmland, but also consider a question with far deeper implications: whether Louisiana's legal system, oil industry, and society at large would accept "America's first negro princess."

The courtroom saga of Joe Herndon and his nephew David H. Raines further illustrated the dangers Black landowners faced as they sought to profit from their property's oil. In 1916, Herndon and Raines agreed to lease their adjacent Caddo Parish farms for oil production, only to find themselves caught between two warring parties of white drillers, each of which claimed to be the rightful lessees. On the surface, this was a dry legal contest over business partnerships and the legitimacy of court documents. But a deeper subtext of racial intimidation permeated the case, with both sides accusing their opponents of threatening violence against these Black men to assure a beneficial legal outcome: accusations that even implicated their own attorneys.

THE LYNCHING OF ISOM MCGEE

As with many Black residents of early twentieth-century North Louisiana, Lillie "Gussie" Taylor's ancestors were among the enslaved laborers who worked the region's vast cotton plantations. Taylor's stepfather, Isom McGee Jr., was born to enslaved parents Eliza Grigsby and Isom McGee Sr., also known as "Kit," on a Claiborne Parish plantation just prior to the Civil War. After Grigsby's death in 1865, Isom Sr. married Sarah Manning, with whom he fathered twelve children.[1] Five years later, the younger Isom, then eighteen years old, was still on the same patch of Claiborne Parish working as a servant for Thornton Bridgeman, a white landowner who employed a long list of Black laborers on his plantation.[2]

In 1889, Bridgeman decided to sell a ninety-one-acre slice of his rural farmland to the younger McGee. In a deed dated January 12 of that year, Bridgeman stipulated a price of $546, or about six dollars per acre.[3] Signatories included Thornton Bridgeman, a notary public named Drew Ferguson, and McGee, who marked his X, likely reflecting an inability to sign his name. To this point, McGee Jr. had been married to Lona Norton for seven years, with whom he had one daughter, Mattie, and one stepdaughter, Lillie, or "Gussie."[4] The identity of Gussie's biological father remained obscure: a biographical detail that would have enormous legal and financial implications.

The same racial violence terrorizing much of North Louisiana and the wider American South struck the McGee-Norton family on July 24, 1896, when a Claiborne Parish lynch mob murdered Isom McGee Jr.[5] His nominal crime was the attempted rape of a white woman, but McGee's actual offense may have been his upward mobility: perhaps this landowning Black man had become too successful in the eyes of his white executioners. Following McGee's violent murder, Gussie promptly fled to Hope, Arkansas, along with her mother and stepsister. Years later, she would emotionally recount having to leave "her native home . . . with my mother and sister . . . at the death of my father," never qualifying Mattie as a *step*sister or McGee as a *step*father.[6]

Succeeding years in Arkansas would only bring more tragedy, with Mattie dying in 1903 and her mother, Lona, in 1905.[7] In December 1899, Gussie married twenty-one-year-old Albert Taylor in Hempstead County, Arkansas.[8] But only one year later, she abruptly appeared as a widow in census records.[9] Despite the brevity of her marriage, Gussie would continue to bear the Taylor surname throughout her adulthood. By 1910, "Lillie G. Taylor" was still living in Hope along with another Black woman listed as her "Companion."[10] At some point during these years, Taylor briefly returned to her family's Claiborne Parish farm, but did not stay as "she did not consider [the land] worth anything." Around 1914, she left the Arkansas countryside for the city of Dallas, where she became a washerwoman for a white family.[11]

Despite Taylor's brief reappearance at her ancestral farm, which was indeed still *her* property, the Bridgeman family felt entitled to resell the same land to a new buyer. In 1914, the descendants of Thornton Bridgeman deeded "The Nail Place," as it was locally known, to a Black man named George West for $637.[12] West proceeded to cultivate a modest farm with his son and wife on the property. It is unclear whether he was aware of its previous occupants. However, as Louisiana's oil boom feverishly spread into Claiborne Parish by the late 1910s, the value of Nail Place suddenly assumed immense value. On January 18, 1919, West signed an oil lease with Gulf Refining Company to drill on his property, or what he believed to be his property. And on December 27 of that year a Nail Place well struck oil.[13]

LILLIE G. TAYLOR V. GEORGE WEST

Taylor heard about the unfolding bonanza from two sources: firsthand from an unnamed cousin, and via a letter from Foster, Looney and Wilkinson, a

Shreveport law firm that offered to "win the suit . . . on [the] basis of fifty, fifty," referring to half of the land's oil royalties.[14] Initially rebuffing the firm's proposal, Taylor went directly to West, offering him essentially the same proposition: to split the royalties fifty-fifty. West refused, and on October 31, 1919, Taylor hired Foster, Looney and Wilkinson and agreed to the firm's terms. The following month, she signed an oil lease with Y. Allen Holman, a livestock salesman from Ozark, Alabama, to drill on eighty of the disputed ninety-one acres.[15] Holman would pay Taylor a cash bonus of $2,080, an additional bonus of $1,000 per acre, and the customary one-eighth royalty of all oil produced, half of which would go to her lawyers in the event of a legal victory, in addition to paying the "expense of litigation."[16] After that, Taylor would later recall, "the fight was on."[17]

In December 1919, Foster, Looney and Wilkinson sued George West in the US District Court for the Western District of Louisiana. Taylor's attorneys asked the court to recognize their client as the true heir to Nail Place and to nullify West's oil leases in favor of Taylor's. Another Shreveport law firm, Blanchard, Goldstein and Walker, represented West's interests, arguing that the Claiborne Parish farm never legally passed down to Taylor. Never contesting McGee's prior ownership of Nail Place, the defense instead scrutinized a seemingly extraneous issue: Taylor's relationship with her mother and stepfather. West's attorneys claimed that she was an illegitimate child and, as such, not eligible to inherit the oil-rich acreage from her mother, Lona Norton, to whom Nail Place had passed after McGee's murder.

On March 16 and 17, 1920, the Shreveport courthouse heard testimony to weigh the question of whether Lona Norton and Isom McGee raised Taylor as their legitimate daughter. A parade of relatives from their respective families came forth to offer recollections, in the process illuminating the grim conditions that much of North Louisiana's rural Black population endured. According to court summonses, only one of the Black witnesses, Henry Matthews, was capable of signing his own name.[18] Most of the documents list vague rural locations such as "7 miles from Homer" or "5 miles SW of Homer" in lieu of addresses. According to Emma Garrett's summons, it took her three days to travel the sixty-four miles from rural Homer to urban Shreveport, an incomprehensible length of time that would suggest both poverty and a lack of access to any reasonable form of transport.[19]

The testimony of these Black Louisianans also revealed a highly regimented economic and racial order in which white employers remained effectively white masters, and a broader society over which slavery continued to cast a long shadow. When defense attorneys asked Willie Norton, half-brother of Lona Norton, how he initially heard about the case, he deferred to his white boss: "I let my employer see my summons before I left home and asked him did he know what it was for." Asked for her specific age, Angeline Allen, Lona Norton's mother, expressed uncertainty: "I don't know; I got my age about two or three year ago from my owner [who] I was raised with," referring to both an enslaved childhood and a continued economic dependence on her former owner.[20]

For George West's legal team, exaggerating the ignorance and social dysfunction of North Louisiana's rural Black population, their own client's community, was a deliberate strategy. Their specific objective was to advance the proposition that McGee and Norton did not raise Taylor as their legitimate child, meaning they would not be eligible to legally bequeath property to her. Testimony probed the details of McGee and Norton's wedding day and, more importantly, whether Taylor was present as a "legitimate" daughter to both parties. Norton's mother, Angeline, despite her advanced age, retained a very specific memory of her infant grandchild's presence during her daughter's wedding: "I had Gussie in my arms." She proceeded to defend her daughter's capabilities as a parent, asserting that Isom and Lona "treated them [Gussie and Mattie] as their own."[21]

Angeline Allen's participation in her granddaughter's case came with a bitter irony. Later proceedings in the Louisiana Supreme Court revealed that she, and not Taylor, would have inherited those coveted ninety-one acres upon her daughter's death were it not for one fact: "Lona McGee was the illegitimate child of Angelina [sic] Allen . . . and was never legitimated." Indeed, Allen "'would have inherited in default of natural children' . . . if she had acknowledged Lona McGee" or if the "father of Lona McGee had acknowledged her."[22] It seems Lona was intent on protecting her daughter from experiencing the same illegitimacy she endured—a decision that would have enormous financial implications for both her daughter and mother.

On March 18, 1920, the US District Court sided with West, ruling that Taylor was not the legitimate daughter of Lona McGee and thus not entitled to inherit from her. The court evidently found Taylor's case unpersuasive, but also seemed unwilling to rely on the testimony of Black witnesses: "the plaintiff has failed to make out its case, even if you believe the testimony of the witnesses."[23] West's victory, however, was short-lived. On April 11, 1920, district judge J. E. Reynolds ruled that Taylor was Norton's legitimate daughter and a legal heir to her estate. Taylor's legal saga continued to advance, and it would only reach its conclusion in the Louisiana Supreme Court the following year.

Meanwhile, the pace of Claiborne Parish's oil boom accelerated, making its land some of the most coveted real estate in the United States. The same ninety-one acres that George West had purchased for seven dollars per acre in 1914 would have fetched more than $3,000 per acre in 1919.[24] Oil production was accordingly plentiful on Nail Place, where Gulf drilled nineteen wells between February and September 1920.[25] Contemporary newspaper accounts were excessively generous in their estimations of Nail Place's value in oil royalties, citing valuations ranging from $8 to $15 million. One 1922 article in *The Appeal*, a Black-run newspaper from St. Paul, Minnesota, placed the figure at a staggering $29 million.[26] However, the actual production totals prior to September 1921 were closer to $3.5 million, a more modest, but still wildly successful, figure for whichever lessor prevailed in the case.[27]

As news of Nail Place's value spread, a flurry of new parties also made claims to being its rightful heir: the attorney general of Louisiana, who argued the state should assume control over the oil leases in the absence of any legal heirs; a child of Homer Scott (Lona Norton's second husband); and the children of Isom McGee Sr. and his second wife, Sarah Manning.[28] Such claims were ultimately unsuccessful, but they still represented additional opportunities for drillers to hedge their bets. Gulf Refining, already in business with George West, penned an additional lease with the state of Louisiana that would have initiated in the event of the attorney general prevailing in court.[29]

Attorneys also flooded into Claiborne Parish in the hope of representing the winner of such a potentially lucrative case. In 1922, *International Petroleum Reporter* reported that Taylor's case was part of a broader "wave of litigation" adjudicating disputes throughout the Caddo and Claiborne Parish oil fields.[30] When Francis Scott Glenn, daughter of Homer Scott, filed her own petition over Nail Place, she also hired Foster, Looney and Wilkinson, which now represented *two* potential title holders of the same land.[31] Such a steady stream of legal conflicts was a boon for Shreveport's lawyers, affording opportunities to place a variety of bets on who would be victorious, and thereby enhancing their own odds of winning a share of the region's explosive oil field wealth. Over the coming decades, attorneys across the broader oil-producing Southwest would benefit enormously from the legal bonanza of land disputes that ensued across Louisiana, Texas, and Oklahoma, all while the local—primarily tenant—farmers saw comparably few opportunities for any oil royalties as the derricks sprouted around them.[32]

WHITE REACTIONS TO AMERICA'S "FIRST NEGRO PRINCESS"

Much of the media coverage surrounding Taylor's case expressed shock and horror over the prospect of a Black washerwoman acquiring such vast wealth. The *New Iberia and Independent Observer* rendered the case as a kind of racial horror story: the "barbaric love that bore a child out of wedlock" that could end with "America's first negro princess."[33] The *Chicago Journal of Commerce* expressed a perverse sympathy for Taylor in a piece that was reprinted in the

Bismarck Tribune. Having "never . . . possessed a thousand dollars . . . in her life," the anonymous writer bemoaned, Taylor would be "totally unfitted [*sic*] to manage the net income of her property." Rather than donate her wealth to "great charities" or "industrial schools," Taylor would "let the millions melt away amidst feathers and furs and jewels galore." Much like a "ten-year-old child," the author concluded, Taylor is "in need of a guardian."[34]

The *New Orleans Item* published a 1921 "history" of Taylor's case that dripped with racist contempt toward the Black woman and her family. The uncredited author began their account with Isom McGee's acquisition of Nail Place, describing McGee as a "shambling, splay-footed . . . negro . . . who never paid a cent on it." Alternating back to the present case, the narrative characterized Taylor as "a skinny negress . . . huddled in a shack" in the "Nigger Hill" section of Dallas, further alluding to her uncertain parentage: "her name is Lillie Taylor. She's the illegitimate . . . child of Lona Norton, negress, by some wandering, wholly forgotten negro." It is this woman who sits before a group of "solemn gentlemen . . . in an impressive court room" seeking title to lands worth untold millions.[35]

Much like other contemporary accounts, the *New Orleans Item* ascribed a juvenile and primitive nature to Taylor, framing her victory as a darkly comic fluke of history. The author allegedly encountered Gussie outside of the courthouse and portrayed her as a "huddled coughing figure of a negress," quoting her as saying she is "'feelin' porely [*sic*] an' ain't mch hand to talk nohow." The article depicted Taylor's case as an astonishing and perturbing inflection point in history: "Will these shack negroes find themselves multi-millionaires by as grotesque a turn of the wheel as history holds?" The author concluded with one final slander, imagining how the murdered McGee would be observing the dramatic case:

> Way up yonder where the souls of lynched negroes go, Isom McGee must be chuckling as he looks at the complication he started when he got himself listed as owner of a property on which he never paid a cent, of which ownership Bridgeman failed to have him divested when the lynching bee was over.[36]

But for all its venomously racist characterizations, the *New Orleans Item* does make one unwittingly prescient observation about the obstacles that stood between Taylor and her property: "Lillie won't have those millions handed to her on a silver platter. Not while there are lawyers and contingent fees. Not a chance."[37]

Another 1921 piece offered one of the only first-person "interviews" that took place with the prospective heiress. A writer allegedly tracked down Taylor at her "typical negro shack" in East Dallas and attributed a variety of dubious quotations to her. "Lawsy, mercy," she is quoted as saying, "dat shore am some money, but I ain't got no time for foolin' wid it now. See dis wash? Well muh, white folks gotta have dese clothes washed and ironed by tomorrow." Taylor is further quoted on the unsolicited attention her case has attracted:

> Dey ain't none of dese pesky niggers seen fit to seek my company when I was washing and cooking cleaning house and keeping de babies for muh white folks, and dey had better not pester me now because I got some money. I wont need no nigger to help me care for dat oil money and it shore aint going to be healthy for them what comes a hankerin' about here.[38]

These quotations reflect the same expectation set forth in the *Chicago Journal of Commerce* and *New Orleans Item* pieces: that if a member of the Black community struck oil, the money would not be reinvested, but rather wasted on juvenile extravagances. White readers surely read these stories with a mix of amusement and horror. Here was the unaccounted underside of a natural resource boom: if truly *anyone* could strike it rich, then even a Black washerwoman could become "America's first negro princess."[39]

This "interview" was, in fact, a complete fabrication. When a writer from the *Dallas Express*, an esteemed, Black-run newspaper, found Taylor at her Dallas home in the spring of 1921, they offered an entirely different account. By Taylor's own words, the *Dallas Express* writer was "the only newspaper man whom I have talked with." Far from a monstrous racial caricature, Taylor appears as a soft-spoken, petite older woman of "5 feet 6 inches, weight about 105 pounds . . . large brown eyes and . . . a pleasing facial complexion."[40]

And in contrast to the racist presumptions about her extravagant ways, the author commended Taylor for her shrewd business ability as president of the Fair Park C.M.W. Church's Stewardess Board and as superintendent of its Sunday school—roles that had earned her a "splendid reputation" in the community.[41] Asked if she would remain in Dallas after the suit, Taylor's reply was emphatic: "No sir! . . . I plan to go home," that is, to Hope, Arkansas. Although she described Homer as her "native home," Taylor's formative years were in Hope, where her family had found refuge from the racial terrorism of North Louisiana.

THE WINNERS OF *LILLIE G. TAYLOR V. GEORGE WEST*

On May 2, 1921, the Louisiana Supreme Court finally affirmed Taylor's heirship to Nail Place and thus to its vast oil wealth.[42] In reporting this remarkable outcome, newspapers alternatively estimated the value of Taylor's bounty to be somewhere between $10 million and $30 million.[43] Another journal projected that Taylor would earn $300,000 annually, lamenting that this Black heiress had likely "never earned or possessed a thousand dollars . . . in her life."[44] Meanwhile, *The Appeal* was exultant: "One of the greatest victories of right over color prejudice has just been won in Louisiana." Despite the numerous efforts that "white men could conjure up . . . to wrest the property from her," Taylor would now become "one of the richest women in the world."[45]

However, behind the dramatic reports of financial windfall lay a far murkier picture, in which the actual scale of Taylor's victory was less clear. The ultimate resolution came when Gulf made a deal with Taylor's legal team to maintain their Nail Place lease, even if West, their lessor, lost in court. Throughout the case, Gulf had been growing anxious over the prospect of losing their rights to such a productive site.[46] Therefore, on September 13, 1921, Gulf entered into a deal with the victorious plaintiffs that would enable them to continue producing on Nail Place via the leases they had originally signed with George West. In exchange, Taylor's side would receive a one-sixth royalty share of Gulf's production plus a $1 million bonus, all of which would be divided among Taylor, her attorneys, Y. A. Holman, and various other stakeholders.[47] Subsequent court documents transcribed the deal, clearly naming the fractional royalty shares that would be paid out to each recipient—except for Lillie Gussie Taylor.

Unlike the other members of her legal team, Taylor's share remained a matter of dispute: her royalty share, one share out of thirty-two, would be credited to "C. W. Lane, or Lillie Gussie Taylor, *if she establishes her ownership of same*" [italics added]. C. W. Lane does not appear in any court records prior to the 1921 agreement, and succeeding documents merely allude to an ongoing legal dispute: "Lillie Gussie Taylor claims to be the owner of the [1/32] royalty interest accredited to C. W. Lane in the Division Order . . . and that she does not waive her right to establish her ownership of said royalty in her pending suit against C. W. Lane."[48] Taylor would therefore have to prevail in yet *another* lawsuit to actually benefit from the production on her own land. Outwardly presented as the victor of such a dramatic legal case, Taylor was the only member of her own team walking away without a clear profit.

Documents from a subsequent court case further confirm that Taylor ultimately received a pittance compared to the other members of her legal team. Following the resolution of Taylor's case, the Holman family engaged in protracted litigation with Foster, Looney and Wilkinson, claiming the 1921 deal with Gulf enriched the law firm more than its clients. In 1935, the US Supreme Court agreed to adjudicate their case in *Holman v. Gulf Refining Company of Louisiana*, the transcripts of which provide a retrospective view of the 1921 deal and its long-term beneficiaries. Gulf's decision to buy out Taylor's side was indeed highly profitable, netting the company $4,964,537.58 in oil revenues as of 1932. Over the same period, Foster, Looney and Wilkinson earned $321,880.68 from its own royalty shares. Even the Holman brothers, to whom Taylor originally leased the land, netted more than $200,000 between them. And how much did Lillie Taylor, the lawful heiress to Nail Place, ultimately earn from its enormously productive oil field? Between $20,000 and $25,000, plus a "lesser royalty interest."[49]

So what happened to the vast fortune that America's first "negro princess" was poised to receive? One possibility is that Taylor *sold* her share prior to the 1921 agreement. According to a 1922 newspaper account, Taylor had already received $40,000 to $50,000 in addition to a forthcoming $75,000 payment "from sale of her royalty rights which she disposed of before the litigation was ended."[50] Documents from *Holman v. Gulf Refining Company of Louisiana* also allude to Taylor "[disposing] of all her interests" prior to the resolution of her case.[51] The documents do not outline to whom she may have disposed her share, but C. W. Lane would be the most plausible candidate. However, the lawsuit that emerged between Taylor and Lane would suggest that Gussie ultimately objected to any such transaction.

It remains unclear whether Taylor sold her royalty shares to C. W. Lane—or *why* Taylor would dispose of such an enormously valuable royalty interest. But circumstantial evidence suggests that Lane was indeed the ultimate recipient of Taylor's share. In the years following his appearance in the 1921 agreement, Lane went on to become a prominent Shreveport investor, particularly in the North Louisiana oil fields. Lane's 1959 obituary described a lifetime of business endeavors, including his role in developing the "Caddo-Pine Island, *Homer*, Haynesville and Smackover oil fields" [italics added].[52] Although the precise details of Taylor's dealings with Lane remain murky, Lane's eventual possession of oil rights in Homer suggests that the white investor may have indeed acquired Nail Place—evidently over Taylor's legal objections.

Given these many ambiguities, who actually *won* the Lillie Gussie Taylor case? The most outright victor was Gulf Refining, which profited enormously from the derricks on Taylor's property. The other major beneficiaries were the attorneys of Foster, Looney and Wilkinson, who managed to siphon off a considerable share of Taylor's interests—far more than their clients ultimately received. During the 1935 *Holman v. Gulf Refining* proceedings, Holman's legal side characterized the Shreveport law firm as being fraudulent self-dealers more intent on acquiring royalties than providing disinterested legal advice. Testimony further revealed how the attorneys had quietly entered into an even earlier 1920 agreement with West's counsel in which they—the *law firm*, and not their clients—would be able to purchase their own one-sixteenth share of Nail Place's oil royalties, *even if their clients lost.*

Neither Taylor nor the Holman brothers were aware that their attorneys would be receiving a one-sixteenth share *in addition* to the royalties they would receive from the 1921 deal. When one of the Holmans' outside attorneys became aware of the 1920 deal and asked FLW partner Frank J. Looney about its details, Looney replied that it was "none of your goddamned business." Indeed, the attorneys at Foster, Looney and Wilkinson were so eager to assure their own oil royalties that they failed to realize their fundamental objective: to establish *Taylor's* legal rights over Nail Place's oil revenues. The 1921 deal with Gulf readily acknowledged that Taylor, ostensibly at the center of the entire case, was still without clear title over the profits of her own land.[53] Although their central client remained under dispute with another party, the partners of Foster, Looney and Wilkinson were still able to handsomely profit.

Taylor's story illuminates the unfortunate need for Black plaintiffs to rely on white counsel to navigate a white legal system: counsel that was very often more intent on enriching themselves. The interests of a Black client were secondary to Foster, Looney and Wilkinson's main goal: firmly establishing the attorneys' own share of Nail Place's abundant production. Isom McGee, Lona Norton, Lillie Taylor, and all their hardships were merely a conduit into North Louisiana's vast oil wealth. But white attorneys still remained essential for Black claimants such as Taylor to compete within a judicial system that was exclusively composed of white judges, white lawyers, and white jurors, even if that white legal counsel was self-interested or corrupted.

The ensuing trajectory of Taylor's life is ambiguous. According to a March 2, 1922, headline, her whereabouts became suddenly unknown following her victory in court: "Disappearance of Heiress Is Mystery." The brief story claimed that Taylor, the "richest negro woman in the world," had vanished and left "no clue to her whereabouts."[54] However, Taylor does briefly reappear in the 1935 *Holman v. Gulf* Supreme Court case, the records of which refer to information she had submitted to the court. Documents from the case further note that Taylor was unable to testify in person due to illness.[55] Taylor henceforth vanishes from census records and does not appear in any further stories about America's wealthiest Black washerwoman.

At first glance, Taylor's story reads as the stunning victory of a humble Black woman over Louisiana's thoroughly white-supremacist economic and legal system. But a closer examination reveals the profound asymmetry of power that still persisted between Taylor and her own legal team. The white actors around Lillie Taylor were the biggest beneficiaries of *her* alleged victory: Gulf Refining; Foster, Looney and Wilkinson; the Holman brothers; and perhaps even C. W. Lane all profited far more than the actual Black landowner. The lack of subsequent newspaper accounts and media attention over America's first "negro princess" only underscores the generational oil wealth that Taylor never received, and that one of "the greatest victories of right over color prejudice" was merely a nominal one for its Black plaintiff.[56]

THE HERNDON-RAINES FAMILY

Taylor was not the only Black landowner to enter such a perilous legal maze over the racial and economic boundaries of North Louisiana's oil boom, nor was she the only one to encounter the threat of white violence and intimidation, either implicit or explicit, as she sought to rightfully profit from her land. In 1916, Joseph H. Herndon and his nephew David H. Raines discovered that their adjacent Caddo Parish farms were atop the Pine Island field, at the time one of North Louisiana's most productive sources of crude oil. In October of that year, Herndon and Raines signed respective oil leases with Dunson, Harrell, Brown and Dyer, a drilling partnership based in Shreveport.[57] There is a dark familial irony to Dunson, Harrell, Brown and Dyer agreeing to terms that would potentially make two Black men millionaires: one of the firm's partners, C. E. (Charles Edward) Dunson, was the father of William H. "Pete" Dunson, the Claiborne Parish oil hand who would be shot and killed by Tom Shannon for attacking a Black worker only a few years later.[58]

Much like Lillie Taylor's ninety-one acres, the Herndon-Raines farms were in a remote section of Caddo Parish where Joseph and David's forebears had been enslaved—and had also owned slaves. Sometime before 1837, a white Virginian named John F. Herndon migrated into Caddo Parish to enter its burgeoning cotton economy. Prior to that, Herndon had been living in Newberry, South Carolina, where he managed a household of twenty enslaved people.[59] But on December 8, 1840, Herndon appeared before the Caddo Parish Police Jury to make what was surely a controversial request:

> Your petitioner a citizen of Caddo Parish respectfully represents to your Honour that he is the owner of a Colored woman named Patsy who from long and faithfull [sic] Services rendered your Petitioner both when he labored under Sickness and been in health, he is anxious and conscientiously believes it to be his duty to set at liberty together with her offspring your Honour will do me the favour to lay this petition before the Police Jury at its next meeting and a subsequent [illegible] and do and perform such other acts and things as may be necessary for the ultimate relief of your and he will ever pray be, Signed, John F. Herndon.[60]

The Police Jury received and eventually adopted the petition, ruling that "the Slave Patsy and her offspring be emancipated for life."[61] Obtaining such a decree within North Louisiana's committed plantation society was nothing short of miraculous, and perhaps an indication of Herndon's local wealth and influence. Following Emancipation, Herndon and Patsy remained on their Caddo Parish farm, now living openly as man and wife during the brief period of Louisiana's Reconstruction that allowed interracial marriage.[62] The erstwhile slave owner and enslaved woman had sixteen children together, including Joseph Herndon Jr., born in 1840, and Mary Ann, born in 1837, who would give birth to David H. Raines in 1860.[63]

By the dawn of the twentieth century, Herndon Jr. and Raines were landowning farmers in the same parish where their forebears had turned their plantation household upside down. In 1900, Herndon farmed a plot of land he owned outright with his wife and stepson.[64] Ten years later, the younger Raines also freely possessed a farm, much of which derived from an unlikely source. On June 28, 1901, President William McKinley conferred Raines just over forty acres of Caddo Parish land in accordance with the Homestead Act of 1862.[65] How the mixed-race grandchild of an enslaved woman in rural North Louisiana could obtain such a coveted federal grant was unclear—perhaps another suggestion of the Herndon family's political influence, or perhaps an indication that Raines, descended from a white man, may have had the capacity to "pass" as white.[66] Those forty acres would ultimately transform from a modest homestead into an oil play with enormous financial value.

D. H. RAINES AND JOE HERNDON V. C. E. DUNSON

By all accounts, the terms of Raines and Herndon's oil leases were ordinary. But when Dunson, Harrell, Brown and Dyer dissolved their firm on May 7, 1917, a gap in their contract with the landowning pair suddenly opened, resulting in a contentious lawsuit. On May 30 of that year, Raines and Herndon filed parallel suits in the First District Court to have their leases dissolved, thereby enabling them to sign new leases with new drillers. The court, however, upheld the original accords, prompting attorneys for Herndon and Raines to appeal to the Louisiana Supreme Court. In the meantime, two significant developments had occurred: the transfer of the original oil lease to Clark and Greer Drilling Company, and the creation of an entirely new lease between Herndon, Raines, and a white driller named R. T. Layne.

The litigation that followed was opaque and dramatic. On September 12, 1917, Raines and Herndon signed identical letters addressed to Barrett and Files, the Shreveport law firm representing them, formally asking the firm to drop the appeal so that they could "obtain immediate development" with Clark and Greer via the original leases. Both copies were notarized and duly filed with the Caddo Parish clerk's office. Then just fourteen days later, both men signed a new letter *retracting* that dismissal request and instead asking their attorneys to proceed with their appeal. Both men claimed to have been "persuaded . . . to sign [the initial dismissal request] . . . without full knowledge of [their] rights in the premises and [without] having consulted" their attorneys.[67] The new statement further asserted that Herndon and Raines would honor a new lease with R. T. Layne, who agreed to pay all legal fees on behalf of the pair.

With the legitimacy of these documents now in question, both sides met in the Louisiana Supreme Court, where accusations of racial intimidation charged the testimony. Each side mutually cast their opponents as canny white oil men coercing simple Black landowners into signing favorable deals. The legal teams alternated between caricaturing and empowering the Black landowners, claiming their opponents had manipulated these poor, uneducated "darkies," only to abruptly elevate the competency of Herndon and Raines when it suited the particulars of their argument.[68]

Testimony began on November 16, 1917, with Herndon and Raines facing questions from opposing counsel, which sought to validate the original dismissal the pair had signed and thereby grant Clark and Greer a new drilling lease on their property. When a lawyer asked Herndon whether he signed "willing and of your own will," he responded in the affirmative.[69] Further asked whether the document was read to him and if he understood it, Herndon again answered yes. But when Raines received the same line of questioning, he equivocated:

Q. Did you sign it willingly and of your own will?
A: Well I wasn't forced into signing it
Q: Didn't you read it
A: Well, yes sir
Q: And you understood what you were signing
A: I suppose so
Q: Didn't you know what you were signing
A: Yes sir, I guess so
Q: Did they use any fraud or persuasion to get you to sign it
A: Not that I know of
Q: You signed it and gave it to them didn't you
A: Yes sir
Q: Of your own free will
A: Well I signed it and thought those things was [*sic*] all right
Q: Didn't you sign it of your own free will?
A: Well I couldn't say that I didn't, I wasn't forced to sign it[70]

Raines's testimony reads like someone sensing danger in every direction. While ultimately affirming the legitimacy of his signature, it appears Raines did not want to choose one side and incur the wrath of the other. As the testimony unfolded, it became evident how much pressure Raines and Herndon faced from all corners, including from their own attorneys.

Counsel for Raines and Herndon characterized the dismissal request as a product of coercion, arguing that Clark and Greer threatened economic and physical harm to get signatures from two vulnerable Black men. White agents of the drilling outfit allegedly made that threat evident by appearing on the Raines-Herndon land alongside Will Caldwell, the cashier of Vivian State Bank, the institution through which the pair would be receiving royalty payments. Testimony revealed an even darker element to the encounter:

Q: The three men that came out [there] that got you to sign the [letter] were white men . . . were they not?

A: Yes sir

Q: Mr. Clark is a good sized man isn't he

A: Yes sir.[71]

Clark and Greer were intimidating Herndon and Raines on two levels: by asserting their authority within the state's financial and legal world, but also by appealing to brute force—both of which they could plausibly wield against these Black men with impunity. The attorneys for Raines and Herndon made that dynamic clear by evoking the image of "white men and shrewd oil operators" looking to perpetrate fraud against "ignorant negroes."[72]

But even the lawyers ostensibly defending Herndon and Raines seemed to be exploiting that same power dynamic. Counsel for Clark and Greer alleged that the Barrett and Files firm leveraged its own legal authority to manipulate its Black clients to the benefit of its other client, R. T. Layne. Under cross-examination, Raines reluctantly admitted that Files threatened him with a "damage suit" if he didn't retract the dismissal. Herndon confirmed the story, recalling Files threatening to do "a good deal of damage," including taking "all our part of the production." Asked whether he would have signed the retraction had Files not leveled those threats, Herndon responded with certainty, "No sir." Even the driller Layne, who was present as Barrett and Files confronted its clients over the dismissal, acknowledged making threats: "when a man does me, takes my money and then tries to turn on me, why I am going after him, sure."[73]

Once again, applications of legal and financial pressure were punctuated by far more ominous threats. Counsel for Clark and Greer asked Raines to confirm a story: that he only retracted the dismissal on behalf of his attorneys and Layne because he was "afraid for [*sic*] them because they were white men and [he was] a negro," to which Raines replied: "I don't remember." But the cross-examining lawyer pressed him, citing a statement that Raines allegedly made declaring that Layne was "the meanest man you ever saw, and was standing there with his hand in his pocket, and you were afraid of him."[74]

Raines never confirmed or denied the story, as his attorneys successfully objected to the line of questioning. But that evocative fragment of testimony revealed the deeper legal objectives animating Barrett and Files: securing drilling rights for R. T. Layne, its white client. As with Lillie Taylor's legal representation, Raines and Herndon's white attorneys only had a tenuous loyalty to their Black clients. When Layne's legal interests no longer aligned with those of Herndon or Raines, Files and Barrett protected its white client without hesitation. And when its Black clients objected or would not comply, the firm was perfectly willing to apply legal or even physical threats against the people it was ostensibly defending.

On April 1, 1918, Judge John R. Land ruled against Herndon, Raines, and Layne, upholding their original request to dismiss the case and granting Clark and Greer full title over the lease. In his ruling, Judge Land accepted the narrative that Herndon and Raines had duly signed the initial request so they could pursue immediate production with Clark and Greer and that "no fraud or persuasion was used to obtain [their] signatures." However, the letter *recalling* that dismissal, Judge Land wrote, was indeed the product of intimidation on the part of R. T. Layne and Barrett and Files, Herndon and Raines's ostensible legal and business partners. The pair had only signed that retraction because their "counsel had said that Mr. Layne could come in and take all of [their] share," adding that Herndon and Raines were "afraid Mr. Layne would take [their] oil and break [them] up."[75] The Barrett and Files firm was very clearly pursuing the profits of its white client over its Black clients, a fact that even a white judge seemed to recognize.

While many details of Herndon and Raines's dealings with these competing drillers remain ambiguous, a broader context emerges from the court records: two groups of white men attempted to leverage their economic, legal, and racial positions to acquire Black-owned mineral rights. As prominent members of the business and legal world, these white actors understood that Herndon and Raines would have little recourse in court or in government. And they also knew that, as white men, they possessed the ultimate leverage in Bloody Caddo, where the promise of lethal violence shadowed every encounter. When R. T. Layne allegedly stood before David Raines "with his hand in his pocket," he exerted a formidable and sinister bargaining position that Raines would have ignored at his own peril.

However, threats and intimidation did not fully encapsulate the lives of Joseph Herndon and David Raines. Herndon, depicted as frail and elderly in the trial transcripts, passed away in 1924 at the age of eighty-four. The much younger Raines went on to live a remarkable life. Despite all the controversy and coercion that surrounded his oil lease, it still paid, and made him very wealthy. By 1920, Raines owned a home on 1419 Peabody Street in Shreveport, where he lived with his wife and two daughters. He may have inherited his grandfather's complexion, as a census taker that year listed him as "white."[76]

Raines shrewdly invested his oil wealth into Caddo Parish real estate, providing himself with a diverse stream of oil royalties and rental money that made him a millionaire by 1936. He also donated a good deal of that money and property toward philanthropic efforts, especially for Shreveport's Black community. Upon his death, Raines bequeathed twenty-two acres, including his Peabody Street home, to become the site of a new center for juvenile delinquents, the David Raines Center, which still serves Shreveport as a community health center.[77] He died in 1945 at eighty-four, the same age his uncle Joseph reached.

However, the affirming final arc of David Raines's life cannot nullify the threats and contempt that he and other Black landowners such as Joseph Herndon and Lillie "Gussie" Taylor faced during North Louisiana's oil boom. But it does make Raines's achievements all the more impressive. It surely took great courage for Raines to attain so much success in Bloody Caddo, where any Black individuals seen to be subverting the racial order, either socially or economically, could be subject to the same murderous violence that stole the life of Isom McGee. At one point during the trial, Raines made that courage apparent before the all-white courtroom. Asked under oath if he feared Layne, he responded thusly: "No sir, I wasn't scare [sic] of Mr. Lane [sic], and am not scared of him now. I don't think I ever say [sic] a man I was afraid of. I might be scared of the law, but not of just the looks of a man."[78]

6 / THE LAND

IN A 1999 INTERVIEW, WALTER DUVALL GEORGE JR., WHOSE father Walter Sr. helped to drill the first oil well in Caddo Parish, could still remember Oil City's distinctively bizarre industrial landscape. When asked, "What's your first recollection of Oil City?" George Jr. responded, "I could smell it."[1] By George's estimation, nearby Caddo Lake was host to at least forty to fifty oil rigs "lined up like soldiers." They leaked so much that swimmers would get "oil up to [their] ankles." And yet the younger Walter still looked back on that extraordinary built environment with a perversely warm nostalgia. Despite the ecological disaster unfolding before their eyes, locals proudly referred to the leaking soldiers as "old payday," because "they could look at it . . . and they knew they was going to get paid."[2]

But George's sanguine memories notwithstanding, the toll of North Louisiana's oil industry on the surrounding landscape was staggering. Oil spillage, saltwater runoff, and calamitous fires were constant features of Oil City's work and home life. Locals recalled an eerie twilight sky that eternally glowed red. Storing oil in open-air earthen pits was common, as was allowing crude to simply flow into adjacent lakes and swamps. Even when the Louisiana Conservation Committee began nominally regulating such waste, enforcement from this poorly funded agency was uneven at best and corrupted at worst. Technological limitations, myopic economic incentives, and poor regulation all collided in North Louisiana's landscape, resulting in untold environmental damage and producing an extraordinarily unusual natural setting in which to live.

THE NATURAL WORLD OF NORTH LOUISIANA

Decades before derricks were blowing oil, gas, and fire hundreds of feet into the air, North Louisiana's landscape presented a daunting picture to visitors.

Thick woods and swamps conjured darkness and isolation, but also quiet abundance and untapped possibilities. In 1898, W. O. Whitaker and Wade Hampton encountered this remote stretch of Louisiana on a hunting trip, which Whitaker recalled in a piece he wrote for *Forest and Stream* in 1907. After leaving by boat from Mooringsport, they traversed a "string of lakes extending from Shreveport, La., to Jefferson, Texas," eventually descending onto what appeared to be Pine Island. Whitaker found the boggy region to be an insalubrious and primitive place:

> After two days we reached the lake and landed on a large island, well wooded, with undergrowth, the moss hanging in long festoons from tree to tree, making it almost impossible for the sun to shine on the ground. It was the most dismal forest we ever saw. Every imaginable vine trailed from one tree to another, making a perfect network overhead. The ground being covered almost entirely with small undergrowth and palmetto fan leaf, and adding the darkness of the woods, it made a disagreeable picture. We did not much mind the looks of the island, for we had been told of the abundance of game that was to be found there. Deer were plentiful and in the great canebrakes the small black bear was anything but scarce.[3]

Though Whitaker and Hampton were seasoned hunters presumably accustomed to forbidding surroundings, they regarded Pine Island as especially "dismal" and "disagreeable." In that unpleasant setting, however, they nonetheless managed to find an abundance of game. They had made a prescient summation of North Louisiana and its landscape: miserable, swampy, and dim, but quietly brimming with natural wealth.

North Louisiana's most lucrative resource lay below the earth's surface: a geological formation known as the Sabine Uplift. Approximately eighty miles in length and sixty-five miles in width, the Sabine is shaped like a rough parallelogram, half of which lies under Northeast Texas and the other half below Northwest Louisiana.[4] Across this formation, an "uplift" creates access to porous, oil-bearing Cretaceous rocks underneath.[5] Prior to the twentieth century, Anglo settlers and Native Americans were aware of this underground reserve, but had little economic incentive to extract and sell it on a large scale. Indigenous Caddo tribespeople would filter oil out of lakes and use the "pitch" to treat skin ailments. Later Anglo settlers used the product to grease their wagon wheels.[6] But as factories, cars, and trains proliferated across an industrializing world, crude oil reservoirs such as the Sabine Uplift became highly sought-after economic assets, prompting Walter Duvall Sr.'s drilling team to spike North Louisiana's first oil well in 1904.

In addition to its oil and gas reserves, North Louisiana also boasted a plentiful array of local cypress trees, an invaluable raw material for the nascent oil business. Prior to 1904, local trees had been grist for a robust sawmilling economy that exported timber across the Southwest. But as oil became the preeminent form of economic production, much of that cypress was transformed into the roads, houses, and equipment that would power a new industry. Local wood contributed to virtually every phase of production: the wheels operating the drill; the small wooden room housing the engine; the derrick tower itself. Cypress trees also were used to construct storage tanks, "corduroy" roads laid over mud, worker houses, and, eventually, the large piers connecting Caddo Lake's overwater rigs to the land.

W. J. "Bill" Snead grew up in Caddo Parish and recalled that "very little iron was used in those days," as the industry drew "from the trees and the logs right there on location." While the nearby wood supplies were indeed highly convenient, their application still required hard manual labor. Teams of men and mules had to drag and raise the enormous logs, some of which were twenty to twenty-five feet long, to fashion a wooden derrick.[7] By the 1920s, metal derricks began to proliferate across the industry, supplanting the need for local wood. But North Louisiana's cypress trees had been a crucial ingredient to the industry's earliest growth, offering an accessible and relatively low-cost means of erecting its infrastructure.

But local topography and hydrology also created enormous obstacles for oil production, transportation, and everyday life. The most immediate challenge was negotiating the unpredictable and watery ground. After visiting the Caddo Parish fields in 1911, geologist Walter E. Hopper described the significant impact of these natural impediments on production:

> The condition of the ground and roads is far from good. The lakes and bayous almost completely surround with water the whole central portion of the field, and make the hauling of pipe and machinery exceedingly hard work. Salt-water ponds and swampy patches occur here and there . . . the surface throughout the whole field presents swamp conditions.[8]

Benedum and Trees employee John Lantz recalled similar conditions on his employer's "impenetrable" Caddo Parish lease: "The ground was treacherous . . . and no matter how solid the surface appeared, there was always a danger that when you took a step you would mire up to your waist." Soil conditions were so unpredictable that employees always traveled in pairs to avoid workers becoming stuck alone: "a man would have been a fool to go in there alone."[9] The lands adjacent to Caddo Lake were also susceptible to sudden rises in water levels, forcing drillers to construct a large "boxlike structure" at the base of their derricks to keep them safely above the high-water mark.[10]

Lacking any decent roads to import tools and workers, oil companies were forced to wade through muck throughout the process of drilling and pumping a well. Transporting heavy oil field materials was especially treacherous, with all-too-common incidents of horse and mule teams being "suddenly swallowed up by the soft earth."[11] Contemporary photographs captured wagons laden with oil field tools submerged in mud. Even the advent of automobiles could not fully overcome such miserable conditions, as photographs from the 1920s portrayed Fords precariously mired in the earthen soup. Oil companies tried to mitigate these conditions by building corduroy roads of wooden planks running parallel over the rutted earth. But they were at best a temporary solution, as each set of lines eventually sank into the ground.[12]

Despite the ubiquity of water in North Louisiana, *potable* water was a scarce commodity. In 1911, a visiting state health official named Oscar Dowling pronounced Oil City's water supplies "not at all satisfactory" and in need of "improvement at once."[13] Dowling further noted the unsanitary prevalence of standing water around the community and the lack of an adequate drainage system. In Oil City, John F. Law's family had to rely on cisterns: "Water was precious," he recalled.[14] Given the low, humid climate, bugs were a constant threat to such improvised water sources. Before drinking from the cistern, Law's family had to drain out mosquito eggs. Harry Davidson grew up in Caddo Parish and experienced the "primitive" conditions of its boomtowns. Davidson could still recall that just across the lake, Mooringsport was able to offer clean water to its residents, further reinforcing the community's social composition of families looking for a relatively wholesome and sanitary place to live.[15]

Caddo Parish's natural conditions even shaped social behavior, breeding a sense of isolation that further encouraged illicit economies of sex and drink to operate. Thick swampland and flood-prone soils made road construction a Herculean task, reducing accessibility to outside communities and to law enforcement. Swaths of North Louisiana became effectively autonomous spaces where violence, drinking, and lax if any policing prevailed. According to Shreveport native Tunnell Day, one particularly rural outpost called Douglas Island was a virtual no man's land where law enforcement rarely trod, in part due to its environmental context.[16] Situated between two bayous, this "heavily wooded" zone formed a "neutral strip between the jurisdictions of [Shreveport] police and the parish sheriff's department," making an otherwise "beautiful sylvan" into the "secluded bowers of assignation."[17] Bootlegging and counterfeiting accordingly flourished along this isolated piece of rural land.

Douglas Island's natural seclusion offered particularly ideal cover for prostitution. Shreveport native R. J. Hughes recalled a mixed-race madam named "Old Fanny Edwards" owning a brothel in Douglas Island that was well patronized by white men.[18] When Shreveport formally banned prostitution in November 1917, many of its sex workers migrated to Douglas Island to keep plying their trade.[19] Tunnell Day retained a vivid memory of traveling out to the Island for a salacious "picnic" with two female sex workers. Made safe by the thick swamp surrounding them, Day used his Kodak camera to snap nude photographs of "Red Headed Madge" and Lois Weber. The racy photographs, copies of which historian and author Goodloe Stuck preserved, captured the women posing in broad daylight, with rural woodland framing the background.[20] But even the environmental and legal isolation that Douglas Island offered had its limits. On March 25, 1914, the *Shreveport Journal* reported that a group of Oil City bootleggers was arrested for violating "the prohibition law on Douglas Island."[21]

DRILLING NORTH LOUISIANA'S LANDSCAPE

North Louisiana's challenging environmental conditions not only raised costs for the oil industry, but also altered the final destination for the money it generated. When Mike Benedum and Joe Trees began drilling on the W. P. Stiles lease, they encountered natural challenges unlike anything they had experienced in previous drilling projects. The region's sandy earth made wells far more susceptible to caving in, and each Caddo Parish well they dug was roughly two to three times deeper than projects they had previously completed in Illinois. North Louisiana's landscape in turn had a dramatic impact on their finances, resulting in costs three to five times higher per well than in comparable investments. Such unforeseen expenses strained company finances and forced its managers, in the words of Joe Trees, to "stretch the lion's skin of credit over an acre of indebtedness and outlay."[22]

The unique challenges of drilling in North Louisiana made access to liquidity all the more essential, dramatically shaping who would ultimately profit from oil production. Benedum and Trees stretched that "lion's skin of credit" to keep the drilling process moving forward. The staggering costs of doing business in Caddo Parish even shaped their eventual decision to accept Standard Oil's buyout offer and pay down their debts.[23] North Louisiana's watery, sandy soils thus had a pronounced impact on who would economically benefit from its oil wealth, pushing cash away from smaller producers and toward the banks willing to extend credit and the cash-rich companies willing to assume the high costs of drilling in such a hostile landscape.

North Louisiana's humidity and swampy soil raised costs for small producers, but also paradoxically created opportunities for local skilled men who had the capacity and the proximity to promptly address their consequences. On the Benedum and Trees lease, the natural humidity of the "low sultry country" resulted in rapid deterioration of pipes and oil field tools, creating significant demand for welders, blacksmiths, and other skilled workers.[24] However, roads were so impassable "you could hardly get in and out," meaning that the companies had to rely on nearby machine shops to repair and maintain its materials. The difficulty of moving people and tools through North Louisiana's mud-laden ground meant that local blacksmiths, boiler men, and carpenters enjoyed a natural monopoly and accordingly strong wages.

The region's sandy and permeable soils were also crucibles for technological innovation. As Benedum and Trees drilled on their Caddo Parish leases, they found the "formations were soft and cavy,"[25] conditions that made underground wells highly susceptible to ruining production. "We just couldn't keep our drill hole clear of cavings," Mike Benedum recalled.[26] After several aborted wells, the drillers were beginning to assume major financial losses, with Benedum remembering that "we were in the red properly."[27] To find a solution, the pair recalled their experiences drilling in West Virginia, where the earth around their oil wells would similarly collapse. At the time, Joe Trees's father, a former millwright, had suggested injecting cement into the well to wall off the fluid sand surrounding it.

The drillers elected to try this "cementing" method in the Caddo Parish oil fields. As they drilled into depths that would previously hit sand, workers poured cement into the well, inserted a hollow steel tube, or "casing," and then waited thirty days for the fixture to dry. What resulted was a stable hole encased in steel and cement, enabling steady production without sand incursion. The first hole that Benedum and Trees cemented in Caddo Parish was stable and flush, producing twenty-five hundred barrels per day. In a 1951 interview, Mike Benedum credited Joe Trees and his "engineering knowledge" with "the cement proposition," a method that "made possible the drilling of oil in the Southwest."[28] In 1921, Erle P. Halliburton patented his own cementing method and proceeded to sell it around the Oklahoma oil fields, making him most prominently associated with the revolutionary technology. But just a few years prior, Benedum and Trees had been experimenting with a proto version made necessary by North Louisiana's sandy geology.

North Louisiana's "soft and cavy" geological formations also greatly enhanced the risk of "blowouts," or the dangerous incursion of high-pressured gas into a well. These incidents had the capacity to send vast columns of gas, oil, and water into the air with awesome force, ruining the well's production and potentially resulting in significant bodily harm to any nearby workers. Prior to the advent of Cameron ram-type blowout preventers in the 1920s, drillers had to work with cable tool drills, blunt instruments that percussed into the earth with little ability to control the flow of gas into a well. "Every time they hit a gas pocket," Mike Benedum recalled, "the well would blow out, tear the hole apart, and frequently rip the derrick to pieces."[29] To be sure, blowouts were a challenge across the early twentieth-century oil industry. But the combination of fragile topography and high-pressured gas under North Louisiana's soil made such catastrophes a uniquely common feature of its oil fields.

The confluence of high-pressured gas and underground water reserves even had the astonishing capacity to liquefy the ground surrounding a blown-out well, animating the solid earth into a horrifying quicksand that could bubble twenty feet in the air before descending into a concave depression. In May 1905, Producers' No. 2 blew out, causing a "boiling, churning motion" so powerful that "the derrick and machinery were engulfed in a mass of mud."[30] The resulting "geyser" of earth and water was so dramatic that it attracted a crowd of curious onlookers. Major Frank M. Kerr, a representative of Louisiana's Conservation Commission, witnessed one such event firsthand and later recounted the otherworldly spectacle:

> A basin or bowl of water some 250 feet in diameter had resulted from the action of the escaping gas and the roll of the waves from the mouth of the orifice toward the rim of the basin, like waves on a sea beach in stormy weather, from the center of which leaps a flame some 30 feet in diameter and equally high. This, with the monster upheaval of water and leaping of spray, presented a spectacle which might readily have been likened to the display of a prismatic fountain of unusual magnitude and superb effects.[31]

These "geysers" of gas and water were powerful enough to permanently reshape the ground. One such event resulted in a crater three hundred feet in width.[32] North Louisiana's oil producers had to constantly account for the volatile geology of their workplace. At any moment, the delicate equilibrium of underground water, gas, and oil could collapse, destroying an oil well and turning solid earth into a "prismatic fountain of unusual magnitude."

The greatest hazard North Louisiana's blowouts posed was their flammability: escaping oil and gas had the capacity to suddenly erupt into a pillar of flames. "If we start driving nails," Benedum recalled, "one spark from the hammer will blow us all to Kingdom Come."[33] Blowout fires could vaporize thousands of barrels of oil within a matter of days—or hours. When Star Oil Company's Loucke No. 3 well near Mooringsport ignited in August 1913, the fire consumed an estimated thirty thousand barrels of oil per day.[34] With a market rate of $0.95 per barrel of crude in 1913, Star Oil was losing $28,500 every day to the flames.[35] A photograph of the blowout captured the horror of such a scene: a widening spire of flames ascending past the tree line with smoke curling even higher above it.[36]

Part of the reason these blazes caused such devastation was the dearth of effective tools or experienced individuals readily available to fight them. Lacking the expertise or technology that a municipal fire force could provide, North Louisiana's boomtowns had to simply improvise with whatever tools or professional expertise they were able to access when fires struck. Harrell's No. 7, a Producer's Oil Company well in the Caddo Parish boomtown of Vivian, ignited on May 11, 1911, severely burning four employees and killing two. The "terrific gas pressure . . . [sent] flames upwards of one hundred feet high, with great volume of black smoke which could be seen for twenty-five miles, seething and roaring continuously." Workers set about repurposing oil field equipment such as boilers, pumps, and pipe to attack the fire with water and steam. They used the pumps to pour water on the fire, and also on each other to keep their own clothes from igniting.[37]

Efforts continued all night, with some men working continuously for thirty hours. One worker fought the blaze even after being "severely scalded by boiling oil."[38] But the Harrell No. 7 continued to burn, leading the workers to attempt ever more novel methods at extinguishing the fire. After locating a Civil War–era bore cannon, workers fired nine shots toward a valve in the hope of severing the pressurized flow of oil fueling the fire. Photographs captured a bizarre scene: oil field workers aiming a diminutive cannon at a massive inferno, looking at once comical and desperate. The cannon not only missed the valve but

FIGURE 6.1. *Workers in Vivian attempting to fight the blaze at Harrell's No. 7, 1911, including with the novel (and ineffective) method of firing a cannon into the inferno.*

also punctured several of the pipelines underneath, further spreading the flames' breadth.

After the cannon's failure, contractor Hardy Haire made another novel, albeit somewhat more practical, suggestion: to build an underground tunnel that would redirect the oil away from the well. A former coal miner turned roughneck named Charles "Dub" Randolph volunteered to perform the task. Producer's Company paid Randolph a dollar an hour on a twenty-four-hour basis, including meals, coffee, a new suit, and a lifetime job with the company, all in addition to the "occasional drink thrown in" according to one retrospective account.[39] Randolph employed his old mining skills to construct a fifteen-foot-deep, fifty-foot-long passageway to the well, successfully rerouting the oil away from the fire. An arresting photograph captured twelve workmen, including a small boy, proudly posing around the tunnel's entrance as smoke billowed over their heads.[40]

Oil well fires were not always unfortunate accidents; sometimes they were products of explicit company policies of "flaring" gas. Underground gas reserves existed in "immense quantities" in North Louisiana—gas was present in far higher proportions than crude oil—and many firms extracted and sold it to nearby cities like Shreveport, Marshall, and Texarkana.[41] However, the costs associated with storing and transporting the gaseous product were comparatively high. Unlike crude, which could sit in a tank or an earthen pit, natural gas needed pressurized storage facilities. And while oil could reach market by mule or truck, natural gas necessitated a pipeline and upfront costs that most smaller firms could not immediately bear.

Despite the relative unprofitability of natural gas, it lay in high-pressure pockets right next to the crude oil, meaning that allowing some of the gas to escape was often essential to accessing the adjacent crude. Neglecting to relieve the gaseous pressure could lead to a disastrous blowout and the destruction of an entire well. Faced with a profuse, less profitable, and potentially dangerous natural resource blocking the more lucrative crude, producers often chose to simply burn or "flare" the gas into the air. The resulting waste was enormous. By one estimation, producers emitted roughly 70 million cubic feet of Caddo Parish natural gas in 1907 alone.[42] Between 1906 and 1913, that figure reached an estimated 200 billion cubic feet.[43] In the short term, flaring gas seemed to be a practical method for accessing the more profitable crude oil lying next to it. But in the long term, this myopic strategy depleted underground pressure, making future extraction of North Louisiana crude costlier and more logistically difficult.[44]

The ubiquitous gas flares not only pumped toxic chemical properties into the air day and night, but also significantly distorted the everyday experience of living in North Louisiana. For people residing in and around the oil fields, the sights and sounds of forever-burning "gassers" became ordinary, if bizarre,

FIGURE 6.2. *Workers, including a young boy, pose around the tunnel that a former coal miner dug to relieve the fire at Harrell's No. 7 in Vivian, 1911.*

features of their natural world. Natives of Oil City recalled an otherworldly sky that eternally burned red, night and day.[45] Driller Carl W. Jones claimed that one could "read a newspaper at night several miles away" from the oil wells.[46] Roughly thirty miles south in Shreveport, Walter Duvall George Jr. remembered "you could see Oil City . . . it would light up the sky at night . . . [a] red sky."[47] Locals even *heard* it. Flared gas escaped from wells with such force that a constant sonic roar was audible for miles around. Oral histories from North Louisiana natives tend to portray the perpetually burning wells as a quaint, even romantic, piece of local history, but having to live under that reddish glow and the sonic pollution which accompanied it would have been undoubtedly surreal.

North Louisiana's burning wells became objects of fascination, and even an unlikely source of tourism. Reflecting public curiosity about these towering columns of fire, contemporary photographers captured numerous images of the burning gas wells, many of them with crowds gawking in the foreground. Although their reddish glow was visible from Shreveport's streets, the actual sight of such towering fires was apparently compelling enough to entice an urbane crowd into the boomtowns as a kind of voyeuristic experience. Enterprising salesmen at the Kansas City Southern Railroad offered one-dollar day trips from the city to go witness the dramatic fires.[48]

The draw to curious onlookers of witnessing the oil industry's astonishing "factoryscape" was hardly unique to North Louisiana: late nineteenth-century tourists had also flocked to experience the "technological sublime" of Western Pennsylvania's oil derricks and the otherworldly new extractive landscape they had wrought.[49] Such trips offered a bizarre and compelling opportunity for middle-class families to take an exotic adventure into the hellish world of oil field boomtowns, many of which, like Caddo Parish, were just a few dozen miles north of Shreveport's comfortable, tree-lined streets.

THE CONSERVATION COMMISSION'S ATTEMPTS AT REGULATION

Gas flaring became so economically and environmentally wasteful that the state of Louisiana, historically loath to regulate business, finally sought to curb the practice. In 1906 the governor, Jared Y. Sanders, signed a law making the wasteful burning of gas illegal. Two years later he created the Louisiana Commission for the Conservation of Natural Resources, or simply the Conservation Commission, to enforce the new law. The commission's 1910 report included a letter from Theodore Roosevelt stressing the importance of such regulatory bodies: "Natural Resources on which the welfare of this Nation rests are becoming depleted, and, in not a few cases are already exhausted." This Rooseveltian ambition of preserving natural resources for future economic betterment permeated the group's work. By the commission's estimation, too many oil men were willing to "waste much to get little."[50] Environmental degradation, while a nominal concern for the commission, was ultimately secondary to an *economic* objective of preventing needless waste of oil and gas commodities.

The commission henceforth deployed a team of government experts to identify and eradicate gas wastage. With Shreveport as its headquarters, the group
fanned out across the North Louisiana oil fields, inspecting wells and looking
for incidents of waste. In addition to making spot inspections, team members
used a variety of other mediums—public meetings, lectures, news releases in
the press—to "bring to the people a greater knowledge and broader apprecia-
tion of what Louisiana possesses in natural resources and the necessity for their
conservation." Their reports even furnished pictures of the *Daisy*, a yacht that
team members used to travel along the Red River and its adjacent bayous. The
commission proudly recounted episodes in which agents successfully applied
their expertise to bring gassers under control and preserve a natural resource
that would otherwise be squandered. In some cases, they discovered firms using
fires promotionally, burning gas solely "for advertisement and for spectacular
effect."[51]

However, from its very conception the Conservation Commission's efforts
were plagued with institutional inertia, poor financial resources, and allegedly
corrupt practices. Even as the commission's annual reports celebrated individual successes in the preservation of oil and gas, they also bemoaned the lack of
money and political will supporting their work. The 1912 statement to the governor assumed a remarkably accusatory tone toward the state government. The
"report for this year will be brief," it began, as the commission's activities had
been "almost completely extinguished by reason of the fact that the appropria-
tion for . . . expenses . . . was not available."[52] The report then bemoaned the
futility of its work given the lack of political and financial support:

> It is a cause of the deepest regret to the Commission that it has been unable
> to do any practical work . . . we are convinced that we could have increased
> the Conservation sentiment among the people by education and by practice
> demonstration. Almost all of the evils which formerly existed in the exploi-
> tation of our natural resources, report in 1910, yet exist. For instance, there
> has been little, if any, attempt on the part of the oil and gas drillers and pro-
> ducers to prevent waste, especially in connection with gas.[53]

The report further defended the Conservation Commission against the accusation that "useless offices and officers" filled its ranks, pleading with the governor to continue funding its agents. However, outside evaluations indicated
that such accusations may not have been unfounded. A 1991 study by the Louisiana Geological Survey described a history of "Inconsistent administration
practices and corruption" afflicting the commission, suggesting that the state's
reluctance to fund their office was perhaps not so misguided.[54] Driller Carl Morris spoke of the Conservation Commission with derision, noting that he could

easily cheat their regulatory hand to cut costs.[55] As a consequence of this anemic state regulation, gas waste and the environmental damage it wrought continued apace.

DRILLING OVER NORTH LOUISIANA'S WATER

Some of Caddo Parish's largest, most alluring reservoirs of crude lay within an even more inaccessible position: under the enormous Caddo Lake, then known as "Ferry Lake." Approximately thirty-two miles long, the lake's forty-five thousand acres straddle the border of Marion County, Texas, and Louisiana's Caddo Parish, making it one of the largest natural freshwater lakes in the American South.[56] Locals began to suspect that oil reserves might lie under its waters as early as 1907, when J. B. McCann, an employee of the J. M. Guffey Petroleum Company, allegedly ignited a gas vapor on one side of the lake and followed the resulting line of flames by boat from one side to the other.[57]

As oil derricks began sprouting around its banks, Caddo Lake was also the site of a parallel boom in pearl hunting. One Japanese immigrant and oil company cook named Sachihiko Ono Murata had discovered the pearl-producing mussels by diving to the lake's bottom in 1909.[58] Murata's discovery prompted an influx of pearl hunters, many of whom set up tents around the lake and tried their luck at diving for the underwater jewels.[59] However, very few were able to replicate Murata's success. Caddo Lake's brief pearl boom permanently ended after the US Army Corps of Engineers dammed the lake between 1910 and 1914.[60] Completed over the objections of local pearl hunters and the Shreveport Chamber of Commerce, the new dam raised the lake to such a high level that diving became impossible, leaving oil production as the only boom taking place in the lake's waters.

Oil production not only transformed the waters of Caddo Lake, but also significantly expanded the political and economic role of the Parish Levee Board that governed it. An ordinarily discreet public entity tasked with administering the Parish's levee system, the board was suddenly responsible for leasing out Caddo Lake's oil-bearing lake bottom to eager drillers. On November 1, 1907, Gulf Refining Company leased twelve sections of lake bed from the Levee Board.[61] In exchange for drilling rights, Gulf would pay the board a cash bonus of $30,000 and the customary one-eighth royalty on the first two hundred barrels produced, followed by a more modest one-sixteenth royalty for all subsequent production.[62] Gulf further agreed to pay the board an additional $70,000 bonus once their production exceeded thirty thousand barrels. In May 1911, Gulf's Ferry Lake No. 1, Caddo Lake's first over-water well, was completed.[63]

Working atop Caddo Lake required elaborate pieces of infrastructure unlike anything that would be necessary on the (comparably) solid land elsewhere in North Louisiana. One of the most immediate challenges was simply getting tools and raw materials to the over-water production sites, many of which were up to a mile away from the shore.[64] To meet these unique challenges, Gulf assembled a fleet of fifty craft, including thirty-six boats, three tugboats, ten barges, and a remarkable floating pile driver.[65] Company boats barged out roughly 140 cypress logs onto the lake, drove them into the most solid ground available, and created foundations for two over-water platforms—one to support the derrick and another, about one hundred yards away, for its accompanying boiler.[66] Gulf successfully constructed a permanent drilling platform every 660 feet, enabling them to drill a well in the middle of individual ten-square-acre grids across their lake bed lease.[67]

Contemporary photographs captured the skillfully improvised pile-driving boat Gulf used to construct the over-water platforms. Fashioned entirely out of wood, the small vessel was scarcely large enough to house the tools and personnel it carried: a crane for lifting the cypress logs, a boiler to power the crane, and six men to operate the machinery. Once the platforms were in place, workers connected them to the lakeshore with a system of wooden boardwalks crisscrossing the lake. Yet again, local cypress trees were crucial to this process, becoming the boats, walkways, and drilling platforms that enabled the elaborate over-water procedure.

Caddo Lake production boomed following the initial success of Ferry Lake No. 1, prompting the neat rows of derricks "lined up like soldiers" on its waters; those "soldiers" continued to consistently produce over the coming decades. By 1950, Gulf Refining Company had drilled 278 lake-bed wells, producing roughly 13,685,000 barrels. However, by that point the Caddo Levee Board had not been reaping the financial benefits of such innovative production for quite some time. In April 1919, the state of Louisiana sued the board to assume control over the lake-bed leasing of Ferry Lake. After two years of litigation, a district judge ultimately ruled in favor of the state of Louisiana, formally stripping the Levee Board of its vast leasing powers in November 1921.[68]

Many historical records and local Oil City monuments credit Ferry Lake No. 1 as the first over-water oil well in the United States—or globally. However, recent scholarship has uncovered even earlier over-water oil production on Ohio's man-made Grand Reservoir around 1891, during which producers used technologies very similar to those that Gulf employed over Caddo Lake. To make the foundation on which the derrick rested, pile drivers on the Grand Reservoir created a "crib 14 feet square" to keep their rigs above water. Even earlier overwater operations may have also occurred in Michigan or Russia, although there is less evidence to validate such claims.[69] So while Gulf's

FIGURE 6.3. *The floating crane workers used to construct oil derricks on Caddo Lake, 1908.*

over-water drilling methods on Caddo Lake were extraordinary and innovative, they do not register as the very first of their kind.

The technological and environmental challenges associated with Caddo Lake's development also had a pronounced economic impact: larger, better-capitalized firms such as Gulf Refining were far better positioned to assume the costs of accessing the underwater crude. According to Walter Hopper's 1908 estimations, a deep well on Caddo field's (relatively) solid ground cost approximately $10,000 to $12,000.[70] Meanwhile, Caddo Lake's over-water derricks cost an estimated $15,000. However, considering all the boats, cypress logs, and infrastructure that were unique to drilling on Caddo Lake, it is remarkable how *small* the financial difference actually was between on-land and over-water drilling. The strikingly similar costs do not diminish the unique challenges of drilling over Caddo Lake, but rather underscore the difficulties of building a deep well on an ordinary Caddo Parish lease: drilling North Louisiana's soft, flood-prone lands was perhaps not radically different from working over an actual lake.

Production alongside or on top of Caddo Lake resulted in enormous consequences for its freshwater and surrounding lands. At best, producers modestly endeavored to prevent oil spillage and conserve their product; at worst, they were indifferent to crude or saltwater runoff and unwilling to invest in preventative methods. Cleo Norris grew up alongside Caddo Lake and remembered pollution in its waters as normal, even innocuous. He recalled an on-land Texaco well blowing out of control, with crude running over "all day and all night . . . into Caddo Lake." And yet as saltwater and oil poured in, Norris continued to catch and consume white perch from the lake, declaring the fish "just as good as it was anywhere."[71] He even swam in its briny waters, rendering himself "just about half covered with crude." Walter Duvall George Jr. corroborated Norris's account: "If you played in Caddo Lake you'd get oil up to your ankles."[72]

Still, Norris dismissed the idea that such practices adversely impacted Caddo Lake's ecology. Even though "every well . . . just dumped their salt water in a creek or in the lake . . . it never hurt fishing."[73] Spillage might kill a few lily pads or trees, but "Mother Nature" being "the best cleaner upper there is," they would grow back. Norris was contemptuous of environmentalists: "I don't believe they know too much." It seemed that many of the early drillers on Caddo Lake shared the same attitude. The 1910 *United States Geological Survey* published an image revealing the impact of such relentless saltwater waste. Alongside an active Caddo Parish well spraying a thick column of saltwater lay a barren cluster of stumps and trees stripped of their leaves.

As over-water rigs generated increasing amounts of crude and saltwater runoff, state regulators were characteristically slow to staunch the environmental wreckage. In its April 1916 report the Conservation Commission described its efforts to eradicate the "very troublesome . . . salt water question" in the oil fields. However, as it was "impossible to continue the production of oil without obtaining some amount of salt water," the author lamented, producers remained in the habit of allowing the runoff to flow into streams and topsoil. The commission did propose a hypothetical, if imperfect, solution: holding "the

FIGURE 6.4. *A 1915 image of the Pine Island field reveals the level of environmental destruction that often accompanied oil production.*

mass of the salt water in pound until such season as it may be allowed to flow into the streams without injury to any one."[74]

By the commission's own admission, however, its ability to enforce even such anemic regulation was limited, given the geographic and financial constraints: "The territory to be covered is large and the funds available for this department are small in comparison." But more importantly, the commission simply lacked the authority to meaningfully curtail the oil companies' behavior. Any compliance would have to be voluntary: it would only be due to the "courtesy of the larger operating companies" and their "desire to . . . strictly comply with the laws" that producers would even consider adopting such regulations.[75] Ultimately, the Conservation Commission could only advise. But with little incentive for firms to incur the costs associated with safely storing their saltwater runoff, the practice largely continued.

Just a few miles to the south of Oil City's mud and fire, Shreveport's local economy paradoxically stood to *benefit* from the boomtowns' atrocious environmental conditions and had a perverse incentive to perpetuate those conditions. With daily train lines running from the growing city into Oil City, Homer, and other North Louisiana boomtowns, Shreveport became a bedroom community for the lawyers, drillers, and other white-collar workers who could afford a refuge away from the crude state of their workplace. Salaried workers preferred Shreveport's tree-lined streets, sewer system, and readily available drinking water. This environmental contrast helped push an economic and social disparity: the wealthiest participants of the oil boom put their resources into making Shreveport a sanitary, comfortable enclave; those investments relied on nearby boomtowns remaining environmentally despoiled, but profitable, centers of extraction. Shreveport's livability thus directly correlated to the oil fields' environmental devastation.

Shreveport's environmental conditions also shaped the racial barriers that governed its urban boundaries. Oil field wealth built mansions along streets like Fairfield Avenue that were set on higher land farther from the Red River. But the lower-lying lands around the "Silver Lake" area remained some of the city's least desirable lots. As the city's urban-industrial economy grew at the turn of the century, Black migrants seeking urban work had to settle in this low-lying district for lack of a more salubrious space to inhabit. Louisiana state politician W. Scott Wilkinson moved to Shreveport as a child in 1900 and had distinct recollections of the lake's environmental—and racial—composition: "I remember well the smell of the water. It wasn't very good. Negroes lived around the banks of it. There were surface toilets, of course, and all of that would wash into Silver Lake."[76] As they did in Oil City, environmental conditions fashioned the social contours of Shreveport's cityscape.

PIPELINES THROUGH THE SWAMP

All the mud, rivers, and swampland encircling North Louisiana's oil rigs made the construction of oil and gas pipelines all the more essential. Efficient underground lines augured an industry in which producers no longer had to rely on teamsters slowly dragging small barrelages of crude by mule or horse through the muck to get their product to market. Although train lines existed from the earliest days of the boom, simply getting the oil from the wells to the loading racks was time-consuming and expensive. And as production expanded, these antiquated methods were becoming increasingly insufficient for operators who wanted to sell their booming supplies as fast and efficiently as possible.

Demand among producers to overcome North Louisiana's landscape translated into an enormous business opportunity for companies with the resources to enact large infrastructure projects. Firms like Standard Oil and Gulf had a unique opportunity to build and, more importantly, *control* a new transportation system for Louisiana's growing oil economy: pipelines. These networks would revolutionize how North Louisiana's producers could get their oil to market, but they came at a premium cost to use. The creation of pipelines thus placed smaller producers in an economic bind: by using these efficient new systems, independents would be enabling Standard Oil and Gulf to further consolidate their control over yet another segment of the oil business. Environmental obstacles effectively resulted in greater economic consolidation.

In 1909, Standard Oil initiated construction on an enormous pipeline that would connect the constellation of North Louisiana's oil fields to Standard's nascent Baton Rouge refinery. The company assembled a "tong gang" of workers with previous experience laying pipe in Pennsylvania, West Virginia, and Ohio.[77] Standard Oil notably sought workers who had experience laying pipelines over rivers, an essential expertise given North Louisiana's watery landscape. The "tough but likeable Irishman" James W. Finnegan would be the team's foreman, in part due to his reputation as the company's "ace river-crossing specialist."[78]

Many of these veteran pipeliners were reluctant to go south and work in the notorious "vast swampland" of Louisiana—and probably for good reason.[79] Much like the oil field workers, the tong gangs were utterly exposed to a ruthless climate. Smith W. Day, who had previously pipelined in New York, distinctly remembered "us Yankees" having to readjust to the brutal conditions.[80] Every day of laying pipe involved walking "ankle deep" through the mud, recalled pipeliner Dale Benroth.[81] One stretch of bayou was too soft for mules to tread, so the men had to manually dig the line, finding the ground "full of snakes and mosquitos" as they worked.[82] Many of the workers fell ill with malaria, including Day. Fred Bimel remembered Louisiana's malarial mosquitos as having almost supernatural strength, claiming, perhaps hyperbolically, that he saw a "swarm of mosquitos . . . raise up and choke a mule to death."[83]

Despite the workers' experiences in other challenging environments, North Louisiana was something entirely new, adding significant costs and time to the labor process. Before work even began, the land's watery volatility had already altered the line's path. With much of the region inaccessible by road and far too swampy to facilitate the transportation of pipelining materials, the pipe would have to parallel existing railroads and their already cleared land, curtailing surveyors' options for prospective routes. Under ordinary circumstances, pipeliners could install a mile of pipe in a ten-hour day. But North Louisiana's swamps, rivers, and uneven terrain frequently prevented workers from even reaching that quotidian benchmark.[84] Harsh weather also slowed work patterns. In the summer of 1909, Louisiana's heat was so extreme that Standard Oil had to hire an extra thirty-five workers to perform the requisite labor.

Though many of the tong men had constructed lines through New York's Hudson River, those experiences still could not prepare them for the Red River's unpredictability. Even Finnegan, the "ace river-crossing" foreman, "never had experiences" with anything like the Red River. When Smith W. Day's team had to place their line across the river, they witnessed its banks gradually shift half a mile from its original boundaries, the points on which they had initially based the line's path. Faced with such unprecedented conditions, Finnegan's men altered the line's contours, putting "[plenty] of curvey [*sic*] in it so it could crawl into the river" and not break apart as the Red River's size naturally ebbed and flowed.[85]

Even as the pipeline companies successfully completed their lines, environmental obstacles did not cease. In 1913, Standard Oil discovered that the very soil protecting their new Louisiana pipeline contained highly acidic properties, corroding major portions of their elaborate new investment. Pipeliners had been aware that such corrosion was possible during the initial construction phase and painted red lead paint over the pipe in an attempt to insulate the steel.[86] But those preventative measures were insufficient against the powerful chemicals that lay within Louisiana's soil. According to an internal Standard Oil report, just five years in the region's acidic earth could end the life of a pipeline.[87]

To reinforce the steel lines and protect the valuable crude oil passing through them, Standard Oil set about hiring hundreds of workers, most of whom were Black, to initiate an elaborate retrofitting process. Those workers faced an arduous sequence of tasks: raising the pipe from the ground, cleaning the pipe, setting wooden frames around the pipe, and finally pouring concrete within the wooden frames, ultimately creating a hard shell one inch thick to protect the line against corrosion.[88] In the wettest and swampiest areas, where the corrosion was most severe, workers had to replace the pipes outright. In addition to the requisite manpower, such retrofitting was materially intensive, requiring enormous amounts of sand and cement.

Two photographs published in a 1919 edition of *The Lamp*, Standard Oil's company newspaper, revealed how elaborate and labor-intensive the process was. The workers look positively diminutive against the swampland enclosing them. In one of the photographs, a Black worker stands waist-deep in the mud, his work smock covered in mud. In the other, a segmented line of newly cemented pipes dissects the pitch-black earth, eventually vanishing into the horizon. By publishing these dramatic photographs in their corporate literature, Standard Oil was celebrating the company's technological prowess and ability to maximize production despite the formidable natural challenges they encountered. But Louisiana's soil had in fact cost the company a great deal in money, labor, and time: workers had to unearth and encase 540 miles of pipeline at a cost of $750,000.[89]

WORLD WAR I AND THE PINE ISLAND DISASTER

As North Louisiana's production figures grew and pipeline networks expanded, its oil fields became an environmental and economic crossroads: a place where the global forces of politics, war, and money collided with local swamps, water, and oil. The entry of American forces into the First World War had particularly seismic implications for the region's oil economy and the landscape that housed it. As the United States mobilized for war, the military became an enormous consumer of crude oil. In 1917, President Woodrow Wilson created the Federal Fuel Administration, an agency tasked with encouraging maximum production and reducing consumer waste, thereby ensuring that the United States would maintain a steady supply of coal and crude to feed its war machine. The US Navy became a particularly major consumer of domestic crude oil, which fed the boilers on its fleet of ships heading to Europe.

These gathering international events had profound economic and environmental implications for North Louisiana. Spiking naval demand for the heavier variety of crude perfectly coincided with the 1917 opening of Pine Island, a new twenty-five-square-mile oil field in Caddo Parish. That "dismal swamp" which W. O. Whitaker and Wade Hampton had encountered twenty years prior on their hunting trip had now become the latest center of North Louisiana production. When blended with higher-quality Mexican crude, Pine Island's heavy oil was ideal for naval boilers. The three biggest pipeline firms, Gulf Oil, Texas Company, and Standard Oil of Louisiana, all entered into the lucrative business of buying and transporting the field's crude to satiate the military's demand. High prices encouraged more drilling, further expanding the field's production. By 1918, Pine Island boasted 140 wells producing an average of 28,000 barrels per day, resulting in an annual total of 11 million barrels.[90]

But the end of World War I meant a commensurate drop in the government's demand for crude, particularly Pine Island's heavy variety. Even prior to the Armistice of 1918, Standard Oil, Gulf, and the Texas Company were already devaluing Pine Island's glutted product with a new price structure, buying heavier crude at $1.55 per barrel instead of the $2.10 to $2.25 per barrel premium they paid at the height of US involvement.[91] Once the war formally ended, the big three had even less appetite, abruptly informing local producers "that they would no longer take, purchase, transport or refine" any Pine Island crude. The pipeline companies ultimately softened their stance and agreed to buy some, but only a pittance: "between 20 and 35 percent of the actual oil production of that field and . . . [refusing] to handle the production of any new wells," estimated a 1919 report written by the precocious young railroad commissioner, Huey P. Long.[92] By the spring of 1919, the price for heavy crude reached a low of $0.50 per barrel.

Despite the collapsing market for crude, Pine Island's producers continued to pump oil, transforming a price slump into an outright economic crisis for the Caddo Parish oil industry. The most immediate motive to keep pumping oil was economic. While some producers plugged their wells to pause production, others remained insistent on getting revenue—any revenue—to pay down their debts and compensate investors. "Rule of Capture" incentives only further enticed producers to match any competitors who continued to pump on adjacent lands. Environmental considerations also discouraged many drillers from stopping outright. Much of Pine Island's crude lay alongside underground reserves of saltwater, which producers feared would bleed through the soft ground and into the wells if production ceased. For these reasons, most producers felt more comfortable simply allowing the oil to flow, even with precious few buyers willing to buy, and with even fewer places to store all the flowing oil.[93]

What started as an economic decline quickly devolved into a dramatic environmental crisis, a consequence of both financial and technological constraints. Pine Island's producers were enduring a soft market in a region with virtually no reliable storage options, and all while they insisted on continuing to pump oil. When prices for their product were high, producers relied on infrastructure controlled by other companies, such as pipelines and railroads, to get their product to market. With so much crude being quickly purchased and moved out of Pine Island, local firms had little incentive to build large-scale storage tanks. But now they were suddenly in desperate and immediate need of storage in an area where none existed. As they so often did, local producers improvised, hastily constructing earthen tanks with capacity of 30,000 to 40,000 barrels, ultimately carving more than a million barrels' worth of storage capacity into the ground.[94]

By the winter of 1919, however, oil production was outpacing the speed at which earthen tanks could be dug, making even more rudimentary and environmentally calamitous storage methods necessary. Many producers dammed up creeks and let the oil flow into the water beds, to be collected later. Others just let oil gather on the ground without constraint. Even the freshly dug earthen tanks often failed to keep the oil in one place. Under ordinary circumstances, companies would line such pits with clay or asphalt to prevent seepage into the surrounding soil. Given Pine Island's severe overproduction, however, operators valued speed over quality and neglected to line the tanks. With nothing enclosing the massive ponds of crude, between 42,500 and 75,000 barrels vanished into the surrounding earth each week.[95]

The environmental toll only worsened as record rainfall gripped North Louisiana during the spring and summer of 1919. That May, drenching rains led many earthen tanks and dammed-up creeks to overflow, sloshing stagnant crude indiscriminately over the land. On June 26 alone, heavy precipitation caused an approximate single-day loss of one million barrels.[96] Dramatic and bizarre scenes of environmental devastation unfolded. As crude indiscriminately washed over the ground, the landscape itself became severely flammable. When

Earl W. Wagy, an inspector of the Federal Bureau of Mines, visited Pine Island in April 1919, he witnessed an "indescribable fire danger . . . which menaces everything . . . including buildings, trees and stored oil."[97] If ever a fire broke out, he further warned, it would "mean a destruction of life" across Caddo Parish. Oil man D. W. Deupre imagined a similar scene:

> A stroke of lightning could set the entire field ablaze and literally wipe out the operations there for the time being and paralyze the industry for weeks at least. Every bayou and creek in that country has been dammed up, and oil turned into it, and large circular vats, resembling water tanks, have been thrown up and oil piped into them.[98]

Thick streams of oil aimlessly snaked across the ground, rolling "wild into the numerous bayous running into the [Red River]." Pine Island's orphaned oil was so abundant that it began reaching communities many miles away from the actual wells. In March 1919, the *Shreveport Times* reported that Pine Island oil had migrated fifty miles down the Red River, where residents of the riverside town of Colfax observed an alarming sight: petroleum in a "quantity . . . so great as to change the color of the river to a yellowish brown," prompting fears "among fishermen that fish in the stream would be killed."[99]

The catastrophic dispersal of oil was particularly devastating for local farmers who relied on the land's fertility. Inspectors from the US Department of the Interior found oil had saturated everything: it had soaked two feet into the ground, gathered in pools some ten inches deep, and even filled the furrows of plowed farmland. As oil seeped from earthen tanks and spilled from creeks, gravity directed it toward the lowest-lying lands, flowing "downward and then laterally on top of the shallow water table towards the lower land elevations." Farmers who had been previously fortunate enough to till the fertile lands along the Red River floodplain now had the distinct misfortune of being a low-lying magnet for the oil flows, even from as much as half a mile away from producing wells. Under ordinary circumstances, springtime would be planting season. However, by that June, news stories estimated that Caddo's agricultural lands had lost $100 per acre in value, with a total loss of $500,000. And unlike the landowning, politically mobilized rice farmers of Acadia Parish, the farmers occupying Caddo Parish's farms were largely tenants, many of them Black, who lacked the economic and political clout of their urban landlords.[100]

The largest voices of protest came from Pine Island's independent drillers, who mobilized to demand legislative relief from the state of Louisiana. During that spring and summer, they formed the Independent Oil Producers' Association of North Louisiana, which lobbied the Railroad Commission, the oil industry's regulator in Louisiana, to intercede and oblige pipeline companies to buy and ship their clients' crude. Fortunately for the association, recently elected Railroad Commissioner Huey Long was not only an oil driller himself, but also an ambitious politician eager to make headlines by jousting with Big Oil in support of fellow independents.[101] Prior to the 1918 election, Louisiana's Railroad Commission had been a quiet state agency that was largely subservient to the industry. However, as commissioner, Long animated the moribund entity into an active regulatory force that fought for lower consumer utility rates and extended railroad service into rural areas, while challenging the oil industry's monopolistic control over Louisiana's pipelines.[102]

On March 25, 1919, Long's commission passed a resolution condemning the "big three" pipeline companies for refusing to buy independently produced North Louisiana oil and demanding legislative action to remedy the crisis. The commission's statement recognized its own political and economic limitations, however, conceding that it was "unable to presently afford any affirmative relief." Instead, it implored the state legislature to enact a series of actions on behalf of the independents: "to force all handlers of crude petroleum to become common purchasers"; to compel "the furnishing of common storage"; and to "[divorce] pipeline companies and refining companies from those producing oils."[103] The environmental impacts of overproduction to North Louisiana, while acknowledged and condemned by the Railroad Commission, were largely secondary to the economic dimensions of conservation, storage, and price.

The political pressures that the Railroad Commission and Independent Oil Producers' Association applied to the big pipeline companies had little impact until August 1919, when Standard Oil agreed to move ten thousand barrels of Pine Island crude per day, paying its producers $0.75 per barrel. While nowhere near robust wartime prices, this new arrangement finally meant an end to untold barrels of oil idly washing through Caddo Parish. As the larger US economy gradually emerged out of a post-World War I recession, demand for oil overall also reemerged, buoying the price for heavy crude up to $2.50 per barrel by the spring of 1920.[104] However, precisely as national crude oil prices were rebounding, the productivity of Pine Island's wells was waning. After reaching a peak of 18 million barrels in 1918, production dropped to less than 6 million barrels in 1921. Once again, short-term decisions to produce quickly resulted in calamitous long-term consequences for the industry in North Louisiana.

The misalignment of local geology and economic demand was catastrophic for North Louisiana, costing its economy and environment dearly: roughly 2,279,000 barrels—or the equivalent of just under ten *Exxon Valdez* spills—went to waste in 1919.[105] The enormity of the overproduction also underscored how the best-capitalized firms shrewdly leveraged Louisiana's arduous landscape into a position of economic dominance over the industry's transportation sector. If the region had not been so laden with swamps, water, and other obstacles, producers would not have become so beholden to the pipelines belonging to Standard Oil, Gulf Oil, and the Texas Company. Natural challenges effectively drained money from smaller local producers and placed more economic power in the hands of large, rich companies.

THE HISTORICAL POWER OF NORTH LOUISIANA'S LANDSCAPE

The natural landscape that oil producers, pipeliners, and roughnecks encountered in North Louisiana was far more than just a daily encumbrance; it wielded a real economic impact on the region's oil industry. Oil production may have been a national and indeed global business by the early twentieth century, but Louisiana's workforce discovered that to succeed in the emergent oil-producing region, it had to contort its practices to meet the unique challenges of its soils and waterways—a global industry assuming a *local* form.

Environmental conditions not only shaped work patterns, but also indirectly impacted who would be the economic winners. Skilled workers with the knowledge and proximity to fix machines corroded by the humid swamp air benefited; meanwhile, larger companies with the resources to build and manage pipelines assumed control over the industry's transportation routes, and distant credit houses in Shreveport or as far away as New York profited handsomely, as the swamp and mud raised costs and impelled more financing to make a project viable. Even bootleggers and sex workers could rely on the thick woods and opaque swamps to provide a safe space in which to conduct business.

North Louisiana's landscape also very much shaped the character of the communities that formed around the oil industry. Living in Oil City meant enduring an eternally red night sky, massive pools of oil or saltwater next door, and all the sounds and smells that accompanied nearly twenty-four-hour production. Those brutal natural conditions also reinforced Shreveport's standing as the oil boom's preeminent economic and social center: a place where the wealthiest could live on handsome, manicured streets that felt far from the oil fields' primitive sights and odors. Oil production churned North Louisiana's boomtowns into a sacrificial landscape for energy extraction; that degradation in turn helped burnish Shreveport's reputation as a refuge away from those degraded conditions.[106]

7 / THE CITY

IN NOVEMBER 1900, CHARLES HOWARD, SPECIAL REPRE-
sentative for the Twelfth US Census, arrived in Shreveport to evaluate the
city's economic present and prognosticate about its future. Howard left with a
very positive impression of the growing North Louisiana city, which had
embraced a forward-looking economic strategy of industrial development:
"Shreveport has the spirit," he told the *New Orleans Daily Picayune*, and is
"imbued with the belief that it takes factories to make up a well-rounded and
prosperous city." Ringed by the fertile Red River valley, the city had become an
agricultural distribution point by the turn of the century, transporting much of
the lumber, cotton, and other raw materials produced by its rural hinterlands.[1]
Shreveport's "progressive spirit" seemed to be advancing toward an ever-
brighter future of factories, wage-earning jobs, and middle-class stability.

Just a decade after Howard's visit, Shreveport had indeed made considerable strides in transforming itself into an urban center of industrial production.
Much of that wealth did not originate in local factories, however, but instead
from the network of oil boomtowns which had germinated across the city's
rural northern frontier. Shreveport offered an ideal geographic vicinity to those
oil fields, enabling commuters to fan out by rail into the boomtowns, work a full
day, and then return home by nightfall. Moreover, Shreveport maintained a
useful proximity to an entire *region* of oil fields spanning North Louisiana,
Oklahoma, Southern Arkansas, and East Texas. Never beholden to one oil field,
Shreveport translated that diversified economic portfolio into steady growth
and a steady population, even as individual boomtowns rose and fell around it.

However, Shreveport's *distance* from the oil fields was just as essential to its
economic growth and civic identity. Oil industry lawyers, land buyers, engineers, and other white-collar professionals populated Shreveport's handsome
tree-lined avenues, where they bought homes, funded civic projects, and sought
to improve the city's quality of life. In turn, Shreveport's political officials largely

privileged the municipal issues of their urban constituents over the social and environmental crises plaguing boomtowns like Oil City. This dynamic only reinforced the enormous chasm in quality of life between the city and the boomtowns of North Louisiana. As Oil City and its surrounding boomtowns were becoming increasingly squalid for the workers who could only afford to pitch a tent alongside the rigs, Shreveport perversely benefited, becoming the urbane antidote to the boomtowns' churned earth and pervasive violence.

Much of Shreveport's money flowed from the violent and dirty tent cities just a few miles north. But once that money arrived in Shreveport, it financed a sanitary, middle-class escape from those primitive boomtown conditions. In contrast to the derelict tents and clapboard saloons that pervaded the boomtowns around Oil City, Shreveport's sturdy brick homes and elaborate office buildings articulated a civic language of comfort and permanence. Shreveport's economy was deeply embedded in both the boomtowns and the oil fields, but its civic and political culture defined itself in *opposition* to the boomtown communities; oil money built an urban refuge away from the very environmental and social depravity its derricks were perpetuating.[2]

SHREVEPORT'S PRE-OIL ECONOMY

Shreveport's early nineteenth-century Anglo settlement was enabled by a remarkable feat of hydrological engineering. When Spanish and French traders attempted to navigate the Red River during the seventeenth and eighteenth centuries, they encountered an enormous natural logjam of wood and debris that made water transport effectively impossible. In times of severe flooding, trees adjacent to the Red River were pulled from their roots and dragged into the river. While most of those trees broke into small parts and drained into the Mississippi, larger and drier pieces became wedged in narrower sections of the waters.[3] These wedged pieces accumulated into enormous natural dams of trapped debris, obstructing massive portions of the Red River.

Following the Jefferson administration's 1803 purchase of the Louisiana Territory, the "Great Raft," as the dam was known, remained a major impediment to transportation and commerce in the region, inhibiting a natural trade route between the fertile Red River valley and the Mississippi River. When renowned Revolutionary War surgeon and colonial agent Dr. John Sibley surveyed North Louisiana in 1805, he witnessed the "great raft or jam of timber" that "chokes the main channel for upwards of one hundred miles by the course of the river."[4] Making the Red River navigable became part of a massive undertaking to integrate Jefferson's newly acquired western expanse into the US market, and thus pacific part of a broader economic and environmental project to make the newly acquired lands amenable to capitalism and slave-produced cotton.[5]

Beginning in 1833, Captain Henry Miller Shreve of the US Army Corps of Engineers was tasked with clearing the Great Raft and opening the Red River to trade. To clear the raft's tree limbs and tree trunks, Shreve placed a jagged, jaw-like device on the bow of his steamboat, the *Heliopolis*.[6] This remarkable apparatus allowed men aboard the ship to pick the wooded refuse right out of the water and then promptly dispose of it using an onboard sawmill. On March 7, 1838, Shreve's team finally severed the head of the raft, allowing the first steamboat to pass in its wake.[7] This was hardly the last time that wood and debris clogged the Red River, as officials had to remain vigilant to keep its waters clear throughout the nineteenth century. But Shreve's efforts were nonetheless transformative for the burgeoning riverside settlement and enabled the city of Shreveport to be formally incorporated in March 1839.[8]

With the Red River cleared for major river traffic, raw materials could now profitably migrate from its alluvial soils to distant markets. Antebellum Shreveport subsequently grew into the central distribution point for North Louisiana's slave-produced agricultural products, in particular its cotton. With North Louisiana's abundant cypress tree population, Shreveport also grew into a major hub for milling and distributing timber, selling into an industrializing national economy hungry for lumber. As one Southern Pacific Railroad official observed, the Shreveport hinterlands remained a "fine agricultural and stock territory . . . [the] principal crop being cotton." But increasingly, "hardwood lumber in large volume is being manufactured at many points on these lines." Steamboats primarily moved goods along the Red River and the Mississippi, but railroad lines also began connecting Shreveport by the dawn of the Civil War, providing a new means of bringing North Louisiana staples to the major cities of the Southwest. The St. Louis Southern Railway, which connected Shreveport to stops across Arkansas and Texas, came to be known as the "Cotton Belt Route" for its critical role in moving North Louisiana's foremost export from farm to market.[9]

Following the Civil War and the end of chattel slavery, Shreveport continued to function as a critical distribution point for the region's cotton and timber products. But the city's urban economy increasingly diverged from the rural hinterlands, which remained largely reliant on natural resource extraction. This rural-urban economic divide was emblematic of the "colonial pattern" afflicting much of the postbellum American South: cheap raw materials flowed from its rural sections to the factories of its urban centers, discouraging the rural South from adopting more innovative, wage-creating industries.[10] Improvements in manufacturing and transportation disproportionately benefited city centers positioned to trade and transport those raw materials. Therefore, as

Shreveport swelled with wage-earning work, the rural hinterlands producing the cotton and lumber that filled the city's railcars remained primarily remote communities of tenant farmers and sawmills.[11]

SHREVEPORT'S URBAN OIL BOOM

By Charles Howard's 1900 visit to Shreveport, the city had indeed become a center of "progressive," middle-class businessmen. The city's rail yards were especially vibrant, providing wage-earning jobs and placing the city at the center of a widening axis of regional production and trade.[12] So when murmurs of oil production in Caddo Parish began to emerge just four years later, the city was well positioned to absorb the influx of prospectors eager for the new business opportunity. With ready access to eight crisscrossing railroad lines, Shreveport became a gateway for investors looking to explore North Louisiana's prospective oil lands.[13] Well-appointed hotels and offices offered spaces to socialize and do business. The city's political role as the seat of Caddo Parish meant that local courts, law firms, and bureaucratic offices would all be essential to transacting land deals and penning oil leases. In short order, the city acquired an economic and cultural reputation as a place that was conducive to doing business in North Louisiana's oil boom.

The nature of Shreveport's urban development reflected the steadier, white-collar work that many of its residents enjoyed, which enabled them a far less migratory existence than the workers who lived by the rig. By the very nature of their work, roughnecks, roustabouts, and teamsters needed to have immediate proximity to the derrick or the well. Consequently, one field's decline in production could mean another migration onto the next boom, as so many had done from Spindletop to Jennings to Oil City and beyond. But an attorney, land buyer, or geologist working across an entire portfolio of oil wells had the luxury of remaining in Shreveport, a center point from which investors and firms could simply pivot from one spot on the oil boom axis to another.

Accordingly, Shreveport became home to "district exploration offices" for the industry, in which ten to thirty employees would use the city as a headquarters from which they could scout for promising new fields across the region.[14] Such corporate structures were crucial to the sustained economic success Shreveport achieved amid such a volatile oil boom. Even as particular boomtowns rose and fell, these "district exploration offices" buoyed real estate values and provided the city with a steadier anchor of people and wealth. Wages from these white-collar professionals manifested into elegant residential areas, notably along Fairfield Avenue, which became one of the city's most sought-after addresses for prosperous industry men.[15] In contrast to Oil City's improvised tent homes and poorly insured clapboard businesses, Shreveport's sturdy brick homes articulated a stronger faith in the city's long-term viability.

Shreveport's economy further benefited from the high up-front costs associated with oil production in North Louisiana—costs that while standard across the industry were also unusually steep in the region's landscape. Drilling a well meant purchasing or leasing an assortment of costly materials: a boiler, a hoisting machine, casing, and pipe in addition to the derrick itself. When geologist Walter Hopper investigated the costs of drilling in Caddo Parish between 1908 and 1909, he estimated that "rigging up" a rotary derrick, including tools and materials, came out to roughly $2,825. This figure did not include the costs of hiring employees, hauling equipment, or penning real estate deals on land worth an estimated $500 to $1,000 per acre by 1910.[16] Nor did it include the challenges that were unique to drilling the swampy Caddo Parish topography, circumstances that Mike Benedum and Joe Trees estimated raised their costs three to five times more per well relative to other North American sites.[17]

These costs created a financial hindrance to aspiring drillers, but also an opportunity for Shreveport's banking institutions offering the liquidity that was so essential to "rigging up" North Louisiana's derricks. As the boom's regional banking center, the city once again leveraged its balance of access and distance to the oil fields. Bankers and investors could easily take a train ride out to Oil City and the surrounding area to inspect a well or make a deal. But they could also maintain a wider portfolio of investments across the region, meaning their institution was not overly exposed to the success or failure of one or two wells, a shrewd hedge given that roughly one in nine wells were successful in that era.[18] That advantageous financial position resulted in significant cash returns. By 1920, the five most prominent Shreveport banks collectively boasted more than $26 million in resources and $43 million in deposits.[19]

Shreveport was also home to a wide variety of legal teams that arbitrated disputes and notarized deals across the region's oil fields. Law firms frequently handled cases that concerned the rural oil fields of Caddo and Claiborne Parish, but they still operated out of their Shreveport offices as they litigated in the city's courthouses. When Lillie "Gussie" Taylor, Joseph Herndon, and David Raines were plaintiffs, they both hired law firms domiciled in Shreveport; Taylor's attorneys even represented multiple clients seeking rights over the same property. By mediating legal cases across the boomtowns, attorneys from the city were able to acquire a sizable portion of the cash being generated in the oil fields via legal fees, yet another financial channel from the surrounding boomtowns into the city's corporate coffers.

Shreveport's financial salesmen even began soliciting to a largely untapped new pool of potential oil field investors: ordinary, middle-class Americans. Just as the Sears Roebuck catalogue was selling products directly to consumers, urban financial brokers began hawking oil field investments as a novel retail opportunity. Advertisements appeared in newspapers across the country imploring average Americans to invest in North Louisiana's wild and lucrative oil boom. Bearing the august-sounding names of Shreveport's financial firms, these announcements projected a language of expertise and insider knowledge. Pitchmen used the city's access to the oil fields as a critical component of the sale, assuring ordinary Americans otherwise unfamiliar with the oil industry that investing in North Louisiana's oil patch would be a safe bet and an exhilarating consumer experience.

In 1919, the New York Brokerage Company of Shreveport asked a tantalizing question to the readers of Arizona's *Bisbee Daily Review*: "Did you ever stop to contemplate that possibility of making money in some other way than by the result of your own daily labors?" The brokerage firm offered shares in North Louisiana lands that were alleged to be "within a few hundred feet of the great Gushers." One need not be a geologist to properly invest: "Let us make a selection for you," the ad reassured; simply "indicate what price you can afford . . . and we will be guided accordingly."[20] Just below these instructions were two boxes asking the prospective oil investor simple questions: What is your name? How much would you like to spend? How many acres? A buyer could simply mail the completed coupons and remit payment to become a bona fide oil investor.

But this generous offer to invest on behalf of less-informed consumers disproportionately benefited the Shreveport financial firms pitching the idea, which could essentially put that money into whatever project they chose. And these investments were far from guaranteed—a fact that the New York Brokerage Company colorfully acknowledged in its advertisement. Rather than obscure the risk inherent to investing in wildcat oil wells, the ad repackaged that peril into a source of excitement and adventure:

> The element of chance is ever-present. Life itself is either "DO" OR "DON'T" . . . there is the dormant uncertainty in nearly everything we do every day of our lives. Nearly everybody who has 'arrived' in life took a chance one way or the other—some WIN, others lose—it is the irrevocable law of chance. . . . But buy today! Tomorrow may be too late! It may mean the turning point in your life![21]

This sharp bit of salesmanship effectively transformed a risky oil investment into an exciting consumer experience: an adventurous departure from the everyday doldrums of middle-class life into the wild, money-crazed boomtowns of North Louisiana. Shreveport's financial class was the engine behind this campaign, selling Americans on their industry knowledge as well as their geographic access to the "great Gushers" of North Louisiana.

Shreveport's well-heeled professionals sought to cultivate an urbane civic experience that was largely abstracted from the boomtowns' churned earth and tent cities. The city's contemporary newspapers made occasional mention of the nearby oil fields that employed so many locals, but primarily followed theater openings, opera performances, and parties held at the homes of prominent citizens.[22] During the spring of 1911, the Harrell No. 7 fire just outside Oil City was "seething and roaring continuously," sending "flames upwards of one hundred feet high" along with a "great volume of black smoke which could be seen for twenty-five miles."[23] But as this catastrophe unfolded just to the north, its flames literally within sight of the city, the *Shreveport Journal* was publishing an "American and Paris Fashion" issue to digest the latest haute couture.[24] These parallel communities developed in opposition to each other: as Oil City's livability devolved, Shreveport's value as its genteel antidote accordingly grew.

THE PEOPLE OF SHREVEPORT

Shreveport functioned as a crucial center for entrepreneurs who would rather sell goods and services into the teeming boomtowns than assume the risks of drilling for oil. Much of Oil City's nonperishable food arrived from Shreveport wholesalers via train, going into two warehouses alongside the Kansas City Southern rail line, from which local grocers would collect items to retail. "Everything we got out of the store we got from Shreveport," recalled local Cleo Norris.[25] One of the individuals emblematic of Shreveport's retail economy was Isaac, or "Ike," Muslow, a remarkable Russian émigré. After completing his odyssey from the Russian Empire to Caddo Parish, Muslow accumulated a diverse array of business interests in the boomtowns. In addition to his investments in farmland and oil leases, Muslow built an oil field hauling business and founded Pine Island Mercantile, which sold food, clothing, and supplies to oil field workers. In 1908, Muslow and several partners also invested in a new thirty-five-room, two-story frame hotel in Oil City.[26]

While Muslow's business interests always revolved around Oil City, the Russian immigrant was increasingly drawn to the comforts of Shreveport as his wealth grew. In his earlier years in Caddo Parish, Muslow's son James recalled, Ike lived right in Oil City and typically commuted to his job sites via horse. But the wealth Muslow acquired eventually allowed him to trade the boomtown for Shreveport, where he took up residence in an "old colonial" hotel. As an affluent urbanite, Muslow could now enjoy the city's comforts and ride the train to inspect his Oil City investments.[27] In 1921 the Shreveport City Directory listed Muslow as an employee of the First National Bank, where he eventually assumed the role of director.[28] Oil production created the conditions for Muslow's success, buoying demand for goods, land, and services. But he was not exclusively reliant on oil production itself; he was betting on *people* to consume clothes, food, housing, and land.

The arc of Isaac Muslow's career reveals a great deal about Shreveport's economic relationship with the oil boomtowns encircling it, and also a broader truth about natural resource extraction. Muslow's success conjures an old adage regarding the true winners of a boom: *you can mine for gold or you can sell pickaxes.* Muslow's son would later credit his father for not falling into the gold rush mentality of trying to strike it rich with one big oil gusher. Many oil fortunes were won and lost, the younger Muslow observed, when people simply put their money right back into risky wildcatting propositions.[29] Muslow did not arrive in Oil City simply to prospect for oil, but rather to sell products to its many prospectors, a shrewd position that allowed him to broadly profit from the boom without being too beholden to its volatility.

Muslow's identity as a Russian émigré was also emblematic of Shreveport's growing community of immigrants, many of whom found similar opportunities in industries that were adjacent to the oil fields. In 1917, Russian-born immigrant Sam Sklar owned a "junk shop" on Shreveport's Texas Avenue along the Kansas City Southern line. Having immigrated in 1904, Sklar was a naturalized US citizen by the time he completed a World War I draft card.[30] A Shreveport City Directory advertisement elaborated that Sklar's "junk shop" was the Louisiana Iron and Supply Company, "Wholesale and retail dealers in Pipe and Machinery, etc."[31]

Subsequent records follow Sklar's remarkable ascent into the middle class. In 1940 he resided in Shreveport, working as the manager of an oil company and earning a comfortable annual salary of $3,600.[32] Thirteen years later, he was in California boarding a boat to Hawaii with his wife, Ida.[33] The oil boom may have drawn Sklar to Shreveport, but he attained his wealth largely by selling supplies into that boom, rather than by wildcatting for the black gold itself. Like Muslow, Sklar profitably sold the proverbial pickax.

Louis David Abramson followed a strikingly similar path into Shreveport's oil industry goods and services economy. After emigrating from Russia to Shreveport in 1904, Abramson became a manager at a dry goods store and bought a home in the city with his Lithuanian wife, Ethel, and three children.[34] Abramson even had enough money to hire a live-in housemaid, an eighteen-year-old "mulatto" woman listed as Elmira Dickson in the 1920 census.[35] However, the next decades revealed leaner times. By 1930, Abramson remained a dry goods store manager, but was renting a home (still in Shreveport) and no longer employed a maid.[36] Ten years later, he was a salesman for a retail clothing company, a position his wife occupied as well.[37] While hardly destitute, Abramson's path was not one of unimpeded growth and success, demonstrating that even industries that only indirectly served the oil industry still remained subject to its economic ebbs and flows.

A striking common denominator among these Shreveport émigrés was the Jewish faith, creating a unique cultural and religious imprint on the otherwise heavily Baptist city. The 1930 census records denoted Sklar's ability to speak Yiddish.[38] Louis David Abramson also maintained his native tongue, and was respectively listed as a "Hebrew" speaker in 1920 and as "Yiddish" in 1930.[39] Jae Bold, a Russian-Jewish immigrant working at a Shreveport oil well supply company, appeared as a "Jewish" speaker in the 1920 census.[40] Shreveport's Jewish population swelled so much during the oil boom that the local Congregation B'nai Zion, which traced its early origins to the 1850s, built a grand new Beaux Arts structure to house its growing ranks.[41] In June 1913, the Caddo Parish Police Jury accepted monetary requests from a number of civic organizations, including a group called Hebrew Ladies Aid.[42] Jewish women were even alleged to have been among the city's class of sex workers.[43] While the religious culture in Shreveport and Caddo Parish remained overwhelmingly Protestant, the city's demographic growth included a dynamic corner of Jewish identity.

Shreveport's Black community also carved out a vibrant corner of the city. Even prior to the advent of oil production, Shreveport had attracted a host of Black migrants looking for wage labor in its burgeoning industrial economy. That community coalesced around the St. Paul's Bottoms district, where Texas Avenue, known colloquially as "The Avenue," came to be the main artery of Black commerce. The Avenue boasted a thriving corridor of Black-run retail shops, insurance agencies, and funeral homes to serve the community. The term "St. Paul's Bottoms" derived from two sources: St. Paul's United Methodist Church, a local parish founded by Black freedmen in 1865; and its geographic position as some of the lowest-lying land by the Red River, making it among the least desirable, least hygienic places to live in the city.[44] The very name of Shreveport's St. Paul's "Bottoms" district thus embodied the precarious social and economic position that its Black community endured: in possession of distinct cultural institutions, and yet still relegated to the least desirable space.

Shreveport was also the headquarters for pioneering Black-owned oil businesses. In 1924, Odessa Strickland, a Black Texan originally trained in architecture, invested in a Claiborne Parish drilling rig, working the project with a group of other Black investors. Six years later, that investment had become the Universal Oil, Gas and Mining Company, headed by Strickland. Headquartered on "The Avenue's" 1000 block alongside Shreveport's other Black-run businesses, Universal was the only Black-owned oil company in the United States at the time.[45] Strickland's corporate mission centered on the economic uplift of his community: to employ local Black workers and to help Black landowners retain and profit from North Louisiana's oil wealth.[46] Universal might have been unique in its racial composition, but it essentially functioned like any other Shreveport-based oil company, using the city as a center point from which to drill wells across North Louisiana and East Texas.

Many of the Black landowners who profited from rural Caddo Parish oil wells also used their royalties to relocate into Shreveport's middle-class residential enclaves. After enduring a harrowing legal battle along with his uncle Joseph Herndon, David Raines was able to enjoy steady royalties from his oil-bearing property just outside Oil City. While Herndon died shortly after the proceedings, Raines was able to invest his earnings in a Shreveport home on 1419 Peabody Street, only steps away from the "Avenue" and its ecosystem of Black-owned businesses. As a Shreveport resident, Raines also funded a variety of civic causes, aimed in particular at the city's Black population: contributing money for the construction of a church and twenty-two acres of land to build a home to rehabilitate juvenile delinquents.[47] Like so many other successful investors of his time, Raines's money originated from the rural oil fields of Caddo Parish but ultimately came to benefit the people and institutions of urban Shreveport, with a particular focus on its Black community.

THE MADAMS AND SEX WORKERS OF SHREVEPORT

Much like in Oil City, an extensive economy of sex workers rose alongside Shreveport's white-shoe law firms and oil industry offices. But unlike the extralegal nature of Oil City's Reno Hill, Shreveport's sex trade was the product of deliberate municipal policy. In 1902, the city council passed a law allowing prostitution, provided it took place within a "segregated" zone: the largely Black St. Paul's Bottoms riverside district.[48] With express legal permission from the city government, an enormous red-light district promptly flourished. By 1917 there were sixty acknowledged houses of prostitution within the area and at least thirty-eight illicit houses outside the "segregated" zone, making St. Paul's Bottoms one of the largest red-light districts in the United States.[49] Brothels employed not only sex workers, but also doctors, housekeepers, and domestic washerwomen. As a child, Louilie McCarty used to help his mother perform such duties, warmly recalling the Shreveport sex workers as being very nice and the daily pay, "about $3 or $4," as competitive.[50]

Bluesman and Caddo Parish native Huddie "Lead Belly" Ledbetter recorded one of the more evocative depictions of the St. Paul's Bottoms red-light district. His lyrics to "Fannin Street," a major thoroughfare running through the "segregated" area, depicted the local sex trade as perilously seductive: "My mama told me/My sister too/Said, 'The Shreveport women, son,/Will be the death of you.'"[51] That enigmatic "Shreveport woman" embodied irresistible danger: "She used to sit down and gamble with/Mr. Buffalo Bill . . . [She] lives back of the jail/Makes an honest livin'/By the wigglin' of her tail." While aspects of "Fannin Street" might have been artfully exaggerated—it's not clear that Buffalo Bill ever gambled in Shreveport—Ledbetter undoubtedly captured the intoxicatingly transgressive atmosphere of St. Paul's Bottoms. He certainly had firsthand knowledge of its establishments, as the iconic bluesman reputedly made some of his earliest performances at Shreveport's brothels.[52]

The same dynamics of geography and infrastructure that made Shreveport an ideal place for the oil industry's professional class also made the city a natural headquarters for sex workers and their presiding madams. Indeed, the sex industry used Shreveport in much the same way as oil companies did: as the center point of an "interrelated community of vice" connecting the city's brothels to nearby boomtowns. As Oil City emerged as a major center of oil production, Shreveport's madams opened up Reno Hill as a "satellite district" to absorb the new business opportunities oil field wages were producing, not unlike a downtown store opening a suburban shopping center.[53] The sex trade often mirrored the mobility of its oil field clients. When Shreveport's oil companies began seeing less production around Caddo Parish and pivoted toward the expanding fields in nearby Claiborne Parish, sex workers began soliciting more patrons from the emergent boomtown of Homer than from Oil City.[54]

Shreveport's access to a variety of train lines crisscrossing the region was critical to bringing so many oil field workers into its red-light district. Once the sun went down, a peculiar reverse commute began: railroad lines that carried middle-class oil industry figures from Shreveport out to the oil fields in the morning transitioned into herding roustabouts, roughnecks, and other oil field hands *into* the city for a night of carousing. The Kansas City Southern railroad provided four daily trains from Oil City into Shreveport, many of which would be standing-room only with oil workers looking for a night out.[55] Even if the KCS could not accommodate any more riders, there were other means of getting into town. An enterprising man by the name of Mitchell used to offer Oil City residents a ride into St. Paul's Bottoms in his Model T for a tidy $1.25 fee.[56]

But if Oil City was a "satellite district," Shreveport remained the home base for the sex work business, especially for its governing madams. And much like the banks providing liquidity to prospective oil drillers across the Sabine Uplift, Shreveport's madams made sure they benefited from every transaction, often using severe methods to do so. Those in charge of sex rings "always kept [their girls] in debt," recalled Caddo Parish public health official Willis Butler.[57] To further control their assets, madams even limited their girls' mobility. According to Butler, a physician who used to visit Shreveport brothels to examine its workers, it "would be hard to get away" if you were a prostitute, adding that madams were "pretty strict about keeping their own."[58] While individual sex workers could earn a wage plying their trade alongside the oil fields, the ultimate beneficiaries remained those who kept them in debt and largely controlled their movement: the madams domiciled in Shreveport.

Sex work even lifted Shreveport's consumer goods market. At the same moment in which white-collar oil industry figures were building elegant homes along Fairfield Avenue, the queens of North Louisiana's sex industry were also acquiring the consumerist trappings of middle-class success. Among the papers left by local madam Nell Jester were 1917 inventories from shopping expeditions at furniture and jewelry stores, where she purchased beds, dressers, rockers, a Victrola, and a sizable record collection, amounting to costs of $394.05.[59] When the notorious and enigmatic Shreveport madam Annie McCune died in 1920, her probate records revealed an impressive portfolio of assets she bought over a lifetime of brokering women: $7,119 in cash, a house and two lots in Shreveport, and $500 in life insurance in addition to a massive array of glass plates, saucers, vases, wine sets, jewelry, and a myriad of other products.[60]

Much like the wealth being generated across North Louisiana's oil belt, the money from sex work performed both in the city and in the boomtowns largely came to reside in Shreveport's banking institutions. Ray Oden, an employee of Ardis Bank, used to receive weekly cash deposits from Nell Jester amounting to roughly $2,000 to $5,000. He estimated that deposits from Annie McCune were even higher. While some people felt that such money was "tainted," Oden quipped that sex trade money was now "mixed with Baptist money [so] no one can tell the difference."[61] Once again, Shreveport benefited by being at the center: the center of the Sabine Uplift and its myriad oil projects, and the center of the booming and equally lucrative "interrelated community of vice" that also served the oil fields.

However, by 1917 Shreveport's thriving red-light district was coming under increasing public scrutiny. That July, the local Rotary Club initiated an anti-vice campaign to shutter the district, formally outlaw prostitution, and bring a more "respectable" atmosphere to the city. Shreveport's city council initially balked at the idea. While not necessarily "pro-vice," the council feared that banning sex work would result in a consummate drop in tax receipts from the expansive nexus of businesses now reliant on the St. Paul's Bottom's brothels: landlords, merchants, domestics, and bankers, in addition to the sex workers themselves. But the anti-vice movement steadily grew as the Rotary Club's campaign attracted the support of other like-minded citizens groups, including the Lions Club, the Advertising Club, and the woman-run Cooperative Protection Association. Meanwhile, church sermons also began denouncing the "low and vile" behavior occurring in the Bottoms district.[62]

US entry into World War I further empowered anti-vice forces. Much as in Oil City's Reno Hill, the presence of federal troops helped spur dramatic changes to the city's urban landscape and underground economy. The Council of the National Defense, a federal wartime entity, expressed concern over young soldiers stationed near Shreveport being exposed to the "largest vice district of any city its size in the country."[63] Fears of racial miscegenation also tinged the anti-vice movement. When reformers spent a night surveying St. Paul's Bottoms, they not only discovered the shocking sight of "Young Men Wearing The Uniform Of Their Country" at such establishments, but also blatant disregard for the "color line": white men patronizing a club full of "colored women" and a Mexican "hot tamale man" plying their trade.[64]

On November 15, 1917, Shreveport's voters ratified a ballot measure that outlawed legal prostitution in the "segregated" zone. The women of St. Paul's Bottoms would have eleven days to vacate and halt their business. With the exception of a few individuals who continued to work freelance across the city, Shreveport's sex industry was effectively closed, an enormous victory for the religious and civic leaders behind the anti-vice campaign.[65] The success of Shreveport's anti-vice campaign underscored the rising political power of the city's white, Christian, middle-class constituents: urban denizens who wanted to promote a wholesome space of abstemious Protestant values, and to draw an ever-clearer distinction between their own community and the vice-ridden boomtowns. Shreveport's anti-vice activists regarded the sexually and racially transgressive atmosphere of St. Paul's Bottoms as fundamentally contrary to those civic ambitions.

CREATING "THE CITY" AND "THE BOOMTOWN"

The dichotomy between Shreveport, the comfortable, safe community, and Oil City, the chaotic, irredeemable boomtown, was never inevitable, but rather the product of deliberate political and economic actions—and *inactions*. While Caddo Parish legislators were keen to deliver safe and sanitary streets to their urban, middle-class constituents, they were largely apathetic toward the boomtowns. Even as violence, lack of potable water, and barely functional roads were consuming Oil City, the minutes of the Caddo Parish Police Jury only scarcely acknowledged the catastrophes unfolding to the city's north. None of the oil fires, saltwater runoffs, gas flares, or general environmental devastation made it to the Police Jury docket. Such decisions made, and not made, only widened the disparities of livability between "the City" and "the Boomtowns."

In contrast to the Spartan resources going into Oil City and its adjacent communities, the Caddo Parish Police Jury invested in elaborate public works projects to enhance Shreveport's economic and cultural vibrancy. In March 1913, Police Jury members allotted money toward the city's "May Carnival," financing an elaborate "illuminated night parade." The carnival would not only "benefit the people of Caddo Parish" but also "illustrate our growth and progress both commercially and ethically; it will promote civic pride and foster a spirit of enterprise." In the same meeting, members would address only one oil field community issue: the problem of companies leaving pipelines "lying on the surface of roads" near the rural oil fields, hardly the most significant issue gripping Oil City and its surrounding boomtowns.[66] While the economic and cultural progress of Shreveport was paramount, rural boomtowns were simply extraction points. Ensuring that Oil City's roads, railways, and pipelines facilitated oil production was the Police Jury's only pressing objective outside of the city; living conditions for actual residents were irrelevant.

One of the most remarkable moments of regulatory indifference came during the Pine Island crisis of 1919, when a post-World War I glut in oil prices resulted in severe overproduction across the North Louisiana fields, leading crude oil to indiscriminately flood across its soil, creeks, and rivers. By that summer, 42,500 to 75,000 barrels had vanished into the earth, ruining crops, polluting water sources, and creating what a federal official deemed an "indescribable fire danger . . . which menaces everything."[67] But when the Police Jury convened on June 12, 1919, the first piece of business was to debate the construction of a "comfort station" [public toilet] to be placed at a particular Shreveport intersection. Members went on to approve the creation of a new road and to announce a vacancy at Louisiana State University. Subsequent meetings on July 10 and 16 continued to disregard the ongoing crisis.[68]

The Caddo Parish Police Jury's determination to prioritize public restrooms in Shreveport over the Pine Island catastrophe underscored that serving their middle-class urban constituents was its primary objective, and that legislators regarded the oil field boomtowns as little more than ephemeral centers of extraction, not habitation. By disregarding the needs of oil-producing communities, the Police Jury, and more broadly Louisiana's regulatory agencies, created a circular chain of events: Oil City did not attract the same resources because it was a boomtown, but it also bore the conditions of a boomtown precisely because of that apathy and lack of resources. Governing bodies such as the Police Jury were not just reacting to Oil City's status as a primitive boomtown, but actively creating and reinforcing it.

The deviating civic paths of Shreveport and Oil City demonstrated that oil-boom communities do not inevitably diverge along "City" and "Boomtown" lines, and that such a disparity was a political and economic creation. Shreveport's business and civic leaders not only benefited from the boomtowns' grim conditions but also perpetuated them. The wages that Shreveport's professional class earned from the oil fields financed a civic respite from the very conditions their industry promulgated, further enhancing the value of living in the city over the actual centers of production. By starving Oil City and other oil-producing communities of desperately needed resources, local politicians ensured that North Louisiana's boomtowns could never improve their conditions or transcend the inevitability of their boomtown status.

Shreveport was deeply integrated into North Louisiana's oil boom—but also intentionally designed to be separate from it. The tony brick homes and elegant office buildings that lined its city streets were totally unlike the tent cities and ramshackle saloons of Oil City. But despite Shreveport's efforts to distance itself from the grime and filth of oil production, the red-orange glow from Oil City's gas flares remained perfectly visible in the city's night sky.[69] The environmental and social costs that North Louisiana's boomtowns bore for Shreveport remained literally within sight, and yet seemed to get further and further away.

EPILOGUE: THE BUST

IN THE SPRING OF 1936, LONGTIME TREES CITY RESIDENT Carrie Duncan Slee spoke at the commemoration of a newly opened schoolhouse that would serve the planned oil field community: "Today, as we come to dedicate this beautiful new school building, I rejoice with all of you . . . It is certainly an improvement to our town and a building that we can point to with pride and say—'This is our school building.'" Looking back across the two decades since the company town's founding, Slee marveled at the variety of social and economic institutions that had blossomed: the bustling town store, the livery service, the hotel, the YMCA, the dance pavilion, and the pool hall, all catering to the "cleanest and most orderly oil field town in [Louisiana]." Two local physicians and a dentist had also served the town. At one time, a local "air dome" even presented films, church services, and school plays.[1] By Slee's telling, Trees City had effectively harnessed the engine of oil production into a thriving and prosperous community that would not endure the same ephemerality as so many other resource-dependent boomtowns.

But just as Slee commemorated the miraculous rise of Trees City, she was also subtly eulogizing its decline. Throughout the speech were latent indications that the handsome company town, a conscious exercise in stable domestic growth that would stand as a counterpoint to riotous boomtowns like Oil City, was beginning to fray. The town dance hall, formerly a "center of attraction—pie suppers, school plays and . . . dances," was torn down "some years ago having outlived its use-fullness." The pool hall that had served as a social hub and de facto post office was recently torn down as well. And when the YMCA, originally erected by Standard Oil at "quite a cost," was "no longer self-supporting," the manager was transferred, leading to the vacant building's ultimate demolition. Indeed, by Slee's own admission, the "population of Trees has been decreased since the early days," further noting that after one Dr. Lawrence left town in 1930 the community was left without any physicians. Even the very building

Slee was inaugurating would soon meet the same fate; a postscript to the speech (which had been transcribed sometime after 1984) outlined: "The population decline continued and soon the school was closed."[2]

The coda to Slee's address proceeded to describe the broader forces of lower demand and declining production that were undermining the civic and economic vitality of oil field communities like Trees City across Caddo Parish: "Oil production continued to decline and men were transfered [sic] to Rodessa, the refinery in Baton Rouge, Oklahoma, Arkansas . . . Only a few houses remain in Trees."[3] Similar dynamics began to corrode the vitality of Oil City, Homer, and Mooringsport as well. External economic forces had brought oil production to these remote corners of Louisiana, along with the money, people, and new work that accompanied it. But now the same national and global forces were exerting the opposite impact: dramatic falls in consumer demand wrought by the Great Depression paired with reduced productivity on local derricks threatened to upend the economic and civic identities of North Louisiana's oil field communities only three decades after they came into existence.

PRICE COLLAPSE

By the dawn of the 1930s, North Louisiana oil's patch began enduring the same crises of overproduction and lagging demand that were plaguing the entire US industry. Driven by Rule of Capture incentives to find the next gusher, producers drilled a series of massive new fields in the late 1920s, even as prices were falling. A "flood of oil . . . seemed to flow unendingly out of the earth," only to encounter a domestic and global market that was teetering into a prolonged economic contraction. Starting in the spring of 1926, the Greater Seminole field in Oklahoma became the scene of "breakneck drilling competition" driven by "wanton and wasteful methods."[4] Aware that Seminole's production was outstripping demand, oilmen in Oklahoma did organize some voluntary efforts to limit their own output.[5] Nonetheless, wasteful production continued to reign. By 1931 an estimated 765 more wells than were necessary for efficient production had been drilled in Seminole, resulting in $70 million of unnecessary drilling costs.[6]

Despite the heedless production taking place in Oklahoma, Texas drillers continued to develop their own ill-advised wells. Even as excess oil streamed out of Seminole, the Yates field was contemporaneously expanding in the Permian Basin of West Texas, contributing an additional 41 million barrels to an already bloated crude market in its peak year of 1929. But neither the Yates nor the Seminole field would compare to the enormity of "Black Giant," a forty-five-mile-long, 140,000-acre East Texas gusher that contributed a daily total of 500,000 barrels in the spring of 1931, a figure which would double by summer's end.[7] All of this occurred as the national price of crude had collapsed to $0.65 per barrel, a precipitous fall from its 1920 high of $3.07 per unit.[8]

Downstream innovations further contributed to the glut of cheap oil flooding the market. A new "cracking" method in refining enabled companies to "crack" (or break down) crude oil with larger, less desirable hydrocarbon properties into smaller molecules that were more amenable to automobile fuel. As a result, refiners doubled their efficiency: one barrel of "cracked" oil could produce as much automobile fuel as two "uncracked" barrels.[9] Consumers even discovered that "cracked" gasoline had superior qualities for their automobiles, further increasing the "cracked" product's share of the fuel market. While the efficiencies of "cracking" methods created a boon to refiners selling into a rising car market, it only deepened the crisis for producers: automobile consumers lifted demand for gasoline, but refiners' demand for crude oil stayed effectively flat.

Among industry leaders and government agencies, no consensus existed on how to stem the falling prices. Collectively, they all agreed that lower production and higher prices were imperative, but the industry's Rule of Capture-driven business climate impelled continual production, especially among smaller independent producers who viewed quick extraction as their only leverage over big companies. When Frederick Godber, an executive at Shell Oil's London office, visited the United States in 1931, he found his American counterparts locked in a precarious state: "there is nothing to do but sit back," he observed, adding that "there is no co-operation from most of the other companies." With little federal regulation governing oil production, each state was left to manage itself, which they did to varying degrees. Even Texas's Railroad Commission, the Populist-backed entity created in 1891 to fight big-moneyed interests, was legislatively prohibited from regulating "economic waste," a consequence of political lobbying from independent producers.[10]

By August 1931, East Texas production had reached more than a million barrels per day, nearly one-half the entire demand of the US oil market. Governor Ross Sterling made the remarkable decision to declare the oil field regions of Texas to be in a "state of insurrection" and "open rebellion," mobilizing National Guardsmen and Texas Rangers to shut down production across its 1,644 wells. The governor also took political action, finally bestowing the Railroad Commission with the power to counter "economic waste" and establish production quotas. These dual political and military actions initially stemmed the tide of East Texas crude, raising prices over the early months of 1932—but only temporarily.[11]

The combination of relatively high production quotas and "hot oil" being illicitly smuggled out of the field meant that the glut in East Texas and, by extension, the United States would persist unabated. Texas overproduction reached such a crisis point by the spring of 1933 that state officials had to swallow their long-standing disdain for federal authority and ask for President Franklin Roosevelt's intervention. Governor Miriam (known colloquially as "Ma") Ferguson sent Harold L. Ickes, the secretary of the interior, an urgent telegram stating that "the situation is beyond the control of the state authorities," further informing Ickes that crude prices in East Texas were presently trading at around four cents a barrel.[12]

As the national and global demand for crude dramatically collapsed, the viability of North Louisiana's remaining oil fields accordingly waned, prompting large migrations away from the oil fields and shaking the civic foundations of Caddo Parish's earliest boomtown communities. As Carrie Duncan Slee was delivering her address to the new Trees City schoolhouse, those same overlapping dynamics were undermining the viability of her modest hometown. The 1930 census records for Slee's area of Trees City revealed a community still deeply reliant on oil: page after page listed individuals employed by "oil wells" or "oil refinery" or "gasoline plant."[13] Although Trees City expressed a civic and economic identity of stability and permanence, the local economy still rested atop a precarious foundation of oil production and its attendant volatility. Trees City had bet its civic and economic future heavily on an industry that, by its very nature, sprouts and withers with little regard to the town hosting it.

While the mobility of oil work had initially benefited North Louisiana with inflows of workers, that same movement of people and capital began to wield the opposite impact. An out-migration now commenced, with many of the individuals drawn to Caddo and Claiborne Parish's oil wages now leaving to pursue the next boom, or to exit the struggling industry entirely. W. J. Snead described his father, Mike, as the classic "boomer," moving away from his central Texas farm to be a mule teamster in the oil fields of Spindletop, Hackberry, and Sour Lake before crossing into Louisiana to work at Jennings and then Oil City. But once Homer rose to the center of North Louisiana oil production, Snead Sr. moved off to adjacent Claiborne Parish, followed by further migration north to Arkansas's El Dorado.[14]

The decline of North Louisiana's first oil boomtowns also reflected their disproportionate reliance on large, highly capitalized companies. When firms like Standard Oil or the Texas Company perceived declining production, they had little compunction about pivoting their resources toward newer and more promising fields. Caddo Parish had been a major point of extraction for Standard Oil, contributing two-thirds of its Louisiana crude. Meanwhile, wells in nearby Homer contributed 20 percent. Between 1919 and 1927, these two North Louisiana oil fields combined to contribute roughly 86 percent of the total production for Standard's Louisiana office, generating profits of $523,000 in 1919 and

$8,454,000 in 1920.[15] However, by the end of 1927 the productivity of Standard's North Louisiana oil fields had begun to diminish, prompting the firm to reduce drilling across the region. Since its earliest days in the state, Standard Oil's Louisiana affiliate had tried to brand itself as a consummately local business eager to provide economic uplift to the rural South.[16] But the bottom line was ultimately paramount: profitability, not civic loyalty, was their animatieng principle.

Given their comparative lack of resources, independent producers were less suited to withstand enormous price declines. Cleo Norris remembered Depression-era Oil City as not "all that booming" anymore and lacking the same number of independent producing outfits that prevailed in earlier, more flush times. The small- to moderate-scale producers that did remain were often "po boy rigs," operations that offered workers a share of future production in lieu of cash: propositions that frequently did not pay. Norris further recalled the accompanying decline of Reno Hill and its sex workforce: "You know the boom is gone when they start pulling up pipe and the prostitutes leave town."[17]

While many oil workers chose to pull up stakes and seek out the next boom-town in East Texas, Oklahoma, or Arkansas, others stayed in place and transitioned to other forms of income. Walter Duvall George Sr., one of the drillers on Caddo Parish's first successful well, had earned enough from the George and Jones Drilling Company in Oil City to move to Shreveport, where he continued to operate his oil business. But in 1930 he moved his family back to rural Caddo Parish, where George ran a two-hundred-acre farm. Using tenant labor, the farm produced cotton, corn, and hay, along with other staples that helped him to "[keep] his head above water during the depression."[18] George apparently did not wholly abandon the city's oil industry, as he was listed as a Shreveport "Oil Broker" in the census records of 1930 and 1940.[19] However, his pursuit of agricultural income underscored the industry's declining profitability at the time: a fate that George was able to mitigate by transitioning back to the farm.

THE BOOMTOWNS' SLOW DECLINE

While Oil City declined, it did not wholly disappear—nor did the town's oil industry. New "acidizing" methods developed in the 1930s and 1940s increased some well productivity and output in Oil City's older fields.[20] Abrupt rises in oil prices during World War II and the OPEC embargo of 1973 also sparked renewed, if brief, spikes in Caddo Parish production. By the mid-twentieth century, local oilman W. C. "Dub" Allen had become the new economic anchor of the city, drilling wells and investing in a collection of new brick buildings along Land Avenue's historic business district, a notable upgrade from the clap-board houses that lined the street during the first decades of the twentieth century. But these momentary spikes notwithstanding, Oil City never attracted the same in-migration or frenzy of economic investment that characterized its early twentieth-century transition from quiet railroad depot to sprawling boomtown.

As Oil City began its slow decline, new boomtowns began replicating many of the same patterns that had birthed North Louisiana's first oil communities. In 1935 and 1936, 268 new oil and gas wells spread across the emerging fields of far Northwest Louisiana, making the towns of Rodessa and Ida the recipi-ents of new workers and jobs, with many of them arriving from Oil City.[21] As Rodessa's population swelled to more than eight thousand new oil field migrants, the same pattern of hasty boomtown development manifested: a mile-long stretch of shops, hotels, and movie theaters arose on the town's main street alongside a collection of rickety shacks housing its workers. By 1939, Rodes-sa's fields had produced more than 93 million barrels of oil, while continuing to contribute more than 58,000 barrels each day. However, the town's popula-tion dwindled back down to four hundred by 1970, making Rodessa another victim of the same process from which it had earlier benefited.[22]

Trees City had offered a tangible alternative to Oil City and the boomtown model with its durable homes, robust civic rules, and wealthy patron, W. P. Stiles. But even with those foundational pillars underlying it, Trees City fell into the same, if not worse, decline as its less-savory counterparts. While Oil City experienced moments of revival in the twentieth century, Trees City saw only decline, with its schoolhouse, doctor's offices, barbershop, homes, and, in 1983, even its post office all vanishing.[23] Today, Oil City has only a fraction of the twenty-five thousand people that once lined its hills, even as the town still bears Dub Allen's line of half-occupied brick businesses along Land Ave-nue. However, nearby Trees City is little more than a dot on the map.[24] Noth-ing remains of the planned community's stately homes; empty streets wind through thick woodland bearing names such as Trees City Road and Stacy Landing Road that evoke bygone communities from the halcyon boom days. Rusted oil tanks and pump jacks along the road stand as vestiges of the town's raison d'être.

As Oil City, Trees City, and North Louisiana's earliest boomtowns looked warily toward an uncertain future, Shreveport's oil-patch professionals simply widened their gaze toward the next opportunity, wherever that might be. Never beholden to one community or one field, the city's managerial class could afford to invest in a large, diversified collection of oil fields beyond Caddo Parish. Accordingly, Shreveport's white-collar workforce was able to steadily benefit

FIGURE 8.1. *Author's photo of Oil City's Land Avenue, November 2014.*

from new oil field discoveries as they unfolded across the Southwest: the 1923 strike in Smackover, Arkansas; the 1927 and 1931 East Texas strikes; and the 1935 Rodessa strike. Even as these new zones of production were drawing workers and interest *away* from Oil City, they were still providing comparably stable revenue streams for Shreveport's land managers, lawyers, drillers, and engineers, who could remain in one place even as the industry evolved.[25] By 1930, Shreveport still boasted 5,700 oil industry employees, sustaining the city's uniquely urban oil "boom" via an ever-changing variety of fields.[26]

Shreveport native Robert Stacey Jr. grew up with an oil industry father who used the city as an anchor point from which to do business across the region. After buying drilling equipment from local machine broker and Russian émigré Sam Sklar in 1932, Robert Sr. ventured into the East Texas fields. Stacey then went on to drill in Haynesville, Louisiana, and later South Arkansas, all the while maintaining Shreveport as his family's home base. In a 2001 interview, Stacey Jr. reflected on how his hometown's access to a wide range of fields really "cushioned" the city during the Great Depression, a fact made evident by Stacey's neighborhood.[27] Dick Norton, their neighbor on Fairfield Avenue, the tony district favored among oil industry figures, was also a successful driller, albeit in the Rodessa fields.[28] The Stacey family's small corner of Shreveport was a microcosm for the city's advantageous economic position: two neighbors, mutually successful in the oil business, but acquiring wealth from different oil fields.

One century after its dramatic rise and slow decline, Oil City continues to be a source of romantic historical drama—and of historical obfuscation. Narratives and memories about the boomtown and its people often transform its brutal violence and lawlessness into quaint, Wild West stories that obscure unpleasant truths: the racial violence, the corrupted law enforcement, and the horrific environmental conditions. When historian John Loos conducted a series of interviews with Louisiana pipeliners, a subject identified as "Mr. Murphy" colorfully recounted the "violence . . . robberies, [and] killings" with dramatic aplomb. Murphy particularly recalled one man named Tom Shannon coming to the Homer field and killing another man "in a gambling game."[29] But this incredible tall tale is only a half truth: Shannon had indeed killed a man named Pete Dunson on the Homer field in 1920, but it was because Dunson was attacking one of Shannon's Black oil field workers.[30] Murphy's idealized recollections had transformed an act of racial violence into a romantic archetype utterly stripped of its historical weight.

This enduring fascination with Oil City and its wild, violent characters is further evident in *Oil City and Some Antidotes* [sic] *from Roughnecks*, a strange piece of historical fiction written by Benjamin Guy (under the pen name B. G. Matheny) sometime before 1988. The author coyly describes "Oil City" as a "composite of all the oilfields along the Gulf Coast in Louisiana and Texas, with a dash of Oklahoma, Arkansas and New Mexico tossed in for flavor." In the book, hard-drinking, violent roughnecks live alongside madams, like Chinese Annie, proprietor of The Joint, a local gambling hall, saloon, and bordello. Oil City's casual violence assumes a comical quality, in which the "hijackers were hijacking each other and then roughnecks began packing so many pistols they looked like a pawn shop window." The roughneck assumes a larger-than-life, mythological status, joining "the ranks of the Indian, the cowboy and the Longhorn steer in fiction."[31] Guy's arch and outlandish rendering of Oil City speaks to the lingering cultural lure of the violent and bygone boomtown world.

By transforming the people and stories of Oil City into such cartoonish tales, these historical productions reduce the boomtown into an ahistorical space, totally abstracted from any of the broader economic or social forces impacting its people. But the rampant gun violence, unending gas flares, and primitive living conditions were deadly serious to the individuals who lived through them. Perhaps the more sanguine, entertaining memories of Oil City were explicit efforts to obscure the stark truth about North Louisiana's oil boom: that its communities were riven with arbitrary killing and death, in large part due to the apathy and incompetence of public officials; and that much of the chaos served to maintain white-supremacist power in Louisiana's workplaces and government. To that end, individuals like Mr. Murphy may have sentimentalized the bleak conditions of North Louisiana's boomtowns to neuter their harsh historical meaning.

Despite their sizable demographic majority, North Louisiana's Black population seems to miraculously vanish in many first-person memories and historical accounts of this pivotal economic moment. Charlie Spikes, who grew up in Trees City, remembered "very, very few Blacks," and "if there were, they were out away from the community," a remarkable statement given Caddo Parish's heavy Black population, or perhaps a reflection of the company town's efforts to racially segregate its people.[32] Contemporary historians all too often engaged in similar forms of Black erasure. When Chuck Smith performed a series of oral history interviews with Oil City natives in 1999, all of them were white.

However, the lack of Black voices within the historical record belies the variety of Black experiences that characterized North Louisiana's oil boom. Extant Black recollections paint a far starker picture, in which economic mobility is hardly as dynamic and the violence and killing is no longer romantic. One descendant of the Herndon-Raines family rendered the oil boom days as a dark period riven with violence and pilfering of Black profit. To this relative of David Raines and Joseph Herndon, their ancestors' court victory paled in comparison to the generational theft that white lawyers broadly perpetrated against their family. Another memory of that era, passed down through the generations, was the image of their barns burning—a warning to the Raines-Herndon family against trying to attain too much economic wealth from their own lands.[33] While the white descendants of North Louisiana's boomtowns had the freedom to remember selectively, its Black population could not forget.

Historical accounts and individual memories of North Louisiana's oil boom also tend to foreground, and to romanticize, the "wild and rowdy" tent cities such as Oil City, depicting the boomtowns right along the derricks as the biggest recipients of economic change. But it was Shreveport, a *city* far from the actual oil fields, that managed to reap the largest and most consistent rewards from North Louisiana's oil boom. While its paved, tree-lined streets looked nothing like Oil City's tents and mud-pit roads, Shreveport was in many ways the biggest and most successful "boomtown" of them all, even if its unassuming corporate offices, law firms, and courthouses do not generate the same historical fascination as Oil City's shootouts, bootleggers, and dramatic gas flares.

Moreover, the perceived gap between "City" and "Boomtowns" in North Louisiana was a deliberate economic, political, and social construction. Shreveport's political and business classes developed their community into a comfortable enclave for white-collar citizens, all the while perpetuating the poor and ephemeral quality of boomtowns such as Oil City. Caddo Parish political figures regarded Shreveport's residents as their prime constituents, placing disproportionate energy and resources into making the city a more livable and economically diverse space. In contrast, oil field boomtowns were regarded as little more than extraction points, where hygienic and environmental conditions were secondary to efficiently producing and moving crude. The oppositional relationship between Shreveport and the oil field communities to its north was therefore not an inevitable circumstance, or an innate component of the oil economy, but rather a direct consequence of economic and political actions, all of which enriched the city over the boomtowns.

Businessmen who prospered during North Louisiana's oil boom also further reinforced that disparity with their wallets. When investors made sufficient money in the oil fields, they typically did not put down roots in boomtowns like Oil City, but rather leveraged that newfound wealth into a middle-class life in nearby Shreveport. The city also hosted many absentee landlords who owned and developed Oil City's businesses from afar, building cheaply and often without insurance, as they expected little from its civic future. As a result, money produced in the boomtowns' oil fields, saloons, and shops rarely improved the conditions of the actual communities around the rigs, but rather flowed into Shreveport schools, homes, and bank accounts. Such economic attitudes may have been a prescient, if callous, strategy, but they also helped ensure that communities like Oil City could never even modestly improve their dilapidated social and environmental state.

WHO MADE OIL CITY?

The poor standards of living that residents of boomtowns such as Oil City endured were in many respects an extension of oil production itself, with its tendency to churn the landscape around the rigs, its economic volatility, and its transient and largely male workforce. But living standards were also the reflection of decisions made and not made: better streets could have been laid out and maintained; law and fire services could have been more accessible and better funded; and Oil City's Land Avenue did not have to consist of largely uninsured, highly flammable structures. The dearth of humane living conditions was a deliberate choice by its landowners, business leaders, and political officials. Moreover, the subtle civic distinctions that existed between Trees City,

Mooringsport, and Oil City further illustrated that boomtowns were not inevitably beholden to one set of conditions: oil field communities could have potable drinking water, sturdy homes, and the relative absence of violence. But political inaction and the perceptions of Oil City as a "boomtown" created a self-fulfilling prophecy that would ensure such places would always have boomtown conditions.

North Louisiana's oil industry could have also fundamentally transformed the trajectory of its sizable Black populace were it not for the embedded racism of "Bloody Caddo." Such abundant natural resources had the capacity to create vast, potentially generational, wealth for North Louisiana's thousands of Black sharecroppers. But white supremacy intervened in the oil fields and in the state government to ensure the boomtowns would remain exclusive founts of wealth for white migrants. Much like the political and economic decisions to not invest in Oil City's livability, white-supremacist ideologies made a pronounced, and largely successful, campaign to keep the boom's abundance away from Black residents. Nonetheless, many Black workers and landowners still managed to acquire their share of North Louisiana's oil wealth: a dramatic challenge to the efforts to engineer a racially segregated outcome to oil production.

Ultimately, oil remained the lifeblood of North Louisiana's boomtowns. Even the efforts by communities such as Trees City and Mooringsport to attract a steadier, longer-term populace were largely unsuccessful once oil lost its profitability. Paved streets and handsome brick homes still don't guarantee a boomtown's civic future: there still needed to be a fundamental economic reason for people to be there. But the varying conditions characterizing the boomtowns of North Louisiana also demonstrated that the primitive standards of living the residents of Oil City experienced were not preordained.

Better investments in the community may not have fully prevented Oil City's eventual decline, but better roads, sturdier homes, and cleaner environmental conditions could have at least created more opportunities for the town to evolve into new forms of production, in addition to simply fostering better standards of living for its boomer populace, if only briefly. And if North Louisiana's political and economic leaders had not been so beholden to the codes of white supremacy, its oil fields might have provided vast economic uplift to a massive Black populace still largely tied to the old plantation economy.

Oil may have brought thousands of new people into North Louisiana's boomtowns, but it remained within the agency of its civic and business leaders to define the social and environmental parameters of those communities. Oil City was not simply a natural reflection of its eponymous business. It was a projection of its people: their ambitions, their hopes, their prejudices, and their competing visions of a new and better future, all made possible by oil.

ACKNOWLEDGMENTS

I BEGAN RESEARCHING THE MATERIALS THAT WOULD BECOME *Oil Cities* at the University of Texas-Austin more than ten years ago as a graduate research seminar project. We were responsible for finding a primary document from the Briscoe Center for American History and writing about its significance. I was immediately drawn to the institute's vast Exxon-Mobil collection, in particular a file on *The Lamp*, an industry newsletter Standard Oil began publishing to promote its various oil field projects across the globe in the early twentieth century.

I discovered one 1919 issue about the firm's investments in Louisiana and was struck by its wistful depictions of the Old South intersecting with industrial modernity: splashy images of cotton fields giving way to refineries; renderings of Standard's plantation-style corporate headquarters; one author even imagining the company's oil pipelines running alongside "Uncle Tom's cabin." I also found an arresting image of Black workers retrofitting a Standard pipeline while waist-deep in mud, surrounded by thick Louisiana swamp in every direction. My research project, and that image in particular, propelled me to learn more about that dynamic collision between the new industrial economy that firms like Standard Oil brought to rural Louisiana and the "Old South" economy, landscape, and society that preceded it.

First and foremost, I would like to sincerely thank Professor Jacqueline Jones, who taught that 2012 graduate research seminar and ultimately became my dissertation adviser. Professor Jones provided outstanding guidance, knowledge, and support as I engaged in the long process of digesting my research and turning it into a coherent dissertation. She especially taught me how to write and assemble disparate sources into a compelling story—an artform she has mastered over her eminent career. Most importantly, Jackie was always willing to sit down and help during times of stress or uncertainty: I still fondly recall the many, many meetings we spent in her office as she patiently addressed my questions or concerns and offered a clear path forward. This book is the result of Dr. Jones's myriad instances of support as a scholar and as a mentor, and I am enormously grateful for it.

This manuscript was also realized through the efforts of my outstanding dissertation committee, which included UT Professors Erika Bsumek and Bruce Hunt, exceptional scholars with a deep understanding of the intersections between scientific, environmental, and social change: an essential perspective for telling this story. *Oil Cities* further benefited from the expertise of Professor Craig Colten and Jason Theriot, outside members of my committee who graciously offered their own time, knowledge, and energy. And as native Louisianans, they also provided firsthand knowledge of the state's inimitable people, culture, and landscapes, something no primary or secondary source can fully replicate.

The University of Texas Press has been instrumental in helping me transform a humble dissertation into this book manuscript, especially during the uncertainty of COVID. My deepest thanks to Robert Devens for his initial vote of confidence in me; to Dawn Durante for her incredible guidance and patience; and to Casey Kittrell for helping me get *Oil Cities* to the finish line. I would not be in this fortuitous position without their talent and support.

There are so many others to thank from the University of Texas history department who made my seven years at the UT so exciting and fulfilling. I am very grateful to the Institute for Historical Studies for supporting my work during my last graduate year and for an additional postdoctoral year, particularly to Professor Seth Garfield for his guidance during that period. I would also like to thank Professor Joan Neuberger, who provided me with an exceptional opportunity to work on her public history project *Not Even Past*, a formative experience that undoubtedly made me a better writer.

Many thanks to UT Professors Bob Olwell and Philippa Levine, under whom I worked as a teacher's assistant and learned so much of what it means to be a great teacher and a great scholar; and a special thanks to Philippa for providing me with the thrilling—and terrifying—experience of performing my first college lecture. Marilyn Lehman was perhaps the single most influential figure in our department during my years at UT, ensuring the trains always ran on time and that each graduate student had the resources they needed to succeed. And every person who passes through the doors of Garrison Hall receives unfailing support and eternal warmth from the peerless Courtney Meador. Thanks to her as well.

Being a graduate student at the University of Texas was intellectually stimulating and a tremendous amount of fun. So many of my colleagues have become lifelong friends well outside of the classroom. Their laughter and knowledge always drove me forward, even during the toughest days of graduate work. My deepest thanks to Eddie, Christina, Jack, Christine, Nick, Adrian, Altina, Brett, Bagman, David, Sinodis, Chloe, Kristie, Sam, Miguel, Jacob, Cris, Vanessa, Mike, Julie, and Robert. I am so thankful to call you my friends—and colleagues—to this day.

My research also benefited tremendously from so many individuals outside of the University of Texas campus. I spent many months at the libraries of Louisiana State University-Shreveport, where Fermand Garlington was an absolutely indispensable resource to me. I am very grateful for his ongoing support. I also benefited from a very insightful correspondence with John Ridge, a Caddo Parish native and local historian with extensive knowledge on Oil City and its surrounding communities. His public history sites, which are cited plentifully throughout *Oil Cities*, offer a terrific window into the fascinating stories and people of North Louisiana.

Stefan Pappius-Lefebvre and Jeffrey Lichtstein, two longtime college friends and esteemed attorneys, kindly provided their legal knowledge—free of charge—as I navigated Lillie Taylor's byzantine courtroom documents. Chris McCall, a friend of more than twenty years, also offered his own lawyerly guidance on the case. I am so grateful to my gracious and talented colleagues at Blackbaud for providing such an enjoyable and rewarding workplace. And I would like to warmly acknowledge Professor Bethel Saler, my major adviser at Haverford College, who inspired my passion in history and helped me realize a lifelong dream of pursuing a doctorate.

And I also must thank the most important supporters, editors, and resources I have in my life, starting with my wife, Nikki. It is difficult to concisely articulate how much you help me in my work and in my life every day. Throughout the past six years your insights, advice, and words of encouragement have fueled me to complete this project, and to write with a spirit of empathy and compassion—values you exemplify. You have helped me become a better writer and a better person. Thank you for your love and support. I am grateful for it every day.

Finally, a deep and heartfelt thanks to my favorite historians: Mom and Dad. From a young age, I have been profoundly inspired by your work and the passion with which you write, research, and pursue the truth. You are my heroes—both professionally and personally. I am the person I am today solely due to the inspiring work you do as authors and the unconditional support you provide as parents. This book is dedicated to you.

NOTES

PROLOGUE: THE SAVAGE-MORRICAL NO. 1

1. Walter E. Hopper, "The Caddo Oil- and Gas-Field, Louisiana," *Bulletin of the American Institute of Mining Engineers* no. 49–54 (1911): 283.
2. "Oil in the Savage-Morrical Well at Caddo City, La.," *Houston Post*, February 5, 1905, 6.
3. Brian Black, *Petrolia: The Landscape of America's First Oil Boom* (Baltimore: Johns Hopkins University Press, 2000), 142.
4. Black, *Petrolia*, 142.
5. Sam Collier, *North Caddo Parish* (Charleston, SC: Arcadia, 2007), 87.
6. Wallace Scot McFarlane, "Oil on the Farm: The East Texas Oil Boom and the Origins of an Energy Economy," *Journal of Southern History* 83, no. 4 (November 2017): 853–888.
7. 1900 US Census, Rusk, Texas, Justice Precinct 4, roll 1667, p. 16B, FHL microfilm 1241667, Ancestry.com.
8. 1920 US Census, Shreveport, Caddo, Louisiana, Precinct 6, Enumeration District 53, roll T625_608, p. 11B, Image 502, Ancestry.com.
9. McFarlane describes a similar dynamic of wealth accumulation during the 1929 East Texas oil boom; see "Oil on the Farm," 853, 860.
10. Black, *Petrolia*, 74, 81.

CHAPTER 1: THE BOOM

1. Robert Wooster and Christine Moor Sanders, "Spindletop Oilfield," The Handbook of Texas, https://www.tshaonline.org/handbook/entries/spindletop-oilfield.
2. Terence Daintith, *Finders Keepers? How the Law of Capture Shaped the World Oil Industry* (Washington, DC: Routledge, 2010), 172.

3. Daniel Yergin, *The Prize: The Epic Quest for Oil, Money, and Power* (New York: Free Press, 2009), 69.

4. Stanley J. Clark, *The Oil Century: From the Drake Well to the Conservation Era* (Norman: University of Oklahoma Press, 1958), 124.

5. Yergin, *The Prize*, 71.

6. Yergin, *The Prize*, 69.

7. Alwyn Barr, *Reconstruction to Reform: Texas Politics, 1876–1906* (Austin: University of Texas Press, 1971), 219.

8. Yergin, *The Prize*, 70.

9. Daintith, *Finders Keepers?* 13.

10. Daintith, *Finders Keepers?* 4.

11. Morgan Downey, *Oil 101* (n.p.: Wooden Table Press, 2009), 83–84. "Rule of Capture" is not universally regarded as having a negative impact on oil production. Many scholars and economists credit the common-law rule for engendering more technological innovation and efficient production in the oil industry (see Daintith, *Finders Keepers?* 4, 11, 412).

12. Yergin, *The Prize*, 72.

13. Yergin, *The Prize*, 71.

14. "Jennings Field—The Birthplace of Louisiana's Oil Industry," *Louisiana Geological Survey*, September 2001.

15. Kenny A. Franks and Paul F. Lambert, *Early Arkansas and Louisiana Oil: A Photographic History* (College Station: Texas A&M University Press, 1982), 17.

16. T. C. Mahaffey, "True History of the First Oil Well in the State of Louisiana," Jennings Carnegie Library.

17. Mahaffey, "True History of the First Oil Well in the State of Louisiana"; 1900 US Census, Jennings, Calcasieu, Louisiana, District 0024, roll 561, p. 5A, FHL microfilm 1240561, Ancestry.com.

18. Franks and Lambert, *Early Arkansas and Louisiana Oil*, 18.

19. Mahaffey, "True History of the First Oil Well in the State of Louisiana."

20. "Jennings Field—The Birthplace of Louisiana's Oil Industry," 2.

21. W. Scott Heywood, *Boom Days and History of the First Oil Field in Louisiana*, Jennings-Heywood Oil Syndicate Records, mss. 3262, Louisiana and Lower Mississippi Valley Collections, Special Collections, Hill Memorial Library, Louisiana State University Libraries, Baton Rouge; "Jennings Field—The Birthplace of Louisiana's Oil Industry," 2; E. L. Hagstetle, "Louisiana's First Oil Field," *Louisiana Conservation Review* (Spring 1939): 11–13.

22. Heywood, *Boom Days*; "Jennings Field—The Birthplace of Louisiana's Oil Industry," 2.

23. G. D. Harris, *Oil and Gas in Louisiana with a Brief Summary of Their Occurrences in Adjacent States* (Washington, DC: Government Printing Office, 1910), 5.

24. "Jennings Field—The Birthplace of Louisiana's Oil Industry," 2.

25. "Jennings Field—The Birthplace of Louisiana's Oil Industry," 2.

26. Heywood, *Boom Days*, 4, 6; Franks and Lambert, *Early Arkansas and Louisiana Oil*, 20.

27. "Jennings Where the Oil Wells Are," *Oil Investors' Journal* 1 (June 7, 1902): 1.

28. "Another Jennings Gusher," *Oil Investors' Journal* 1 (June 7, 1902): 1.

29. "Comparing Texas and Louisiana Oil Fields," *Oil Investors' Journal* 1 (September 15, 1902): 6.

30. "Oil Fields of Louisiana," *Oil Investors' Journal* 1 (June 21, 1902): 1.

31. "Jennings Where the Oil Wells Are."

32. "Another Jennings Gusher."

33. Lewis Gould, *Progressives and Prohibitionists: Texas Democrats in the Wilson Era* (Austin: University of Texas Press, 1973), 5–6.

34. Gould, *Progressives and Prohibitionists*, 9.

35. Barr, *Reconstruction to Reform*, 105–106.

36. Gould, *Progressives and Prohibitionists*, 35–36.

37. Barr, *Reconstruction to Reform*, 219; Gould, *Progressives and Prohibitionists*, 10.

38. Gould, *Progressives and Prohibitionists*, 18; Yergin, *The Prize*, 77, 81; Kenneth E. Hendrickson Jr., *The Chief Executives of Texas: From Stephen F. Austin to John B. Connally, Jr.* (College Station: Texas A&M University Press, 1995), 143.

39. Barr, *Reconstruction to Reform*, 217.

40. Gould, *Progressives and Prohibitionists*, 9, 20.

41. Perry H. Howard, *Political Tendencies in Louisiana* (Baton Rouge: Louisiana State University Press, 1971), 152, 153, 163–165.

42. Henry C. Dethloff and Robert R. Jones, "Race Relations in Louisiana, 1877–98," *Louisiana History: The Journal of the Louisiana Historical Association* 9, no. 4 (Autumn 1968): 302, 308.

43. Dethloff and Jones, "Race Relations in Louisiana, 1877–98," 315–16.

44. "The State's First Refinery," *Jennings Daily News*, June 1963.

45. "Completion of C. B. and B. Pipe Line," *Oil Investors Journal* 3 (May 18, 1905): 8.

46. "Completion of C. B. and B. Pipe Line," 8.

47. "Completion of C. B. and B. Pipe Line," 6, 8.

48. *Mineral Resources of the United States*, 1901, 57th Cong., 1st sess., House Document No. 17, 561–568.

49. Henry LeRoy Riser, "The History of Jennings, Louisiana" (master's thesis, Louisiana State University, 1947), 561–568.

50. Jason P. Theriot, "Louisiana's Legacy Lawsuits," *Louisiana History* 58, no. 4 (Fall 2016): 413.

51. "A New Gusher at Jennings," *Oil Investor's Journal* 1 (July 5, 1902).

52. *New Orleans Times-Democrat*, September 28, 1901.

53. Riser, "The History of Jennings," 561–568.

54. Theriot, "Louisiana's Legacy Lawsuits," 414.

55. Theriot, "Louisiana's Legacy Lawsuits," 415; P. B. Lang to Alba Heywood, December 12, 1906, box 4, folder 217, Heywood Papers, Louisiana State University.

56. Letter to W. J. Patterson, May 6, 1909, Jennings-Heywood Collection, Louisiana State University.

57. "Complaints against Salt Water," *Lower Coast Gazette*, July 24, 1909.

58. Theriot, "Louisiana's Legacy Lawsuits," 417; P. B. Lang to Alba Heywood, December 12, 1906.

59. W. Scott Heywood, "Autobiography of an Oil Man," Jennings-Heywood Oil Syndicate Records, mss. 3262, p. 7, Louisiana and Lower Mississippi Valley Collections, Special Collections, Hill Memorial Library, Louisiana State University Libraries, Baton Rouge.

60. Riser, "The History of Jennings," 561–568.

61. Riser, "The History of Jennings," 561–568.

62. "The City of Jennings, Louisiana," 1903, p. 3, available in Jennings Carnegie Library.

63. J. M. Hoag, interview with Keith A. Darce, December 2, 1980, in "Reflections of Historic Jennings," 3, 5, available in Jennings Carnegie Library.

64. "Jennings: The Rice and Oil City of Southwestern Louisiana," p. 1 (unpaginated), available in Jennings Carnegie Library.

65. "Jennings: The Rice and Oil City of Southwestern Louisiana."

66. Hoag interview, 5.

67. Brian Black, *Petrolia: The Landscape of America's First Oil Boom* (Baltimore: Johns Hopkins University Press, 2000), 173.

68. "Steam, Gas and Hot Air," *Oil Investors' Journal* 9 (August 6, 1909): 22.

69. "Jules Clement Jr.," Find a Grave, https://www.findagrave.com/cgi-bin/fg.cgi?page=grandGRid=26120669andref=acom; Marie Morvant, *Crowley Daily Signal*, April 3, 1957.

70. 1920 US Census, Acadia Parish, Louisiana, Police Jury Ward 4, District 9, roll T625_603, p. 5A, Ancestry.com; 1940 US Census, Acadia Parish, Louisiana, District 9, image 406, Ancestry.com; 1940 US Census, Acadia Parish, Louisiana, District 1–16, roll T627_1377, p. 19B, Ancestry.com.

71. E. L. Hagstetle, "Louisiana's First Oil Field," *Louisiana Conservation Review* (Spring 1939): 11–13.

CHAPTER 2: THE COMMUNITIES

1. 1900 US Census, Caddo Parish, Louisiana, Police Jury Ward 2, District 028, roll 559, p. 3A, FHL microfilm 1240559, Ancestry.com.

2. Kenny A. Franks and Paul F. Lambert, *Early Arkansas and Louisiana Oil: A Photographic History* (College Station: Texas A&M University Press, 1982), 35.

3. Caddo Parish Clerk of Court, Conveyance Records, Book #33, 602–611.

4. 1900 US Census, Joplin, Jasper, Missouri, Ward 4, District 0039, roll 865, p. 10A, FHL microfilm 1240865, Ancestry.com; Port Arthur, Texas, City Directory, 1929, in U.S. City Directories, 1822–1995, Ancestry.com; "U.S., School Catalogs, 1765–1935," Illinois, University of Chicago, 1876, in US, School Catalogs, 1765–1935, Ancestry.com.

5. "Oil in the Savage-Morrical Well at Caddo City, La.," *Houston Post*, February 5, 1905, 6.

6. Walter E. Hopper, "The Caddo Oil- and Gas-Field, Louisiana," *Bulletin of the American Institute of Mining Engineers* no. 49–54 (1911): 283.

7. "Oil in the Savage-Morrical Well."

8. Hopper, "The Caddo Oil- and Gas-Field, Louisiana," 283.

9. Hopper, "The Caddo Oil- and Gas-Field, Louisiana," 413; Daniel Yergin, *The Prize: The Epic Quest for Oil, Money, and Power* (New York: Free Press, 2009), 69; "Caddo Now Center of Interest," *Oil Investors' Journal* 8 (April 10, 1910).

10. C. Lane Sartor, "Early History of the Caddo-Pine Island Field," *Oil Industry History* 4, no. 1 (2003).

11. 1900 US Census, Caddo Parish, Louisiana, Police Jury Ward 3, District 0029, roll 559, p. 14B, FHL microfilm 1240559, Ancestry.com; Louisiana, U.S., State-wide Death Index, 1819–1964, Ancestry.com.

12. Plat of Oil City, filed and recorded March 10, 1908, Caddo Parish Clerk of Court, Plat #50, 76–77.

13. JS Noel to JK Norman, filed and recorded April 12, 1911, Caddo Parish Clerk of Court, Conveyance Records, Book #65, 653.

14. John F. Law, interview by Chuck Smith, 1999, Louisiana State Oil and Gas Museum.

15. Claude R. McFarland, interview by Lillian J. Hall, January 7, 1987, Collection OH, Item OH114, LSUS Archives Oral History Collection, Special Collections Department, Louisiana State University-Shreveport.

16. Sam Thomas Mallison, *The Great Wildcatter* (Charleston, WV: Education Foundation of West Virginia, 1953), 185.

17. Martin Schwartz, "Caddo-Pine Island Oil Boom," *Louisiana Endowment for the Humanities*, Fall 2004, 81.

18. Cleo Norris, interview by Chuck Smith, 1999, Louisiana State Oil and Gas Museum.

19. Tonja Koob Marking and Jennifer Snape, *Louisiana's Oil Heritage* (Charleston, SC: Arcadia, 2012), 109.

20. Florence Hartman, interview by Chuck Smith, 1999, Louisiana State Oil and Gas Museum.

21. Marking and Snape, *Louisiana's Oil Heritage*, 109.

22. Franks and Lambert, *Early Arkansas and Louisiana Oil*, 54.

23. Tom Moore, interview by Chuck Smith, 1999, Louisiana State Oil and Gas Museum.

24. [No headline], *Winslow Dispatch*, January 22, 1909; John Ridge, "Notable People, Lost Tales, and Forgotten Facts of Oil City, Louisiana," http://people-tales-facts -of-ocla.blogspot.com/2016/02/oil-city-burning.html.

25. "Small Louisiana Town Burned," *Thibodaux Sentinel*, December 9, 1911, Image 1; Ridge, "Notable People."

26. "Fire at Oil City, Causes Losses around $100,000," *Baton Rouge State Times*, August 10, 1922, 1; Ridge, "Notable People."

27. "Heavy Loss in Oil City Night Fire," *Monroe News Star*, September 21, 1926; Ridge, "Notable People." Brian Black also notes the prevalence of fires in

nineteenth-century Pennsylvania's oil boomtowns in *Petrolia: The Landscape of America's First Oil Boom* (Baltimore: Johns Hopkins University Press, 2000), 167.

28. "Fire at Oil City"; "Heavy Loss in Oil City"; Ridge, "Notable People."

29. "Strikers Assist in Extinguishing Blaze at Oil City," *New Orleans Times-Picayune*, November 4, 1917, 2; Ridge, "Notable People."

30. "Loss Set at $50,000 in Fire at Oil City," *New Orleans Times Picayune*, December 5, 1936, 1; Ridge, "Notable People."

31. A. B. Hanner, "Oil City Now a Better Place to Live—Hanner," *Caddo Citizen*, July 3, 1975.

32. Black, *Petrolia*, 144–146.

33. Black, *Petrolia*, 146.

34. Walter Duvall George Jr., interview by Chuck Smith, 1999, Louisiana State Oil and Gas Museum.

35. Goodloe Stuck, *Annie McCune: Shreveport Madam* (Baton Rouge: Moran Publishing Corporation, 1981), 64.

36. Moore interview.

37. Margaret Bateman (née Pace), interview by Chuck Smith, 1999, Louisiana State Oil and Gas Museum.

38. Mallison, *The Great Wildcatter*, 195.

39. Stuck, *Annie McCune*, 63.

40. Mallison, *The Great Wildcatter*, 194.

41. Dr. Willis P. Butler, interview by Dalton I. Cloud, March 15, 1977, p. 88, LSUS Archives Oral History Collection, Special Collections Department, Louisiana State University-Shreveport.

42. Frances Davis Brougher, *Pink Taylor: Cattleman and Lawman* (Austin, TX: self-published, copy available at Louisiana Oil and Gas Museum, 1986), 26.

43. Law interview.

44. Moore interview.

45. United States, Officer Down Memorials, 1791–2014, http://www.odmp.org /officer/5386-deputy-sheriff-will-george.

46. Harvard College Class of 1897, *Fourth Report* (Cambridge, MA: Rockwell and Churchill Press, 1912), 219; Ridge, "Notable People."

47. "Oil City Project," p. 3, Department of Sociology, Centenary College, Louisiana State University-Shreveport Special Collections; Stuck, *Annie McCune*, 61; Moore interview.

48. "Small Louisiana Town Burned"; Ridge, "Notable People."

49. D. R. Beamer, interview by Goodloe Stuck, February, 1976, Goodloe Stuck Papers, box 14, folder 129, pp. 7–8, Louisiana State University-Shreveport.

50. Norris interview.

51. "Oil City Trouble," *The Caucasian*, November 17, 1910.

52. "Outlaws Shoot Up Town," *True Republican*, November 19, 1910.

53. "Oil City Trouble."

54. Mallison, *The Great Wildcatter*, 194.

55. Moore interview.

56. Beamer interview, 1.

57. "Bootlegging Charges Pile Up in a Hurry," *Shreveport Journal*, March 25, 1914.

58. Stuck, *Annie McCune*, 63.

59. Alex Rice, interview by Goodloe Stuck, June 24, 1973, Goodloe Stuck Papers, box 14, folder 129, p. 4, Louisiana State University-Shreveport.

60. Law interview.

61. Hartman interview.

62. W. J. "Bill" Snead, interview by Chuck Smith, 1999, Louisiana State Oil and Gas Museum.

63. Snead interview.

64. Marking and Snape, *Louisiana's Oil Heritage*, 106.

65. George Beck and Kim McGee, interview by Henry Wiencek, Oil City, Louisiana, February 3, 2015; John Ridge, interview by Henry Wiencek, Austin, Texas, September 11, 2015.

66. 1920 US Census, Caddo Parish, Louisiana, Police Jury Ward 3, District 38, roll T625_607, p. 9A, Image 788, Ancestry.com.

67. Snead interview.

68. Lutille Beck, interview by Chuck Smith, 1999, Louisiana State Oil and Gas Museum; Lou Bell, interview by Chuck Smith, 1999, Louisiana State Oil and Gas Museum.

69. Sam Collier, *North Caddo Parish* (Charleston, SC: Arcadia, 2007), 87.

70. Snead interview.

71. "Friends of the Gideons," *Monroe News Star*, September 24, 1912, 6; Ridge, "Notable People."

72. "Conference Notes," *Monroe News Star*, December 12, 1912, 8; Ridge, "Notable People."

73. Malachi 4:1 (King James Version).

74. Mallison, *The Great Wildcatter*, 194.

75. Mike Benedum, interview by Allan Nevins, Frank Ernest Hill, and Sam Mallison, p. 9, Benedum and the Oil Industry Project, 1951, Butler Library, Columbia University.

76. Mallison, *The Great Wildcatter*, 194.

77. McFarland interview.

78. Marking and Snape, *Louisiana's Oil Heritage*, 111.

79. "Trees City, LA: An Oil Field Boom Town's Buildings," pamphlet, Louisiana Committee for the Humanities; Carrie Duncan Slee, "History of Trees," 1–3, Trees City Vertical File, Louisiana State University-Shreveport.

80. Keenan Gingles, "Trees Losing Post Office," September 30, 1983, n.p., Louisiana State University; "Trees City," Trees City Vertical File, Louisiana State University-Shreveport.

81. Slee, "History of Trees."

1. Cleo Norris, interview by Chuck Smith, 1999, Louisiana State Oil and Gas Museum.

2. Norris interview.

3. Perry W. Howard, *Political Tendencies in Louisiana* (Baton Rouge: Louisiana State University Press, 1971), 163–164.

4. Howard, *Political Tendencies in Louisiana*, 164.

5. Howard, *Political Tendencies in Louisiana*, 164–165; Roger W. Shugg, *Origins of Class Struggle in Louisiana: A Social History of White Farmers and Laborers during Slavery and After, 1840–1875* (Baton Rouge: Louisiana State University Press, 1972), 241.

6. Howard, *Political Tendencies in Louisiana*, 165–167; Shugg, *Origins of Class Struggle in Louisiana*, 241.

7. Walter E. Hopper, "The Caddo Oil- and Gas-Field, Louisiana," *Bulletin of the American Institute of Mining Engineers* no. 49–54 (1911): 287, 301. Figures reflect wages for white workers; Black oil field workers earned significantly less.

8. John F. Law, interview by Chuck Smith, 1999, Louisiana State Oil and Gas Museum.

9. Wallace Scot McFarlane, "Oil on the Farm: The East Texas Oil Boom and the Origins of an Energy Economy," *Journal of Southern History* 83, no. 4 (November 2017): 857; Steven Hahn, *The Roots of Southern Populism: Yeoman Farmers and the Transformation of the Georgia Upcountry, 1850–1890* (New York: Oxford University Press, 1983), 186.

10. Carl W. Jones, interview by Hubert Humphreys, September 21, 1977, *Louisiana State University Oral History Collection* no. 9, 8.

11. McFarlane, "Oil on the Farm," 857.

12. Photograph, Mooringsport Mini Museum, Mooringsport, Louisiana, in Kenny A. Franks and Paul F. Lambert, *Early Arkansas and Louisiana Oil: A Photographic History* (College Station: Texas A&M University Press, 1982), 60.

13. 1900 US Census, Travis, Texas, Justice Precinct 6, Enumeration District 0115, roll 1673, p. 3B, FHL microfilm 1241673, Ancestry.com.

14. 1920 US Census, Shreveport, Caddo, Louisiana, Precinct 7, Enumeration District 56, roll T625_608, p. 8A, Image 613, Ancestry.com. The census record appears to read, "drugs oil field."

15. Louisiana, U.S., Statewide Death Index, 1819–1964, Ancestry.com; "Sebron Travis Sneed Sr.," https://www.findagrave.com/memorial/25654579/sebron-travis-sneed.

16. Gregory et al. v. Standard Oil Co. of Louisiana, *Southern Reporter* 91 (1922): 717.

17. Gregory et al. v. Standard Oil Co. of Louisiana, 717–718.

18. 1930 US Census, El Dorado, Union, Arkansas, Enumeration District 0013, roll 96, p. 7B, Image 544.0, FHL microfilm 2339831, Ancestry.com.

19. 1910 US Census, Caddo Parish, Louisiana, Police Jury Ward 2, District 0030, pp. 5, 6, Ancestry.com.

20. Tom Moore, interview by Chuck Smith, 1999, Louisiana State Oil and Gas Museum.

21. W. J. "Bill" Snead, interview by Chuck Smith, 1999, Louisiana State Oil and Gas Museum.

22. Gladys Thornton, "Jim Dunman Was Best 16-up Mule Team Driver," *Caddo Citizen*, July 3, 1975.

23. G. D. Harris, *Oil and Gas in Louisiana with a Brief Summary of Their Occurrences in Adjacent States* (Washington, DC: Government Printing Office, 1910), 130.

24. Hopper, "The Caddo Oil- and Gas-Field, Louisiana," 305–307.

25. Jones interview, 8, 13.

26. Snead interview.

27. "Small Louisiana Town Burned," *Thibodaux Sentinel*, December 9, 1911, image 1; John Ridge, "Notable People, Lost Tales, and Forgotten Facts of Oil City, Louisiana," http://people-tales-facts-of-ocla.blogspot.com/2016/02/oil-city-burning.html.

28. 1910 US Census, Caddo Parish, Louisiana, Police Jury Ward 2, Enumeration District 0030, roll T624_510, p. 2B, FHL microfilm 1374523, Ancestry.com.

29. 1910 US Census, Caddo Parish, Louisiana, Police Jury Ward 2, Enumeration District 0030, roll T624_510, p. 2B, FHL microfilm 1374523, Ancestry.com.

30. Sam Collier, *North Caddo Parish* (Charleston, SC: Arcadia, 2007), 76.

31. 1910 US Census, Caddo Parish, Louisiana, Police Jury Ward 2, Enumeration District 0030, roll T624_510, p. 3B, FHL microfilm 1374523, Ancestry.com.

32. U.S., World War I Draft Registration Cards, 1917–1918, Harris County, TX, Draft Board 3, roll 1953564, Ancestry.com.; Death Certificates, 1903–1982, Texas, Ancestry.com.

33. 1910 US Census, Caddo Parish, Louisiana, Police Jury Ward 2, Enumeration District 0030, roll T624_510, p. 3B, FHL microfilm 1374523, Ancestry.com.

34. James Muslow, interview by Chuck Smith, 1999, Louisiana State Oil and Gas Museum.

35. Lou Bell, interview by Chuck Smith, 1999, Louisiana State Oil and Gas Museum.

36. 1930 US Census, Caddo Parish, Louisiana, Police Jury Ward 2, Enumeration District 0006, p. 28B, FHL microfilm 2340521, Ancestry.com.

37. Tonja Koob Marking and Jennifer Snape, *Louisiana's Oil Heritage* (Charleston, SC: Arcadia, 2012), 43.

38. 1910 US Census, Caddo Parish, Louisiana, Police Jury Ward 2, Enumeration District 0030, roll T624_510, p. 2B, 5–6, FHL microfilm 1374523, Ancestry.com.

39. Tunnell Day, interview by Goodloe Stuck, February 6, 1976, box 14, folder 129, p. 8, Louisiana State University-Shreveport.

40. Ray Oden, interview by Goodloe Stuck, February, 1975, Goodloe Stuck Papers, box 14, folder 129 (no pagination), Louisiana State University-Shreveport.

41. Bob Anderson, interview by Goodloe Stuck, January 17, 1974, Goodloe Stuck Papers, box 14, folder 129, p. 13, Louisiana State University-Shreveport.

42. D. R. Beamer, interview by Goodloe Stuck, February, 1976, Goodloe Stuck Papers, box 14, folder 129, p. 9, Louisiana State University-Shreveport.

43. D. R. Beamer, interview by Goodloe Stuck, February, 1976, Goodloe Stuck Papers, box 14, folder 129, p. 9, Louisiana State University-Shreveport.

44. Alex Rice, interview by Goodloe Stuck, June 24, 1973, Goodloe Stuck Papers, box 14, folder 129, p. 5, Louisiana State University-Shreveport.

45. Anderson interview, 13.

46. Beamer interview, 7.

47. Beamer interview, 7.

48. Norris interview.

49. James C. Maroney, "The Texas-Louisiana Oil Field Strike of 1917," in *Essays in Southern Labor History: Selected Papers*, ed. Gary M. Fink and Merl E. Reed (Westport, CT: Greenwood Press, 1976), 161.

50. John Ridge, "Military Occupation of the Caddo Oil Fields 1917–1918," *North Caddo Parish*, http://north-caddo-parish.blogspot.com/2015/06/military-occupation-of-caddo-oil-fields.html; Harvey O'Connor, *History of Oil Workers International Union (CIO)* (Denver: Oil Workers International Union [CIO], 1950), 271, 281–282, 300–301, 384–385.

51. O'Connor, *History of Oil Workers International Union (CIO)*, 281–282, 351–352.

52. Clayton D. Laurie and Ronald H. Cole, *The Role of Federal Military Forces in Domestic Disorders, 1877–1945* (Washington, DC: Center of Military History, US Army, 1997), 250, 164.

53. "Seventeen Texas and Louisiana Oil Fields Affected by Union Strike," *Tulsa Daily World*, November 2, 1917; Laurie and Cole, *The Role of Federal Military Forces in Domestic Disorders, 1877–1945*, 250.

54. "Strikers Hear from President," *Evening Star*, November 16, 1917.

55. "Soldiers Left Last Night for Louisiana," *Vicksburg Herald*, November 2, 1917, 5.

56. "Guards on Watch in Louisiana Oil Fields," *San Antonio Express*, November 12, 1917.

57. "Oil Workers on Strike," *New York Times*, November 1, 1917.

58. Ridge, "Military Occupation of the Caddo Oil Fields 1917–1918"; Laurie and Cole, *The Role of Federal Military Forces in Domestic Disorders, 1877–1945*, 250–251.

59. *New Orleans Item*, November 17, 1917, 4; Ridge, "Military Occupation of the Caddo Oil Fields 1917–1918."

60. "Vice Districts of Oil Field Closed," *New Orleans Daily States*, November 5, 1917; Ridge, "Military Occupation of the Caddo Oil Fields 1917–1918."

61. "Vice Districts of Oil Field Closed"; Ridge, "Military Occupation of the Caddo Oil Fields 1917–1918."

62. "Louisiana Oil Town Threatened by $20,000 Fire," *Paris Morning News*, November 4, 1917, 1.

63. "Vice Districts of Oil Fields Closed."

64. Laurie and Cole, *The Role of Federal Military Forces in Domestic Disorders, 1877–1945*, 250.

65. "Methodist Ladies to Supply Soldiers with Thanksgiving Goodies," *Shreveport Times*, November 26, 1917.

66. Laurie and Cole, *The Role of Federal Military Forces in Domestic Disorders, 1877–1945*, 252.

67. Laurie and Cole, *The Role of Federal Military Forces in Domestic Disorders, 1877–1945*, 252.
68. Maroney, "The Texas-Louisiana Oil Field Strike of 1917," 164–165.
69. Maroney, "The Texas-Louisiana Oil Field Strike of 1917," 167; Laurie and Cole, *The Role of Federal Military Forces in Domestic Disorders, 1877–1945*, 252.
70. Wallace Scot McFarlane argues that a similar dynamic took place in the East Texas oil boom of 1929; see McFarlane, "Oil on the Farm," 860.
71. Dr. Willis P. Butler, interview by Dalton I. Cloud, March 15, 1977, 91, LSUS Archives Oral History Collection, Special Collections Department, Louisiana State University-Shreveport.
72. "Back to Soil Make Good Crop," *Shreveport Times*, January 1, 1909.
73. Sam Thomas Mallison, *The Great Wildcatter* (Charleston, WV: Education Foundation of West Virginia, 1953), 185.
74. Walter Duvall George Jr., interview by Chuck Smith, 1999, Louisiana State Oil and Gas Museum.
75. Mallison, *The Great Wildcatter*, 185.
76. Harris, *Oil and Gas in Louisiana with a Brief Summary of Their Occurrences in Adjacent States*, 132.
77. "Good Money from the Trees No. 4," *Oil Investors' Journal* 8 (March 20, 1910).
78. Mallison, *The Great Wildcatter*, 197.
79. "Good Money from the Trees No. 4."
80. "Caddo Production," *Oil Investors' Journal* 8 (January 6, 1910).
81. Mike Benedum, interview by Allan Nevins, Frank Ernest Hill, and Sam Mallison, Benedum and the Oil Industry Project, 1951, Butler Library, Columbia University; Mallison, *The Great Wildcatter*, 199–200.
82. Daniel Yergin, *The Prize: The Epic Quest for Oil, Money, and Power* (New York: Free Press, 2009), 29; Ron Chernow, *Titan: The Life of John D. Rockefeller, Sr.* (New York: Random House, 1998), 164.
83. Mallison, *The Great Wildcatter*, 200–201.
84. Mallison, *The Great Wildcatter*, 201.
85. Mallison, *The Great Wildcatter*, 201, 209–211.

CHAPTER 4: THE RACIAL VIOLENCE OF "BLOODY CADDO"

1. Campbell Robertson, "History of Lynchings in the South Documents Nearly 4,000 Names," *New York Times*, February 10, 2015, http://www.nytimes.com /2015/02/10/us/history-of-lynchings-in-the-south-documents-nearly-4000 -names.html.
2. William I. Hair, "Plundered Legacy: The Early History of North Louisiana's Oil and Gas Industry," *North Louisiana Historical Association* 8 (Fall 1977): 181.
3. Dr. Willis P. Butler, interview by Dalton I. Cloud, March 15, 1977, 93, LSUS Archives Oral History Collection, Special Collections Department, Louisiana State University-Shreveport.

4. Willie Burton, *The Blacker the Berry: A Black History of Shreveport* (Shreveport, LA: The Times, 2002), 3; Joseph Karl Menn, *The Large Slaveholders of Louisiana* (New Orleans: Pelican, 1964), 36.

5. Maude Hearn-O'Pry, *Chronicles of Shreveport and Caddo Parish* (Shreveport, LA: Journal Printing Company, 1928), 144.

6. Gilles Vandal, "The Policy of Violence in Caddo Parish, 1865–1884," *Louisiana History: The Journal of the Louisiana Historical Association* 32, no. 2 (1991): 171, 173.

7. Gilles Vandal, "'Bloody Caddo': White Violence against Blacks in a Louisiana Parish, 1865–1876," *Journal of Social History* 25, no. 2 (Winter 1991): 373–388.

8. Vandal, "The Policy of Violence in Caddo Parish, 1865–1884," 159–160, 175.

9. Vandal, "'Bloody Caddo': White Violence against Blacks in a Louisiana Parish, 1865–1876," 373–388.

10. Vandal, "The Policy of Violence in Caddo Parish, 1865–1884," 161, 164–166.

11. Vandal, "'Bloody Caddo': White Violence against Blacks in a Louisiana Parish, 1865–1876," 379.

12. Burton, *The Blacker the Berry*, 3; Menn, *The Large Slaveholders of Louisiana*, 18.

13. Vandal, "The Policy of Violence in Caddo Parish, 1865–1884," 171.

14. "Citizens Hunt Negro Murderer. Determined to Burn at the Stake Fellow Who Killed Foster," *Idaho Statesman*, June 14, 1901, 1.

15. "News of the Day," *Alexandria Gazette*, June 21, 1901, 2.

16. "Natives of Texas," *Idaho Statesman*, June 14, 1901, 1.

17. "Maddened Men," *Fort Worth Register*, June 14, 1901, 2.

18. Brief of Counsel for Frances S. Glenn, Alleged Heir, Lillie G. Taylor v. Angeline Allen, State of Louisiana, no. 24, p. 209, Supreme Court of Louisiana, 1922, Special Collections, University of New Orleans.

19. Michael James Pfeifer, *Rough Justice: Lynching and American Society, 1874–1947* (Urbana: University of Illinois Press, 2004), 161. Newspaper accounts and court records relating to Lillie Taylor often incorrectly cite 1897 as the year of Isom McGee's murder.

20. "World's Richest Negro Woman Lives in Dallas," *Dallas Express*, May 14, 1921, 2.

21. Carl B. King and Howard W. Risher Jr., "The Negro in the Petroleum Industry," Industrial Research Unit, Wharton School of Finance and Commerce, University of Pennsylvania, distributed by University of Pennsylvania Press, 1969, 1, 13, 26.

22. King and Risher, "The Negro in the Petroleum Industry," 22.

23. Joe W. Specht, "Oil Well Blues," *East Texas Historical Journal* 49 (2011): 83.

24. Pfeifer, *Rough Justice*, 9, 22, 67.

25. Pfeifer, *Rough Justice*, 141.

26. Pfeifer, *Rough Justice*, 144.

27. Pfeifer, *Rough Justice*, 142–144.

28. Pfeifer, *Rough Justice*, 144, 146. Between 1918 and 1919 there were sixteen acts of lynching in Louisiana, largely relating to the tensions over Black citizenship and military service following the First World War.

29. Interview with Mike Benedum, p. 81, Benedum and the Oil Industry Project, 1951, Butler Library, Columbia University.

30. Benedum interview, 81–82.

31. State v. Shannon, no. 24283, Supreme Court of Louisiana, 1921, *Southern Reporter* (West Publishing Company, 1921), 500.

32. "Deputy Found Guilty," *News Scimitar*, July 9, 1920, 3.

33. Certificate of Death, William Hardy Dunson, Louisiana State Board of Health, Bureau of Vital Statistics, May 21, 1920.

34. State v. Shannon, 500–502.

35. State v. Shannon, 500–502.

36. David Mark Chalmers, *Hooded Americanism: The History of the Ku Klux Klan* (New York: New Viewpoints, 1976), 59.

37. "Mapping the Second Ku Klux Klan," Virginia Commonwealth University, http://labs.library.vcu.edu/klan.

38. Chalmers, *Hooded Americanism*, 60.

39. Chalmers, *Hooded Americanism*, 59.

40. W. Scott Wilkinson, interview by Hubert Humphreys, October 26, 1976, p. 12, Louisiana State University-Shreveport Oral History Project, Special Collections, Louisiana State University-Shreveport.

41. Wilkinson interview, 12.

42. Chalmers, *Hooded Americanism*, 59, 60–64.

43. Chalmers, *Hooded Americanism*, 64.

44. John F. Law, interview by Chuck Smith, 1999, Louisiana State Oil and Gas Museum.

45. Walter Duvall George Jr., interview by Chuck Smith, 1999, Louisiana State Oil and Gas Museum.

46. "Black Hanged for Attack on White Woman," *Pine Bluff Daily Graphic*, August 27, 1917, 1; "Mob at Vivian Lynches Negro," *Shreveport Times*, August 27, 1916, 3.

47. "Black Hanged for Attack on White Woman," 1; "Mob at Vivian Lynches Negro," 3.

48. "Black Hanged for Attack on White Woman," 1; "Mob at Vivian Lynches Negro," 3.

49. "Mob at Vivian Lynches Negro," 3.

50. J. B. Barnett, interview by John Loos, 1957, p. 4, John Loos Materials, Louisiana State University.

51. John Loos, *Oil on Stream! A History of Interstate Oil Pipe Line Company, 1909–1959* (Baton Rouge: Louisiana State University Press, 1959), 13.

52. Barnett interview, 5.

53. Loos, *Oil on Stream!* 25.

54. Barnett interview, 1.

55. John Crump, interview by John Loos, 1957, p. 2, John Loos Materials, Louisiana State University.

56. Loos, *Oil on Stream!* 23.

57. "Mr. Bowie," interview by John Loos, 1957, p. 3, John Loos Materials, Louisiana State University.

58. Fred Bimel, interview by John Loos, 1957, p. 3, John Loos Materials, Louisiana State University.

59. Bimel interview, 12.

60. Barnett interview, 10.

61. Bimel interview, 9.

62. Smith W. Day, interview by John Loos, 1957, p. 26, John Loos Materials, Louisiana State University.

63. Day interview, 26.

64. Bimel interview, 9.

65. Specht, "Oil Well Blues," 94; Paul Oliver, *The Story of the Blues* (Boston: Northeastern University Press, 1998), 116.

66. Noah Moore, "Oil City Blues," lyrics in Specht, "Oil Well Blues," 94.

67. Bob Anderson, interview by Goodloe Stuck, January 17, 1974, p. 2, Goodloe Stuck Papers, Special Collections Department, Louisiana State University-Shreveport.

68. W. H. Griffin, interview by Goodloe Stuck, June 31, 1973, p. 7, Goodloe Stuck Papers, Special Collections Department, Louisiana State University-Shreveport.

69. O. B. Johnson, interview by Goodloe Stuck, Goodloe Stuck Papers, n.d., p. 1, Special Collections Department, Louisiana State University-Shreveport.

70. Griffin interview, 7.

71. Johnson interview, 1, 8.

72. Butler interview, 8.

73. Anderson interview, 16–17.

74. Wallace Scot McFarlane, "Oil on the Farm," *Journal of Southern History* 83, no. 4 (November 2017): 885–886.

CHAPTER 5: THE COURTS OF BLOODY CADDO

1. Alice McGee v. George West et al., no. 5421, Third District Court, Claiborne Parish, September 20, 1921, [no pagination], Special Collections, University of New Orleans.

2. 1880 US Census, Claiborne, Louisiana, Ward 3, Enumeration District 011, roll 451, p. 274B, Ancestry.com.

3. Thornton Bridgeman Deed to Isom McGee, Lillie G. Taylor v. George West, no. 1235, US Circuit Court for Fifth Circuit and Western District of Louisiana, 1920, p. 1, National Archives, Fort Worth, Texas.

4. Lona is also listed as "Onie" in census records.

5. Michael James Pfeifer, *Rough Justice: Lynching and American Society, 1874–1947* (Urbana: University of Illinois Press, 2004), 161.

6. "World's Richest Negro Woman Lives in Dallas," *Dallas Express*, May 14, 1921, 2.

7. Petition of Lillie G. Taylor, Lillie G. Taylor v. Angeline Allen, no. 1235, US District Court for Fifth Circuit and Western District of Louisiana, June 23, 1920, [no pagination], National Archives, Fort Worth, Texas.

8. Arkansas, County Marriages Index, 1837–1957, Ancestry.com.

9. 1900 US Census, Hope, Hempstead, Arkansas, Enumeration District 0044, p. 14, FHL microfilm 1240060, Ancestry.com.

10. 1910 US Census, Hope, Hempstead, Arkansas, Ward 1, Enumeration District 0076, roll T624_52, p. 6B, FHL microfilm 1374065, Ancestry.com. The woman listed as her companion was "Annie Wheaton."

11. "World's Richest Negro Woman Lives in Dallas," 2.

12. Defendant's Bill of Exceptions, Lillie G. Taylor v. George West, no. 1235, US District Court, Western District of Louisiana, August 23, 1920, p. 2, National Archives, Fort Worth, Texas. West was deeded the land by "T. C. Bridgeman, under tutor for minor heirs of George L. Bridgeman and agent for Mrs. Ada Bridgeman." The question of who had legal authority to deed Nail Place became the subject of a legal dispute within the Bridgeman family.

13. Holman et al. v. Gulf Refining Co. of Louisiana et al., no. 7449, Circuit Court of Appeals, Fifth Circuit, March 20, 1935, *Leagle*, http://www.leagle.com/decision/193517076F2d94_1140/HOLMAN%20v.%20GULF%20REFINING%20CO.%20OF%20LOUISIANA.

14. "World's Richest Negro Woman Lives in Dallas," 2. The 1935 Supreme Court case Holman v. Gulf Refining Co. of Louisiana would later note that Taylor learned about Nail Place's oil via "the efforts of one Green, negro, employed by Foster, Looney and Wilkinson to locate the heirs of Isom McGee." Petition for Writ of Certiorari, in *Holman v. Gulf Refining Co. of Louisiana, U.S. Supreme Court Transcript of Record with Supporting Pleadings*, ed. Geo H. Klein and H. L. Stone (Farmington Hills, MI: Gale, US Supreme Court Records, 2011,) 4.

15. Holman v. Gulf, 2. Taylor leased the remaining eleven acres of Nail Place to Charles P. Clayton.

16. Holman v. Gulf, 2; Petition for Writ of Certiorari, Holman v. Gulf, 4–5.

17. "World's Richest Negro Woman Lives in Dallas," 2.

18. Witness Certificate of Henry Matthews, Lillie G. Taylor v. George West, no. 1235, US Circuit Court for Fifth Circuit and Western District of Louisiana, 1920, National Archives, Fort Worth, Texas.

19. Witness Certificate of Angeline Allen and Witness Certificate of Emma Garrett, Lillie G. Taylor v. George West, no. 1235, US Circuit Court for Fifth Circuit and Western District of Louisiana, 1920, National Archives, Fort Worth, Texas.

20. Note of Evidence, Lillie G. Taylor v. George West, no. 1235, US District Court, Western District of Louisiana, Shreveport Division, March 18, 1920, pp. 7, 30, National Archives, Fort Worth, Texas. Allen estimated her age to be seventy-two or seventy-three.

21. Note of Evidence, Taylor v. West, 4, 20.

22. Opinion and Judgement, Lillie G. Taylor v. Angeline Allen, George West, State of Louisiana, no. 24, 209, Supreme Court of Louisiana, April 29, 1921, pp. 2–3, Special Collections, University of New Orleans.

23. Note of Evidence, Taylor v. West, 44.

24. Petition, Lillie G. Taylor v. George West, no. 1235, US Circuit Court for Fifth Circuit and Western District of Louisiana, December 5, 1919, [no pagination], National Archives, Fort Worth, Texas.

25. Petition for Writ of Certiorari, Holman v. Gulf, 7.

26. *The Appeal*, February 11, 1922, 2.

27. Petition for Writ of Certiorari, Holman v. Gulf, 15.

28. Alice McGee et al. v. George West et al., no. 5421, Third Judicial District Court, September 20, 1921, p. 4, Special Collections, University of New Orleans.

29. Holman v. Gulf, 3.

30. "Louisiana Land Suits Cause Rush to Homer," *International Petroleum Reporter*, January 18, 1922.

31. Defendant's Bill of Exceptions, Lillie G. Taylor v. George West, no. 1235, US District Court, Western District of Louisiana, August 23, 1920, [no pagination], National Archives, Fort Worth, Texas.

32. Wallace Scot McFarlane, "Oil on the Farm," *Journal of Southern History* 83, no. 4 (November 2017): 861–862.

33. "Negro Girl, State Claim Oil Millions," *New Iberia Enterprise and Independent Observer*, August 21, 1920, 7.

34. "Lillie Taylor's Case," *Bismarck Tribune*, March 21, 1922, 4.

35. "Ghost of Negro Lynched in 1897 Is Hoodoo [*sic*] in Suit for Oil Millions," *New Orleans Item*, 2. The author falsely notes that McGee bought Nail Place in 1896. Taylor lived on South Hill Avenue in the largely Black East Dallas neighborhood.

36. "Ghost of Negro Lynched in 1897 Is Hoodoo in Suit for Oil Millions," 2.

37. "Ghost of Negro Lynched in 1897 Is Hoodoo in Suit for Oil Millions," 2.

38. "A Most Sensible Colored Woman Washing Clothing," *Eagle*, 4.

39. "Negro Girl, State Claim Oil Millions," 7.

40. "World's Richest Negro Woman Lives in Dallas," 2.

41. "World's Richest Negro Woman Lives in Dallas," 2.

42. Holman v. Gulf, 3.

43. "Ghost of Negro Lynched in 1897 Is Hoodoo in Suit for Oil Millions," 2; *The Appeal*, February 11, 1922, 2; "Millions Awarded to Negress," *Keowee Courier*, March 8, 1922; "World's Richest Negro Woman Lives in Dallas," 2.

44. "Lillie Taylor's Case," *Bismarck Tribune*, March 21, 1922, 4.

45. *The Appeal*, February 11, 1922, 2.

46. Brief in Support of Argument, in Klein and Stone, *Holman v. Gulf Refining Co of Louisiana U.S. Supreme Court Transcript of Record with Supporting Pleadings*, 37.

47. Petition for Writ of Certiorari, Holman v. Gulf, 13.

48. Exception of State of Louisiana, Francis Scott Glenn v. George West et al., no. 5114, Third District Court, Claiborne Parish, November 21, 1921, [no pagination], Special Collections, University of New Orleans.

49. Petition for Writ of Certiorari, Holman v. Gulf, 15.

50. "Negro Heiress Gets Fortune," *Weekly Iberian*, March 18, 1922.

51. Petition for Writ of Certiorari, Holman v. Gulf, 6.

52. "Final Rites Saturday for C. W. Lane Sr.," *Shreveport Times*, August 1, 1959, 2-A.

53. Petition for Writ of Certiorari, Holman v. Gulf, 9, 14–16.

54. "Disappearance of Heiress Is Mystery," *East Oregonian*, March 2, 1922.

55. Petition for Writ of Certiorari, Holman v. Gulf, 15–16.

56. *The Appeal*, February 11, 1922, 2.

57. Exhibit No. 1, D. H. Raines v. C. E. Dunson et al., no. 22607; Joe Herndon v. C. E. Dunson et al., no. 22608, Supreme Court of Louisiana, 1918, p. 1, Special Collections, University of New Orleans.

58. Certificate of Death, William Hardy Dunson, Louisiana State Board of Health, Bureau of Vital Statistics, May 21, 1920.

59. 1830 US Census, Newberry, South Carolina, series M19, roll 171, p. 93, FHL microfilm 0022505, Ancestry.com.

60. W.P.A. Collection, Historical Records Survey Transcriptions of Louisiana Police Jury Records, Caddo Parish, 1840–1940, December 8, 1840, Louisiana State University.

61. W.P.A. Collection, Historical Records Survey Transcriptions of Louisiana Police Jury Records, Caddo Parish, 1840–1940.

62. 1880 US Census, Caddo Parish, Louisiana, Ward 2, Enumeration District 013, roll 449, p. 172C, Ancestry.com.

63. 1880 US Census, Caddo Parish, Louisiana, Ward 2, Enumeration District 013, roll 449, p. 172C, Ancestry.com.

64. 1900 US Census, Caddo Parish, Louisiana, Police Jury Ward 2, Enumeration District 0028, p. 18, Ancestry.com.

65. Federal Land Patents, State Volumes, Homestead Certificate No. 3648, Application 6155, June 28, 1901, Bureau of Land Management, General Land Office Records, Washington, DC.

66. Raines appears as "Mulatto," "Black," and "White" in the census records of 1880, 1910, and 1920 respectively; the 1901 homestead grant does not list his race.

67. Appeal from the Parish of Caddo State of Louisiana, D. H. Raines and Joe Herndon v. C. E. Dunson, no. 22840, Supreme Court of Louisiana, 1918, p. 14, Special Collections, University of New Orleans.

68. Appeal from the Parish of Caddo State of Louisiana, Raines and Herndon v. Dunson, 15.

69. Appeal from the Parish of Caddo State of Louisiana, Raines and Herndon v. Dunson, 23.

70. Appeal from the Parish of Caddo State of Louisiana, Raines and Herndon v. Dunson, 24.

71. Appeal from the Parish of Caddo State of Louisiana, Raines and Herndon v. Dunson, 30.

72. Appeal from the Parish of Caddo State of Louisiana, Raines and Herndon v. Dunson, 25.

73. Appeal from the Parish of Caddo State of Louisiana, Raines and Herndon v. Dunson, 28, 32, 37.

74. Appeal from the Parish of Caddo State of Louisiana, Raines and Herndon v. Dunson, 28–29.

75. Opinion and Judgement, D. H. Raines and Joe Herndon v. C. E. Dunson, no. 22840, Supreme Court of Louisiana, 1918, p. 4, Special Collections, University of New Orleans.

76. 1920 US Census, Shreveport, Caddo, Louisiana, Precinct 7, Enumeration District 56, roll T625_608, p. 10B, Image 618, Ancestry.com.

77. Willie Burton, *The Blacker the Berry: A Black History of Shreveport* (Shreveport, LA: The Times, 2002), 27–28.

78. Appeal from the Parish of Caddo State of Louisiana, Raines and Herndon v. Dunson, 28–29.

CHAPTER 6: THE LAND

1. Walter Duvall George Jr., interview by Chuck Smith, 1999, Louisiana State Oil and Gas Museum.

2. George interview.

3. W. O. Whitaker, "Hunting in Louisiana," *Forest and Stream* 69, no. 16 (October 19, 1907): 614; John Ridge, "Notable People, Lost Tales, and Forgotten Facts of Oil City, Louisiana," http://people-tales-facts-of-ocla.blogspot.com/2015/05/hunting-in-area-pre-1900.html.

4. Sidney Powers, "The Sabine Uplift, Louisiana," *Bulletin of the American Association of Petroleum Geologists* 4, no. 2 (1920): 117.

5. Walter E. Hopper, "The Caddo Oil- and Gas-Field, Louisiana," *Bulletin of the American Institute of Mining Engineers* no. 49–54 (1911): 290.

6. William I. Hair, "Plundered Legacy: The Early History of North Louisiana's Oil and Gas Industry," *North Louisiana Historical Association* 8 (Fall 1977): 179–184.

7. W. J. "Bill" Snead, interview by Chuck Smith, 1999, Louisiana State Oil and Gas Museum.

8. Hopper, "The Caddo Oil- and Gas-Field, Louisiana," 294.

9. Sam Thomas Mallison, *The Great Wildcatter* (Charleston, WV: Education Foundation of West Virginia, 1953), 187.

10. Kenny A. Franks and Paul F. Lambert, *Early Arkansas and Louisiana Oil: A Photographic History* (College Station: Texas A&M University Press, 1982), 37.

11. Franks and Lambert, *Early Arkansas and Louisiana Oil*, 43.

12. Mallison, *The Great Wildcatter*, 187, 192.

13. "General Clean Up of Oil City Has Been Ordered by State Health Officer Oscar Dowling," *Shreveport Journal*, April 11, 1911.

14. John F. Law, interview by Chuck Smith, 1999, Louisiana State Oil and Gas Museum.

15. Harry Davidson, interview by Judge Gayle Hamilton and Dr. Alan Thompson, January 17, 1995, Louisiana State University-Shreveport.

16. Tunnell Day, interview by Goodloe Stuck, February 6, 1976, p. 9, Louisiana State University-Shreveport.

17. Goodloe Stuck, *Annie McCune: Shreveport Madam* (Baton Rouge: Moran Publishing Corporation, 1981), 101.

18. R. J. Hughes, interview by Goodloe Stuck, February 3, 1975, p. 2, Louisiana State University-Shreveport.

19. Stuck, *Annie McCune*, 101.

20. Goodloe Stuck Collection, folder 128, Louisiana State University-Shreveport.

21. "'Bootlegging' Charges Pile Up in a Hurry," *Shreveport Journal*, March 25, 1914.

22. Mallison, *The Great Wildcatter*, 187, 198, 206.

23. Mallison, *The Great Wildcatter*, 201.

24. Interview with Mike Benedum, p. 80, Benedum and the Oil Industry Project, 1951, Butler Library, Columbia University; Mallison, *The Great Wildcatter*, 196.

25. Mallison, *The Great Wildcatter*, 188.

26. Mallison, *The Great Wildcatter*, 188.

27. Benedum interview, 39.

28. Benedum interview, 40, 47.

29. Benedum interview, 188.

30. G. D. Harris, *Oil and Gas in Louisiana with a Brief Summary of Their Occurrences in Adjacent States* (Washington, DC: Government Printing Office, 1910), 136.

31. Harris, *Oil and Gas in Louisiana*, 136.

32. Hair, "Plundered Legacy," 180.

33. Mallison, *The Great Wildcatter*, 190.

34. "Huge oil gusher at Mooringsport, La. A monstrous column of roaring flame, Star Oil Co. Loucke no. 3, on fire since Aug. 7," *Louisiana Mooringsport*, c. 1913, photograph, https://www.loc.gov/item/97514401.

35. "U.S. Crude Oil First Purchase Price," *U.S. Energy Information Administration*, https://www.eia.gov/dnav/pet/hist/LeafHandler.ashx?n=pet&s=f000000__3&f=a.

36. "Huge oil gusher at Mooringsport, La."

37. R. C. Linderman, "Fearful Fight with Oil Fire," *Technical World Magazine* 16, no. 4 (December 1911): 410–411.

38. Linderman, "Fearful Fight with Oil Fire," 411.

39. "Harrell No. 7 Well Put Vivian on Map," *Caddo Citizen*, July 3, 1975, 2-C.

40. Franks and Lambert, *Early Arkansas and Louisiana Oil*, 40.

41. *Report of the Louisiana Conservation Commission of 1910* (New Orleans: Louisiana Commission for the Conservation of Natural Resources, 1910), 18.

42. *Report of the Louisiana Conservation Commission of 1910*, 37.

43. Hair, "Plundered Legacy," 180.

44. Dianne M. Lindstedt, Lori L. Nunn, Joseph C. Holmes Jr., and Elizabeth E. Willis, *History of Oil and Gas Development in Coastal Louisiana* (Baton Rouge: Louisiana Geological Survey, 1991), 17.

45. Oil City locals alternatively recalled the sky as either burning red or orange.

46. Carl W. Jones, interview by Hubert Humphreys, September 21, 1977, no. 9, p. 8, Louisiana State University-Shreveport Oral History Program.

47. George interview.

48. Tonja Koob Marking and Jennifer Snape, *Louisiana's Oil Heritage* (Charleston, SC: Arcadia, 2012), 39.

49. Brian Black, *Petrolia: The Landscape of America's First Oil Boom* (Baltimore: Johns Hopkins University Press, 2000), 174–180.

50. *Report of the Louisiana Conservation Commission of 1910*, 3, 8.

51. *Report of Conservation Commission of Louisiana, 1912–1914* (New Orleans: Louisiana Commission for the Conservation of Natural Resources, 1914), 5, 29.

52. *Report of the Louisiana Conservation Commission of 1910–12* (New Orleans: Louisiana Commission for the Conservation of Natural Resources, 1912), 3.

53. *Report of the Louisiana Conservation Commission of 1910–12*, 5.

54. Lindstedt et al., *History of Oil and Gas Development in Coastal Louisiana*, 18.

55. Carl E. Morris, interview by Chuck Smith, 1999, Louisiana State Oil and Gas Museum.

56. Claudia Clawson, "Indians Thought Bubbly Gas Good for Medicinal Purposes," *Caddo Citizen*, July 3, 1975, 4-C.

57. Franks and Lambert, *Early Arkansas and Louisiana Oil*, 37.

58. J. L. Wilson, "The Pearl Hogs," *Shreveport Times*, February 27, 1977; Margaret Pace Weaver Bateman, interview by Chuck Smith, 1999, Louisiana State Oil and Gas Museum.

59. Wilson, "The Pearl Hogs."

60. Eric Brock, *Eric Brock's Shreveport* (Gretna, LA: Pelican, 2001), 79–81.

61. C. Lane Sartor, "Early History of the Caddo-Pine Island Field," *Oil Industry History* 4, no. 1 (2003): 7; Caddo Parish Levee Board Minutes, November 1, 1910, Louisiana State University-Shreveport.

62. Franks and Lambert, *Early Arkansas and Louisiana Oil*, 41; Brock, *Eric Brock's Shreveport*, 80. Brock lists the initial bonus as $35,000, while Franks and Lambert put the figure at $30,000.

63. Franks and Lambert, *Early Arkansas and Louisiana Oil*, 41; Judith L. Sneed, "The First Over Water Drilling: The Lost History of Ohio's Grand Reservoir Oil Boom," *Oil Industry History* 6, no. 1 (2005): 50.

64. Franks and Lambert, *Early Arkansas and Louisiana Oil*, 41.

65. Brock, *Eric Brock's Shreveport*, 80.

66. Franks and Lambert, *Early Arkansas and Louisiana Oil*, 41.

67. Brock, *Eric Brock's Shreveport*, 80.

68. Brock, *Eric Brock's Shreveport*, 81; State v. Standard Oil Co., 164 La. 334, 113 So. 867 (1927).

69. Sneed, "The First Over Water Drilling," 50.

70. Hopper, "The Caddo Oil- and Gas-Field, Louisiana," 308.

71. Cleo Norris, interview by Chuck Smith, 1999, Louisiana State Oil and Gas Museum.

72. George interview.

73. Norris interview.

74. *Report of the Conservation Commission of Louisiana* (New Orleans: Louisiana Commission for the Conservation of Natural Resources, 1916), 75.

75. *Report of the Conservation Commission of Louisiana*, 75.

76. W. Scott Wilkinson, interview by Hubert Humphreys, October 26, 1976, p. 1, Louisiana State University-Shreveport Oral History Program.

77. W. B. Fulton, "Down the Trail of Evangeline," *The Lamp* 20 (April 1938): 22, Briscoe Center for American History, Exxon-Mobil Collection, University of Texas at Austin.

78. John Loos, *Oil on Stream! A History of Interstate Oil Pipe Line Company, 1909–1959* (Baton Rouge: Louisiana State University Press, 1959), 8.

79. Loos, *Oil on Stream!* 8.

80. Smith W. Day, interview by John Loos, 1957, p. 146, John Loos Materials, Louisiana State University.

81. Dale Benroth, interview by John Loos, 1957, p. 3, John Loos Materials, Louisiana State University.

82. Day interview, 146.

83. Fred Bimel, interview by John Loos, 1957, p. 81, John Loos Materials, Louisiana State University.

84. Loos, *Oil on Stream!* 9, 16.

85. Day interview, 151–152.

86. Loos, *Oil on Stream!* 17.

87. C. K. Clarke, "Pipe Lines in the South," *The Lamp* (January 1919): 22, Briscoe Center for American History, Exxon-Mobil Collection, University of Texas at Austin.

88. Loos, *Oil on Stream!* 9, 41.

89. Clarke, "Pipe Lines in the South," 9; Loos, *Oil on Stream!* 40.

90. Mary Barrett, "Post-World War I Overproduction and Crude Oil Loss, Caddo-Pine Island Field, LA," *Oil Industry History* 2, no. 1 (2001): 10.

91. Barrett, "Post-World War I Overproduction," 11.

92. "Railroad Commission Adopts Recommendation Regarding Conditions in Pine Island," *Shreveport Times*, March 26, 1919.

93. Brady M. Banta, "The Pine Island Situation: Petroleum, Politics, and Research Opportunities in Southern History," *Journal of Southern History* 52, no. 4 (November 1986): 592–594.

94. Barrett, "Post-World War I Overproduction," 12.

95. Barrett, "Post-World War I Overproduction," 11–12.

96. Barrett, "Post-World War I Overproduction," 13.

97. "U.S. Inspector Amazed by Oil Waste in Caddo," *Shreveport Times*, April 9, 1919.

98. "Says Danger of Fire Grave in Pine Island," *Shreveport Times*, March 29, 1919.

99. "Says Danger of Fire Grave in Pine Island."

100. Barrett, "Post-World War I Overproduction," 12–13.

101. Banta, "The Pine Island Situation," 596.

102. Richard White, *Kingfish: The Reign of Huey P. Long* (New York: Random House, 2006), 47–48; Banta, "The Pine Island Situation," 596.

103. "Railroad Commission Adopts Recommendation."
104. Barrett, "Post-World War I Overproduction," 15.
105. Barrett, "Post-World War I Overproduction," 12.
106. Black, *Petrolia*, 74.

CHAPTER 7: THE CITY

1. "Louisiana Industries Will Make a Fine Census Show," *Daily Picayune*, November 22, 1900.
2. Andrew Needham describes a similar dynamic of urban centers benefiting from energy production while obscuring their environmental costs in the twentieth-century American Southwest: Needham, *Power Lines: Phoenix and the Making of the Modern Southwest* (Princeton, NJ: Princeton University Press, 2014).
3. Maude Hearn-O'Pry, *Chronicles of Shreveport and Caddo Parish* (Shreveport, LA: Journal Printing Company, 1928), 5, 8.
4. Hearn-O'Pry, *Chronicles of Shreveport and Caddo Parish*, 8.
5. Walter Johnson, *River of Dark Dreams: Slavery and Empire in the Cotton Kingdom* (Cambridge, MA: Belknap/Harvard University Press, 2013), 3–8.
6. "Henry Miller Shreve," http://www.pbs.org/wgbh/theymadeamerica/whomade/shreve_hi.html.
7. Hearn-O'Pry, *Chronicles of Shreveport and Caddo Parish*, 8.
8. Eric J. Brock, "Shreveport: A Brief History," City of Shreveport, Louisiana, https://web.archive.org/web/20090608103601/http://www.ci.shreveport.la.us/history.htm.
9. Hearn-O'Pry, *Chronicles of Shreveport and Caddo Parish*, 129–130.
10. C. Vann Woodward, *Origins of the New South, 1877–1913* (Baton Rouge: Louisiana State University Press, 1951), 186.
11. Hearn-O'Pry, *Chronicles of Shreveport and Caddo Parish*, 139–140.
12. "Louisiana Industries Will Make a Fine Census Show."
13. Marguerite R. Plummer and Gary D. Joiner, *Historic Shreveport-Bossier: An Illustrated History of Shreveport and Bossier City* (San Antonio: Historical Publishing Network, 2000), 53.
14. Lane Sartor, "Oil and Gas in the Ark-LA-Tex: Its Influence on Shreveport's Development," speech to Leadership Shreveport, 1987.
15. Frank Hood Goldsberry Jr., interview by Chuck Smith, 1999, Louisiana State Oil and Gas Museum.
16. Walter E. Hopper, "The Caddo Oil- and Gas-Field, Louisiana," *Bulletin of the American Institute of Mining Engineers* no. 49–54 (1911): 298, 294.
17. Sam Thomas Mallison, *The Great Wildcatter* (Charleston, WV: Education Foundation of West Virginia, 1953), 198.
18. Walter Duvall George Jr., interview by Chuck Smith, 1999, Louisiana State Oil and Gas Museum.
19. "Tells Wonders of Oil Fields in Louisiana," *Bisbee Daily Review*, March 7, 1920, 6.

20. "Big Fortunes in LA Oil Leases" [advertisement], *Bisbee Daily Review*, November 16, 1919.

21. "Big Fortunes in LA Oil Leases."

22. *Shreveport Journal*, April 4, 1911.

23. R. C. Linderman, "Fearful Fight with Oil Fire," *Technical World Magazine* 16, no. 4 (December 1911): 410.

24. *Shreveport Journal*, April 7, 1911.

25. Cleo Norris, interview by Chuck Smith, 1999, Louisiana State Oil and Gas Museum.

26. "Caddo Oil Shipments," *Atlanta News* 8, no. 35 (April 16, 1908).

27. James Muslow, interview by Chuck Smith, 1999, Louisiana State Oil and Gas Museum.

28. Shreveport, Louisiana, City Directory (1921), U.S. City Directories, 1822–1995, Ancestry.com.

29. Muslow interview.

30. World War I Registration Cards, 1917–1918, Shreveport, Caddo County, Louisiana, Draft Card S, roll 1685021, Ancestry.com.

31. Shreveport, Louisiana, City Directory (1921), 98.

32. 1940 US Census, Shreveport, Caddo, Louisiana, Enumeration District 9–70, roll T627_1388, p. 4A, Ancestry.com.

33. *Passenger Lists of Vessels Arriving at Honolulu, Hawaii, Compiled 02/13/1900–12/30/1953*, National Archives Microfilm Publication A3422, roll 268, Record Group 85, Records of the Immigration and Naturalization Service, 1787–2004, National Archives and Records Administration (NARA).

34. 1920 US Census, Shreveport, Caddo, Louisiana, Precinct 6, Enumeration District 32, roll T625_608, p. 3B, Image 468, Ancestry.com.

35. 1920 US Census, Shreveport, Caddo, Louisiana, Precinct 6, Enumeration District 52, roll T625_608, p. 3B, Image 468, Ancestry.com.

36. 1930 US Census, Shreveport, Caddo, Louisiana, Enumeration District 0040, roll 787, p. 21A, Image 416.0, FHL microfilm 2340522, Ancestry.com.

37. 1940 US Census, Shreveport, Caddo, Louisiana, Enumeration District 9–23, roll T627_1386, p. 11B, Ancestry.com.

38. 1930 US Census, Shreveport, Caddo, Louisiana, Enumeration District 0055, roll 787, p. 8B, Image 884.0, FHL microfilm 2340522, Ancestry.com.

39. 1920 US Census, Shreveport, Caddo, Louisiana, Precinct 6, Enumeration District 52, roll T625_608, p. 3B, Image 468, Ancestry.com; 1930 US Census, Shreveport, Caddo, Louisiana, Enumeration District 0040, roll 787, p. 21A, Image 416.0, FHL microfilm 2340522, Ancestry.com.

40. 1920 US Census, Shreveport, Caddo, Louisiana, Precinct 8, Enumeration District 59, roll T625_608, p. 8B, Ancestry.com.

41. "A Finding Aid to the Shreveport, Louisiana—Congregation B'nai Zion Records, Manuscript Collection No. 651," Jacob Rader Marcus Center of the American Jewish Archives, http://collections.americanjewisharchives.org/ms/ms0651/ms0651.html.

42. W.P.A. Louisiana Historical Records Survey Louisiana Police Jury Minutes Transcriptions, June 12, 1913, mss. 2984, Louisiana and Lower Mississippi Valley Collections, vol. 10B, reel #71, LSU Libraries, Baton Rouge.

43. W. H. Griffin, interview by Goodloe Stuck, June 31, 1973, Goodloe Stuck Papers, box 14, folder 129, p. 4, Louisiana State University-Shreveport.

44. Willie Burton, *The Blacker the Berry: A Black History of Shreveport* (Shreveport, LA: The Times, 2002), 30, 36–40, 143.

45. Burton, *The Blacker the Berry*, 32, 30; Plummer and Joiner, *Historic Shreveport-Bossier*, 53; William D. Reeves, *Historic Louisiana: An Illustrated History* (Historical Publishing Network, 2003), 59.

46. Burton, *The Blacker the Berry*, 34.

47. Burton, *The Blacker the Berry*, 27.

48. "When Prostitution Was Legal," *Shreveport Journal*, December 31, 1976, Goodloe Stuck Collection, folder 127, Louisiana State University-Shreveport; Goodloe Stuck, *Annie McCune: Shreveport Madam* (Baton Rouge: Moran Publishing Corporation, 1981), 10.

49. Stuck, *Annie McCune*, 3, 85.

50. Rev. James Austin, interview by Goodloe Stuck, April 29, 1976, Goodloe Stuck Papers, box 14, folder 129, p. 2, Louisiana State University-Shreveport; Loulie [Louie?] McCarty, interview by Goodloe Stuck, May 3, 1976, Goodloe Stuck Papers, box 14, folder 129, p. 1, Louisiana State University-Shreveport.

51. Lead Belly, "Fannin Street," https://genius.com/Lead-belly-fannin-street-lyrics.

52. Charles Wolfe and Kip Lornell, *The Life and Legend of Leadbelly* (Boston: Da Capo Press, 1999), 28; Jim Montgomery, "Leadbelly, and a Lively Era," *Shreveport Times*, June 8, 1980.

53. Stuck, *Annie McCune*, 59.

54. S. J. Yealock, interview by Goodloe Stuck, December 31, 1975, Goodloe Stuck Papers, box 14, folder 129, p. 14, Louisiana State University-Shreveport.

55. Alex Rice, interview by Goodloe Stuck, June 24, 1973, Goodloe Stuck Papers, box 14, folder 129, p. 1, Louisiana State University-Shreveport.

56. D. R. Beamer, interview by Goodloe Stuck, February, 1976, Goodloe Stuck Papers, box 14, folder 129, p. 4, Louisiana State University-Shreveport.

57. Willis Butler, interview by Goodloe Stuck, Fall, 1972, Goodloe Stuck Papers, box 14, folder 129, p. 14, Louisiana State University-Shreveport.

58. Butler interview, 14.

59. Red-light District Materials, Goodloe Stuck Papers, folder 126, Louisiana State University-Shreveport.

60. Annie McCune's will, court cases, notes, Goodloe Stuck Papers, folder 125, Louisiana State University-Shreveport.

61. Ray Oden, interview by Goodloe Stuck, February, 1975, Goodloe Stuck Papers, box 14, folder 129 [no pagination], Louisiana State University-Shreveport.

62. Stuck, *Annie McCune*, 91, 89.

63. Stuck, *Annie McCune*, 88.

64. "U.S. Soldiers and Boys Take St. Paul's Bottom Saturday Night, Is Report of Survey," *Shreveport Times*, November 4, 1917.

65. Stuck, *Annie McCune*, 97, 99.

66. W.P.A. Louisiana Historical Records Survey Louisiana Police Jury Minutes Transcriptions, March 13, 1913, mss. 2984, vol. 10B, reel #71, LSU Libraries, Baton Rouge.

67. Mary Barrett, "Post-World War I Overproduction and Crude Oil Loss, Caddo-Pine Island Field, LA," *Oil Industry History* 2, no. 1 (2001): 13.

68. W.P.A. Louisiana Historical Records Survey Louisiana Police Jury Minutes Transcriptions, June 12, 1919, mss. 2984, Louisiana and Lower Mississippi Valley Collections, vol. 12, reel #73, LSU Libraries, Baton Rouge.

69. George interview.

EPILOGUE: THE BUST

1. Carrie Duncan Slee, "History of Trees," pp. 1–4, Trees City Vertical File, Louisiana State University-Shreveport.

2. Slee, "History of Trees," 1–4.

3. Slee, "History of Trees," 4.

4. Daniel Yergin, *The Prize: The Epic Quest for Oil, Money, and Power* (New York: Free Press, 2009), 223, 250.

5. Stanley J. Clark, *The Oil Century: From the Drake Well to the Conservation Era* (Norman: University of Oklahoma Press, 1958), 177–178.

6. Terence Daintith, *Finders Keepers? How the Law of Capture Shaped the World Oil Industry* (Washington, DC: Routledge, 2010), 8.

7. Daintith, *Finders Keepers?* 247, 257.

8. "U.S. Crude Oil First Purchase Price," U.S Energy Information Administration, https://www.eia.gov/dnav/pet/hist/LeafHandler.ashx?n=pet&s=f000000_ _3&f=a.

9. Yergin, *The Prize*, 111, 223.

10. Yergin, *The Prize*, 249–250.

11. Yergin, *The Prize*, 250, 251; Julia Cauble Smith, "East Texas Oilfield," The Handbook of Texas, https://tshaonline.org/handbook/online/articles/doc01.

12. Yergin, *The Prize*, 250, 254.

13. 1930 US Census, Caddo Parish, Louisiana, Jury Ward 2, Enumeration District 0006, roll 786, p. 23A, Images 299.0, 300.0, and 301.0, FHL microfilm 2340521, Ancestry.com.

14. W. J. "Bill" Snead, interview by Chuck Smith, 1999, Louisiana State Oil and Gas Museum.

15. George Sweet Gibb and Evelyn H. Knowlton, *The Resurgent Years 1911–1927: History of Standard Oil Company (New Jersey)* (New York: Harper, 1956), 410, 414.

16. "An Entente Cordial," *The Lamp* (January 1919): 12, Briscoe Center for American History, Exxon-Mobil Collection, University of Texas at Austin.

17. Cleo Norris, interview by Chuck Smith, 1999, Louisiana State Oil and Gas Museum.

18. Walter Duvall George Jr., interview by Chuck Smith, 1999, Louisiana State Oil and Gas Museum.

19. 1930 US Census, Shreveport, Caddo, Louisiana, Enumeration District 0045, roll 787, p. 16A, Image 603.0, FHL microfilm 2340522, Ancestry.com; 1940 US Census, Shreveport, Caddo, Louisiana, Enumeration District 9–65, roll T627_1388, p. 4B, Ancestry.com.

20. James Muslow, interview by Chuck Smith, 1999, Louisiana State Oil and Gas Museum.

21. Harry Blackburn Hill and R. K. Guthrie, *Engineering Study of the Rodessa Oil Field in Louisiana, Texas, and Arkansas* (Washington, DC: US Bureau of Mines, 1943), 9, online at University of North Texas Digital Libraries, digital.library.unt .edu/ark:/67531/metadc38414.

22. Bryant, "Well Discovered in 1935 Ignited Rodessa Boom," *Caddo Citizen*.

23. Keenan Gingles, "Trees Losing Post Office," *Times of Shreveport*, September 30, 1983.

24. Trees City appears as "Trees, Louisiana" on contemporary maps.

25. Lane Sartor, "Oil and Gas in the Ark-LA-Tex and Its Influence on Shreveport's Development," speech to Leadership Shreveport, 1987.

26. Debra Kay McGinnis-Helton, "The Impact of the Oil Boom on Caddo Parish Louisiana, 1900–1939" (master's thesis, Louisiana Tech University, 1999), 63.

27. Robert Stacey, interview by Autumn Grant, November 11, 2001, Natchitoches, Louisiana, p. 1, Oral History Collection, Louisiana State University-Shreveport.

28. 1930 US Census, Shreveport, Caddo, Louisiana, Enumeration District 0052, roll 787, p. 9B, Image 814.0, FHL microfilm 2340522, Ancestry.com.

29. "Mr. Murphy" interview by John Loos, 1957, p. 3, John Loos Materials, Louisiana State University.

30. "Deputy Found Guilty," *News Scimitar*, July 9, 1920, 3.

31. *Oil City and Some Antidotes from Roughnecks*, Louisiana State University Special Collection, p. 1, Noel Memorial Library, Louisiana State University-Shreveport.

32. Author interview with Charlie Spikes, February 5, 2015.

33. Author interview with Mark Tyson, September 13, 2015.

INDEX

Page numbers in italics denote images.

Abramson, Louis David, 126–127
agriculture. *See* farmers/farming
"Alboleum," 9
Allen, Angeline, 79
Allen, W. C. "Dub," 139–140
Anderson, Bob, 44, 71–72
antebellum plantation economy, 57
anti-trust legislation, ix, 7
Atchafalaya River (Louisiana), 9
"The Avenue" (Shreveport), 127, 128–129
Aycock, Elmer, 64

Bailey, Senator Joseph, 7
Barnett, J. B., 68
Barrett and Files, law firm of, 87, 89–90
Beamer, D. R., 27, 28, 45
Bell, Annie, 43
Bell, William Thomas, 43
Benedum and Trees: "Bloody Caddo,"
    in, 63; financial success(es) of, 49–53;
    Oil City violence, 25; Stacy's
    Landing, 21–22; Standard Oil,
    transactions with, 51–52; Stiles'
    leased property, drilling on, 20–21,
    49, 50–51, 97–98; Trees City, LA, 31
Benedum, Mike, 21. *See also* Benedum
    and Trees
Benroth, Dale, 111

Bimel, Fred, 69–70
Black community: Caddo Parish, in,
    xiv–xv; "Jim Crow" segregation,
    8, 62, 73; music and songs of,
    70–71; Oil City, LA, in, 143; oil
    millionaires, 75; Shreveport, LA,
    in, 110, 127–128; violence against.
    See also Black workers; racial violence
Black workers, 60–63; Claiborne
    Parish, in, 55; emancipated labor,
    57–60; enslaved labor, 57; pipelines,
    on, 68–71; sex workers, 71–73.
    See also sex trade/workers
Blanchard, Goldstein and Walker, law
    firm of, 78
"Bloody Caddo," xiv–xv, 55–56, 145;
    courts of, 75–91; oil fields of, 60–68;
    reform efforts, 61–62. *See also* court
    cases
"blowouts," 98–103
Bootlegging: Douglas Island, on, 96;
    Reno Hill (Oil City), in, 27–28
"Bourbon" Democratic politics, 7–8
Bridgeman, Thornton, 76–77, 81
"bust" of boomtowns: price of oil,
    collapse of, 136–139; slow decline,
    139–142; Trees City, LA, 135–136, 138
Butler, Dr. Willis P., 26, 56, 64

Caddo Lake ("Ferry Lake") over-water well, 105–110
Caddo Levee Board, 50, 105–106
Caddo Parish: Black community in, xiv–xv. *See also* "Bloody Caddo"
Caddo Parish Police Jury, 132
Caracristi, C. F. Z., 6
Christian revivalism, xiii, 30–31
Claiborne Parish: Black investors in, 127; Black millionaires in, 86; Black workers in, 55; emerging "boomtowns" in, xii, 79–80; Isom McGee, lynching of, 76–77; litigation concerning the oil fields in, 123; migration to and out-migration from, 138; "Nail Place," 77, 78, 79–80; sex trade/workers in, 129. *See also* Homer, LA; *Lillie G. Taylor v. George West*
Clark and Greer Drilling Company, 87–90
Clement, Jules, 4, 15–16, 50
Conservation Commission: Frank M. Kerr, representative on, 99; regulation attempts, 103–105; salt-water problem, efforts to eradicate, 108–109
court cases: *D. H. Raines and Joe Herndon v. C. E. Dunson*, 87–91; *Holman v. Gulf Refining Company of Louisiana*, 83–86. *See also Lillie G. Taylor v. George West*
"cracking" methods, 137
Crump, John, 68

Davidson, Harry, 96
Day, Smith W., 111–112
Day, Tunnell, 96, 97
Democratic politics: "Bourbon," 7–8; Texas (late 19th century), 6–7
D. H. Raines and Joe Herndon v. C. E. Dunson, 87–91
Douglas Island (Caddo Parish), 96–97

Douglas, J. Stuart, 66
Dowling, Oscar, 96
drilling: "blowouts," 98–103; "cementing" method of, 98; North Louisiana landscape, in, 97–103; over the water, 105–110
drinking water, 96
Dunman, Jim Douglas, 40–41
Dunn, Frank, 61
Dunson, C. E, D. H. Raines and Joe Herndon v., 87–91
Dunson, William H. "Pete," 63–65

economic creations, oil-field communities as, 17–18
El Dorado, Arkansas, xv, 39, 41–42, 138

farmers/farming: Jennings, LA, in, 11–13; oil "boom" as an economic lifeline for, 11–12, 35, 36–41; Oil City, LA, in, 36–41
Federal Fuel Administration, 113
Ferguson, Texas Governor Miriam "Ma," 138
Finnegan, James W., 111–112
Flournoy, Sheriff James Patteson, 28
Foster, John Gray, 59–60
Foster, Looney and Wilkinson, law firm of, 77–78, 80, 83–85
Fuqua, Louisiana Governor Henry, 66

George, Martha "Effie," 66–67
George, Walter Duvall Jr., xi, 25, 66, 93, 102, 108
George, Walter Duvall Sr., xi, xiv, 36, 66, 93, 139
George, Will, 26
Glenn, Francis Scott, 80
Godber, Frederick, 137
"Great Raft," 57, 120–121
Gregory, Roy A., 39–40
Griffin, W. H., 71, 72

Grigsby, Eliza, 76
Gulf Refining Company, 50, 77, 80,
 83–85, 105–106, *107*, 107

Hackberry, Texas, 41, 138
Haire, Hardy, 101
Halliburton, Erle P., 98
Hammett, Jesse, 66–68
Hampton, Wade, 94, 113
Hanner, A. B., 25
Harrell No. 7 well, 100–101, *100*,
 102, 125
Hartman, Florence, 22, 29
Herndon, Joe, 76. *See also* Herndon-
 Raines family
Herndon-Raines family, 86–87, 143;
 *D. H. Raines and Joe Herndon v. C. E.
 Dunson*, 87–91
Heywood, W. S. (Walter Scott), 3, 4, 13
Hickey, Thomas, 27
Hoag, J. M., 15
Hogg-Swayne oil syndicate, 7
Hogg, Texas Governor Jim, 6–7
Holladay, Thomas Jefferson, 30
*Holman v. Gulf Refining Company of
 Louisiana*, 83–86
Holman, Y. Allen, 78, 83–85
Homer, LA: "bust" of boomtown of,
 109; center of oil production, as the,
 138; as a growing "boomtown," 109;
 killing of William H. "Pete" Dunson
 in, 63–64; Klu Klux Klan in, 65;
 lynching of Isom McGee, Jr., 76–77;
 migrants to, xii, 41; racial violence
 in, 60, 65; sex trade/workers in, 129.
 *See also Lillie G. Taylor v. George
 West*
Hopper, Walter E., 19, 95
Hosston, LA, xii
"houses of ill repute." *See* sex trade/
 workers
Howard, Charles, 119, 122
Hughes, Howard, Jr., 26
Hughes, Howard R., Sr., 26

Hughes, R. J., 97
Hughes, Tom, 47
Humble Oil and Refining Company, 46
hydrology. *See* landscape of North
 Louisiana

Ida, LA, xii, 140
Independent Oil Producers' Association
 of North Louisiana, 115–116
Industrial Workers of the World
 (IWW), 46
International Brotherhood of Oil and
 Gas Well Workers, 45

Jackson, Dorothy, 28
Jaenke, F. R., 3
Jeem's Bayou (Caddo Parish), 21,
 30, 51
Jefferson, "Blind Lemon," 70
"The Jennings Gusher Fire," *10*,
 10–11
Jennings, LA, 3–6; end of oil "boom"
 in, 13–16; farming in, 11–13; "mad
 dog" epidemic in, 15; oil "boom" in,
 3–4; people of, 11–13; pipelines for,
 9–10; promotional pamphlets for,
 14–15; "Rule of Capture" doctrine
 in, 6, 16; violence in, *5*, 13–14
Jennings Oil Company, 3–4
Jester, Nell, 130
"Jim Crow" segregation, 8, 62, 73
J. M. Guffey Petroleum Company,
 45, 105
Jones, Carl W., 37, 41

Kansas City Southern Railway, xi,
 18–19, 21–22, *24*, 26, 41, 51, 103,
 125–126, 129
Ku Klux Klan, 65–66

labor unions, 45–49
Land Avenue (Oil City), 22–25; fires
 in, 22–25; living quarters/standards
 in, 22

landscape of North Louisiana, 93; Conservation Commission's attempts at regulating, 103–105; historical power of, 117; natural landscape, 93–97. *See also* drilling
Lane, C. W., 83–85
Lantz, John, 95
Law, John F., 20, 26, 66, 96
"Law of Capture." *See* "Rule of Capture" doctrine
Layne, R. T., 87–91
Ledbetter, Huddie "Lead Belly," 128–129
Lillie G. Taylor v. George West, 77–80; winners of, 82–86
Lomax, John A., 70
Long, Huey Pierce, 66, 113
Looney, Frank J., 85
lynching(s), 56, 58–60; Isom McGee, Jr., of, 76–77; Jesse Hammet, of, 66–68. *See also Lillie G. Taylor v. George West*; racial violence

Mahaffey, Thomas Clayton "T.C.," 3
Marks, Mary "Baby Jane," 72
Matheny, B. G., 142–143
Matthews, Henry, 78
McCann, J. B., 105
McCarty, Louilie, 128
McCune, Annie, 130
McDonald, H. A., 64
McFarland, Claude, 20, 31
McGee, Isom, Jr., 60; lynching of, 76–77; "Nail Place" and, 81, 85. *See also Lillie G. Taylor v. George West*
McGee, Isom, Sr., 76, 80
McGee, Lona (Norton), 76–81, 85
McGee, Mattie, 77, 79
McGee, Sarah (Manning), 76, 80
McLand, F. D., 59
migrants, 35; Claiborne Parish, to and from, 138; Homer, LA, to, xii, 41; Mooringsport, LA, to (from Oil City), 29–30; Oil City, LA, to, 35, 36–43; Shreveport, LA, to, 125–127

Mikoff, Theodore, 42
Moore, Noah, 70–71
Moore, Tom, 22, 25–28, 40
Mooringsport, LA: migration from Oil City to, 29–30; Oil City, compared, xiii, 29–30, 33; religion in, 30; Star Oil "blowout" in, 99–100; Trees City, compared, 33
Moran, Patrick, 42
Morrical, Dr. Frank H., 18
Morris, Carl, 104–105
Murata, Sachihiko Ono, 105
music of the Black community, 70–71
Muslow, Isaac "Ike," 42–43, 125–126

"Nail Place" (Homer), 77, 78, 79–80. *See also Lillie G. Taylor v. George West*
Noel, John S., 19–20
Norman Hotel (Oil City), 42, 43–44
Norman, Ida, 20
Norman, James K., 20
Norris, Cleo, 36, 108, 125, 139
Norton, Dick, 141–142

Oil City and Some Antidotes [sic] from Roughnecks (Matheny), 142–143
Oil City, LA, xiii, 17–18; birth of, xii, 18–20; Black community in, 143; decline of, 139–141; Depression-era, 139; economic opportunity in, 36–41; enduring fascination with, xv, 142–144; "escaping," 29–31; farmers/farming in, 36–41; living quarters/standards in, 20–22, 144–145; men of, 42–43; migrants to, 35, 36–43; Mooringsport, compared, xiii, 29–30, 33; Norman Hotel, 42, 43–44; people of, 35–53; racial violence in, 56; religion in, 30; Shreveport, LA, compared, 120, 144; Trees City, compared, 33; violence in, 25–26; who made, 144–145; winners of the "new economy" in,

49–53; women of, 43–45. *See also*
"Bloody Caddo"; Land Avenue
(Oil City); Reno Hill (Oil City)
Oil Workers International Union
(OWIU), 46
"Oklahoma Mamie," 45
"Old Fanny Edwards," 97
"Old Henry Lowry," 70
organized labor, 45–49

Parker, Louisiana Governor John M.,
65–66
Pine Island, LA: environmental
destruction of, *109*; landscape of, 94;
post-WWI disaster, 112–117, 132
Pine Island Mercantile, 43, 125
pipelines: Black workers on, 68–71; first
pipeline, 9; Jennings, LA, for, 9–10;
Standard Oil, of, *69*, 111–112;
swamps, through the, 110–112
Pixley, Burt, 64
"Police Juries," 9; Caddo Parish Police
Jury, 132
politics: oil-field communities as
political creations, 17–18. *See also*
Democratic politics
postbellum plantation economy, 57–60
potable water, 96
price of oil, collapse of, 136–139
Producer's Oil Company, 50, 100
prostitution. *See* sex trade/workers

racial segregation, 8, 62, 73
racial violence: Homer, LA, in, 60; Ku
Klux Klan, 65–66; Oil City, LA, in,
56; Reconstruction-era Louisiana, in,
58–60. *See also* "Bloody Caddo";
lynching(s)
Raines, David H., 76. *See also*
Herndon-Raines family
Randolph, Charles "Dub," 101
Reavis, Holland S., 11
Reconstruction-era Louisiana, 58–60
"Red Headed Madge," 97

religion: Christian revivalism, xiii,
30–31; Mooringsport, LA, in, 30;
Oil City, LA, in, 30; Trees City,
LA, in, 30–31
"Reno Hill" (Oil City), 26–29;
bootlegging in, 27–28; decline of,
139; eradication of, 48–49; sex trade/
workers in, 27, 28–29
Reynolds, T. A., 64, 65
Rice, Alex, 44
Rodessa, LA, 41, 136, 140–142
Roosevelt, President Franklin Delano,
138
Roosevelt, President Theodore, 51–52,
103
"Rule of Capture" doctrine, 2, 5; falling
oil prices and, 136; Jennings, LA, in, 6,
16; offset wells around Stiles property,
50; Pine Island producers, 114

Sabine Uplift, 94
"St. Paul's Bottoms" district
(Shreveport), 127, 128–129, 131
Sanders, Louisiana Governor Jared Y.,
103
S.A. Spencer Company, 3
Savage (J. S. and W. A.) brothers, xi,
18–19
Savage-Morrical No. 1, xi–xvi, *xii*, 19
segregation, 8, 62, 73
sex trade/workers: Black sex workers,
71–73; Claiborne Parish, in, 129;
Douglas Island, on, 97; Homer, LA,
in, 129; Oil City, LA, in, 44–45;
Reno Hill (Oil City), in, 27, 28–29;
Shreveport, LA, in, 72, 128–131
Shannon, Tom, 63–64, 142
Shreve, Captain Henry Miller, 121–122
Shreveport, LA, 119–120; Black
community in, 110, 127–128;
"boomtown" of, 131–133; continuing
economic success of, 110, 140–142, 143;
creating "the city" of, 131–133; "district
exploration offices" in, 122–125;

Shreveport, LA, (*continued*)
"Great Raft," 120–121; migrants to, 125–127; Oil City, LA, compared, 120, 144; people of, 125–128; post-oil "boom" economy of, 122–125; pre-oil economy of, 120–123; "St. Paul's Bottoms" district, 127, 128–129, 131; sex trade in, 72, 128–131. *See also Lillie G. Taylor v. George West*
Sibley, John, 120
Sklar, Sam, 126
Slee, Carrie Duncan, 135–136
Smith, Frank "Prophet," 59
Snead, Mike, 41
Snead, W. J. "Bill," 95
Sneed, Sebrone "Sebe," 38
social creations, oil-field communities as, 17–18
songs of the Black community, 70–71
Sour Lake, TX, 18, 41, 138
Southern Pacific Railroad, 5, 121
Spencer, S. A., 3
Spikes, Charlie, 30–31, 143
Spindletop oil field (Texas), 1–3
Stacey, Robert, Jr., 141
Stacey, Robert, Sr., 141
"Stacy's Landing" (Caddo Parish), 21–22
Standard Oil, ix; Benedum and Trees, transactions with, 51–52; monopolistic, as, 7, 9; Pine Island, on, 116; pipeline construction, 69, 111–112; worker deaths, 68; workers' injuries, compensation for, 39
Star Oil "blowout," 99–100
Sterling, Texas Governor Ross, 137
Stiles, William Pierce (W. P.), 20–21, 32–33; financial success of, 49–50, 52, 53; leased property, drilling on, 20–21, 49, 50–51, 97–98
Strickland, Odessa, 127

Taylor, Albert, 77
Taylor, Lillie "Gussie," 60; "first negro princess," white reactions to America's, 80–82
Taylor, Pinckney "Pink," 26–28
Texas Fuel Company (later "Texaco"), 7
topography. *See* landscape of North Louisiana
transporting petroleum: barging routes, 9. *See also* pipelines
Trees City, LA, 31–33; decline of, 135–136, 138, 140; Mooringsport, compared, 33; Oil City, compared, 33; religion in, 30–31
Trees, Joe, 21, 25, 49, 97–98, 123. *See also* Benedum and Trees

unionism, 45–49
Universal Oil, Gas and Mining Company, 127

violence: Jennings, LA, in, 5, 13–14; Oil City, LA, in, 25–26. *See also* racial violence
Vivian, LA, xii, 30, 37, 46, 65–67, 100, *100*

Wagy, Earl W., 115
Washington-Youree Hotel (Shreveport), 72
Waters-Pierce, 7
Weber, Lois, 97
West, George. *See Lillie G. Taylor v. George West*
Whitaker, W. O., 94, 113
White League, 58
white supremacy, 8–9; Ku Klux Klan, 65–66. *See also* racial violence
Wilkins, Avery, 3
Wilkinson, Louisiana State Representative W. Scott, 65, 110
women: Oil City, LA, of, 43–45. *See also* sex trade/workers
Wood, Benjamin F., 43